Digital PSAT

8/9

Prep 2024-2025

6 Full – Length
Practice

Maximize Your Score with 6 Practice Tests and Targeted Strategies
for the Digital Test

DOY PUBLICATIONS

Legal & Disclaimer

The contents and information contained in this book has been compiled from reliable sources, which are accurate based on the knowledge, belief, expertise and information of the Author. The author cannot be held liable for any omissions and/or errors.

Thank you for this purchase!

Please let us know how you like it!

Thank you in advance

We are passionate about designing and creating educational study guides that will help you through your study, and gives you an inspiration and hope to pass your exams excellently.

TABLE OF CONTENTS

INTRODUCTION

Embarking on the journey of standardized testing can be a daunting prospect, especially when the stakes seem so high. As you stand at the precipice of your high school career, the PSAT 8/9 is a significant milestone. It's more than just a test; it's an opportunity to gauge your academic prowess, identify areas for growth, and prepare for the challenges ahead. This study guide is your trusted companion, meticulously crafted to illuminate the path to success on the PSAT 8/9.

The PSAT 8/9, or Preliminary Scholastic Aptitude Test for 8th and 9th graders, is a standardized test administered by the College Board, the same organization behind the renowned SAT. It serves as a valuable precursor to the SAT, offering a glimpse into the types of questions and testing formats you'll encounter on the actual college entrance exam. Think of it as a dress rehearsal, a chance to hone your skills and build the confidence you'll need to excel on the SAT and beyond.

However, the PSAT 8/9 is not merely a practice run for the SAT. It's a powerful tool for self-assessment, providing valuable feedback on your strengths and weaknesses in critical areas such as reading, writing, and math. By identifying your areas for growth early on, you can tailor your learning strategies and focus your efforts on the areas where you need the most improvement. This personalized approach to learning will not only enhance your performance on the PSAT 8/9 but also lay a solid foundation for academic success throughout high school and beyond.

Moreover, the PSAT 8/9 can open doors to a wealth of opportunities. High scores can qualify you for prestigious programs like the National Merit Scholarship Program, providing recognition and financial assistance for your academic achievements. It's a chance to showcase your potential and gain a competitive edge as you embark on your educational journey.

This study guide is your key to unlocking the secrets of the PSAT 8/9. It's a comprehensive resource, meticulously crafted to provide you with the knowledge, strategies, and practice you need to conquer the exam. Within its pages, you'll find:

In-depth content review: A thorough exploration of the key concepts tested in each section of the PSAT 8/9, ensuring you have a solid grasp of the essential knowledge.

Effective test-taking strategies: Expert guidance on how to approach different question types, manage your time effectively, and avoid common pitfalls.

Abundant practice questions: A wealth of practice opportunities to reinforce your learning, build confidence, and hone your test-taking skills.

Detailed answer explanations: Clear and concise explanations for every practice question, helping you understand the reasoning behind the correct answers and learn from your mistakes.

This guide is not just a collection of facts and figures; it's a roadmap to success, designed to empower you with the tools and strategies you need to navigate the PSAT 8/9 with confidence. It's a testament to the power of preparation, dedication, and a growth mindset.

As you embark on this journey, remember that the PSAT 8/9 is not just a test of your academic abilities; it's a reflection of your commitment to learning and your willingness to embrace challenges. Approach this exam with a positive attitude, a thirst for knowledge, and an unwavering belief in your potential. With hard work and dedication, you can achieve your goals and unlock a future filled with endless possibilities.

CHAPTER 1: WELCOME TO THE DIGITAL PSAT 8/9

WHAT IS THE PSAT 8/9 AND WHY SHOULD YOU CARE?

The PSAT 8/9 is a standardized test administered by the College Board, the same organization behind the SAT, PSAT 10, and PSAT/NMSQT. It's designed to assess your skills in reading, writing, and math, giving you a glimpse into your academic strengths and areas for improvement. While it doesn't directly impact college admissions, it serves as a valuable practice run for the SAT and helps you prepare for the rigors of college-level coursework.

Think of the PSAT 8/9 as a stepping stone in your educational journey. It's an opportunity to familiarize yourself with the types of questions and testing formats you'll encounter on the SAT, which is a crucial component of college applications. By taking the PSAT 8/9, you gain valuable insights into your academic abilities, allowing you to focus your efforts on specific areas where you need to improve.

The PSAT 8/9 can help you gauge your college readiness. It provides a benchmark for your academic performance, allowing you to compare your scores with those of other students nationwide. This information can help you set realistic goals for your future academic pursuits and make informed decisions about your educational path.

In addition to its academic benefits, the PSAT 8/9 can also open doors to scholarship opportunities. High scores on the PSAT 8/9 can qualify you for programs like the National Merit Scholarship Program, which provides financial assistance to high-achieving students. This can be a significant advantage when applying for colleges and universities.

BENEFITS OF TAKING THE PSAT 8/9 IN 8TH OR 9TH GRADE

Taking the PSAT 8/9 in 8th or 9th grade offers several advantages. It allows you to get a head start on your college preparation by familiarizing yourself with the standardized testing format and identifying areas where you need to improve. This early exposure can reduce anxiety and boost your confidence when taking the actual SAT later in high school.

Moreover, taking the PSAT 8/9 early gives you ample time to work on your weaknesses and improve your scores. You can use the feedback from the test to focus your studies and develop effective test-taking strategies. This can lead to better performance on the SAT and increase your chances of getting into your dream college.

Another benefit of taking the PSAT 8/9 early is that it can help you qualify for scholarships and other academic opportunities. Some programs, like the National Merit Scholarship Program, consider PSAT 8/9 scores when awarding scholarships. By taking the test early and achieving high scores, you can increase your chances of receiving financial aid for college.

HOW THE DIGITAL PSAT 8/9 IS DIFFERENT FROM THE PAPER TEST

The most significant change in the PSAT 8/9 is the transition from a paper-based test to a digital format. This means you'll now take the test on a computer or tablet instead of using pencil and paper. This shift brings several key differences that you need to be aware of:

- **Digital format:** The digital PSAT 8/9 is administered on a computer or tablet, providing a more interactive and engaging testing experience. The online interface allows for features like highlighting, answer elimination, and a built-in calculator, which can enhance your test-taking strategies.

- **Adaptive testing:** The digital PSAT 8/9 uses adaptive testing, which means the difficulty of the questions adjusts based on your performance. If you answer a question correctly, the next question will likely be more challenging. Conversely, if you answer incorrectly, the next question will likely be easier. This approach provides a more personalized assessment of your abilities.

- **Shorter test:** The digital PSAT 8/9 is shorter than the paper-based version, with fewer questions and a reduced testing time. This change reflects the adaptive nature of the test, which allows for a more efficient assessment of your skills.

- **New question types:** The digital PSAT 8/9 may introduce new question formats that take advantage of the digital interface. These could include interactive questions, drag-and-drop activities, or multimedia-based scenarios. Familiarizing yourself with these new question types is essential for success on the digital test.

NAVIGATING THE DIGITAL TEST INTERFACE: A STEP-BY-STEP GUIDE

The digital PSAT 8/9 features a user-friendly interface designed to make your test-taking experience smoother and more efficient. Here's a step-by-step guide to help you navigate the digital test interface:

1. **LOG IN:** You'll begin by logging into the testing platform using your College Board credentials. Make sure you have your username and password readily available.

2. **SELECT YOUR TEST:** Once logged in, you'll choose the PSAT 8/9 from the list of available tests.

3. **FAMILIARIZE YOURSELF WITH THE INTERFACE:** Before starting the test, take a moment to explore the interface. You'll see various tools and features, such as a timer, a navigation bar, a built-in calculator, and highlighting options.

4. **ANSWER QUESTIONS:** As you progress through the test, you can use the mouse or touchpad to select your answers. The interface allows you to mark questions for review, eliminate answer choices, and use a built-in calculator for the Math section.

5. **REVIEW YOUR ANSWERS:** At the end of each section, you'll have the

opportunity to review your answers and make any changes. Use this time wisely to ensure you've answered all questions to the best of your ability.

6. **SUBMIT YOUR TEST:** Once you've completed all sections and reviewed your answers, you'll submit your test for scoring.

UNDERSTANDING ADAPTIVE TESTING: HOW IT WORKS AND WHAT IT MEANS FOR YOU

The digital PSAT 8/9 employs adaptive testing, a unique approach that tailors the difficulty of the questions to your performance. This means the test adjusts in real-time based on your answers, providing a more personalized assessment of your abilities.

Here's how it works:

- **INITIAL QUESTIONS:** You'll start with a set of questions of average difficulty.
- **ADJUSTING DIFFICULTY:** As you answer questions, the test measures your performance and adjusts the difficulty of subsequent questions accordingly. If you answer correctly, the next question will likely be more challenging. If you answer incorrectly, the next question will likely be easier.
- **PERSONALIZED ASSESSMENT:** This adaptive process continues throughout the test, creating a customized experience that accurately reflects your strengths and weaknesses.

What does this mean for you?

- **ACCURATE MEASUREMENT:** Adaptive testing provides a more precise evaluation of your skills, as the questions are tailored to your specific level of ability.
- **EFFICIENT TESTING:** The adaptive format allows for a shorter test with fewer questions, as the test focuses on your specific skill level rather than covering a broad range of difficulty.
- **STRATEGIC APPROACH:** Understanding adaptive testing can help you approach the test strategically. It's important to answer each question to the best of your ability, as your performance on earlier questions influences the difficulty of later questions.

CHAPTER 2: HOW TO USE THIS BOOK TO MAXIMIZE YOUR SCORE

This chapter serves as your guide to effectively utilizing this PSAT 8/9 prep book, ensuring you gain the most from its features and strategies. It offers a roadmap to navigate the book's content, create a personalized study plan, set achievable goals, track your progress, and stay motivated throughout your preparation journey.

FEATURES OF THIS BOOK AND HOW THEY CAN HELP YOU SUCCEED

This book is meticulously crafted to provide you with a comprehensive and effective PSAT 8/9 preparation experience. It incorporates several key features designed to help you succeed on the exam:

- **COMPREHENSIVE CONTENT REVIEW:** The book covers all the essential topics and concepts tested on the PSAT 8/9, including reading comprehension, writing and language skills, and math fundamentals. Each chapter provides in-depth explanations, examples, and practice questions to reinforce your understanding and build a strong foundation in each subject area.

- **EFFECTIVE TEST-TAKING STRATEGIES:** Mastering test-taking strategies is crucial for maximizing your PSAT 8/9 score. This book equips you with proven techniques and approaches to tackle different question types, manage your time effectively, and avoid common pitfalls. You'll learn how to identify trap answers, make educated guesses, and approach each section with confidence.

- **PRACTICE TESTS:** The book includes practice tests that simulate the actual exam, allowing you to assess your readiness and identify areas for improvement. These tests are designed to mimic the digital format of the PSAT 8/9, providing a realistic testing experience.

- **DETAILED ANSWER EXPLANATIONS:** Each practice question comes with detailed answer explanations, helping you understand the reasoning behind the correct answer and learn from your mistakes. These explanations reinforce your understanding of the concepts and strategies applied in solving the questions.

- **ONLINE RESOURCES:** The book also offers access to online resources, including additional practice questions, video tutorials, and personalized study plans. These resources complement the book's content and provide further opportunities to reinforce your learning and track your progress.

CREATING A STUDY PLAN THAT WORKS FOR YOU

A well-structured study plan is essential for making the most of your preparation time and staying on track with your PSAT 8/9 goals. Here's a step-by-step guide to help you create a personalized study plan that works for you:

1. **ASSESS YOUR CURRENT SKILLS:** Begin by taking a diagnostic test to evaluate your strengths and weaknesses in each subject area. This will help you identify the areas where you need to focus your efforts.

2. **SET REALISTIC GOALS:** Determine your target PSAT 8/9 score and break down your preparation into smaller, achievable goals. This will help you stay motivated and track your progress effectively.

3. **ALLOCATE YOUR TIME:** Consider your available time and create a schedule that allows for consistent and focused study sessions. Be realistic about how much time you can dedicate each day or week and stick to your schedule as much as possible.

4. **PRIORITIZE YOUR TASKS:** Based on your diagnostic test results and your target score, prioritize the topics and concepts you need to review. Focus on the areas where you have the most room for improvement.

5. **CHOOSE YOUR STUDY MATERIALS:** Select the study materials that best suit your learning style and preferences. This could include textbooks, online resources, practice tests, or a combination of different materials.

6. **INCORPORATE BREAKS AND REWARDS:** Regular breaks and rewards

are essential to maintain focus and avoid burnout. Schedule short breaks during your study sessions and reward yourself for achieving your goals.

7. **REVIEW AND ADAPT:** Periodically review your study plan and make adjustments as needed. Your plan should be flexible and adaptable to your changing needs and progress.

SETTING REALISTIC GOALS AND TRACKING YOUR PROGRESS

Setting realistic goals and tracking your progress are crucial for staying motivated and achieving your desired PSAT 8/9 score. Here's how to approach this aspect of your preparation:

- **START WITH A BASELINE:** Take a diagnostic test to establish your current skill level and identify areas for improvement. This will serve as your baseline for setting realistic goals.
- **SET SMART GOALS:** Your goals should be Specific, Measurable, Achievable, Relevant, and Time-bound. For example, instead of setting a vague goal like "improve my math score," set a specific goal like "increase my math score by 20 points within two months."
- **BREAK DOWN YOUR GOALS:** Divide your larger goals into smaller, more manageable milestones. This will make your preparation less daunting and help you track your progress more effectively.
- **MONITOR YOUR PROGRESS:** Regularly assess your performance on practice tests and quizzes to track your improvement. This will help you identify areas where you need to focus your efforts and adjust your study plan accordingly.
- **CELEBRATE YOUR ACHIEVEMENTS:** Acknowledge and celebrate your progress, no matter how small. This will boost your confidence and keep you motivated throughout your preparation journey.

MAKING THE MOST OF THE PRACTICE TESTS

Practice tests are invaluable tools for assessing your readiness and identifying areas for improvement. Here's how to make the most of the practice tests in this book:

- **SIMULATE TEST CONDITIONS:** Take the practice tests under conditions that mimic the actual exam. This includes adhering to the time limits, using the digital interface, and minimizing distractions.

- **ANALYZE YOUR PERFORMANCE:** After completing each practice test, carefully review your answers and identify your strengths and weaknesses. Focus on understanding the reasoning behind the correct answers and learning from your mistakes.

- **TRACK YOUR PROGRESS:** Monitor your scores on the practice tests to track your improvement over time. This will help you gauge the effectiveness of your study plan and make adjustments as needed.

- **USE THE TESTS STRATEGICALLY:** Don't just take the practice tests to get a score; use them strategically to identify areas where you need to focus your studies and develop effective test-taking strategies.

TIPS FOR STAYING MOTIVATED AND FOCUSED

Staying motivated and focused throughout your PSAT 8/9 preparation can be challenging, but it's essential for achieving your goals. Here are some tips to help you stay on track:

- **FIND A STUDY BUDDY:** Studying with a friend or classmate can provide support, accountability, and motivation.

- **CREATE A POSITIVE STUDY ENVIRONMENT:** Choose a quiet and comfortable study space free from distractions.

- **TAKE REGULAR BREAKS:** Short breaks during your study sessions can help you stay refreshed and focused.

- **REWARD YOURSELF FOR YOUR ACHIEVEMENTS:** Celebrate your progress and reward yourself for reaching your goals.

- **VISUALIZE YOUR SUCCESS:** Imagine yourself acing the PSAT 8/9 and achieving your desired score.
- **STAY POSITIVE:** Maintain a positive attitude and believe in your ability to succeed.

- **REMEMBER YOUR GOALS:** Keep your PSAT 8/9 goals in mind and remind yourself why you're taking the test.
- **DON'T GIVE UP:** Even if you encounter setbacks, don't give up on your preparation. Persevere and stay committed to your goals.

CHAPTER 3: READING

3.1 MASTERING READING COMPREHENSION

Reading comprehension is a critical skill for academic success, and it plays a vital role in your performance on the PSAT 8/9. This section delves into the strategies and techniques to effectively comprehend the passages you'll encounter on the exam. It covers identifying main ideas and supporting details, making inferences and drawing conclusions, understanding vocabulary in context, and analyzing text structure and author's purpose.

Identifying Main Ideas and Supporting Details

The main idea of a passage is the central point or message the author wants to convey. It's the overarching theme that ties all the other elements of the passage together. Supporting details are the facts, examples, and evidence that the author uses to illustrate and reinforce the main idea.

To effectively identify the main idea and supporting details, follow these steps:

1. **READ THE PASSAGE CAREFULLY:** Start by reading the passage attentively, paying attention to the author's tone, style, and the overall flow of ideas.

2. **IDENTIFY THE TOPIC:** Determine the general subject matter of the passage. What is the passage primarily about?

3. **LOOK FOR THE THESIS STATEMENT:** The thesis statement is a concise summary of the main point of the passage. It's often found in the introduction or conclusion, but it can appear anywhere in the passage.

4. **PAY ATTENTION TO SUPPORTING DETAILS:** As you read, identify the details that support the main idea. These could include facts, statistics, examples, anecdotes, or expert opinions.

5. **SUMMARIZE THE PASSAGE:** After reading, try to summarize the passage in your own words, focusing on the main idea and the key supporting details

Making Inferences and Drawing Conclusions

Inferences are educated guesses or conclusions that you draw based on the information provided in the passage. The author may not explicitly state every detail, but you can use your reasoning and background knowledge to infer meaning and draw conclusions.

To make inferences and draw conclusions effectively, follow these steps:

1. **READ ACTIVELY:** Engage with the passage actively, asking yourself questions and making connections between the ideas presented.

2. **CONSIDER THE AUTHOR'S PERSPECTIVE:** Pay attention to the author's tone, style, and the overall message they want to convey.

3. **LOOK FOR CLUES:** Identify clues and hints within the passage that suggest a deeper meaning or implication.

4. **USE YOUR BACKGROUND KNOWLEDGE:** Combine the information from the passage with your own background knowledge and experiences to draw logical conclusions.

5. **SUPPORT YOUR INFERENCES:** Ensure that your inferences are supported by evidence from the passage. Avoid making assumptions or drawing conclusions that are not backed by the text.

Understanding Vocabulary in Context

The PSAT 8/9 often includes vocabulary questions that assess your ability to determine the meaning of words in context. The meaning of a word can change depending on the surrounding words and sentences, so it's crucial to consider the context when answering vocabulary questions.

To effectively understand vocabulary in context, follow these steps:

1. **READ THE SURROUNDING SENTENCES:** Pay attention to the sentences before and after the word in question. The context can provide clues to the word's meaning.

2. **IDENTIFY CLUES:** Look for clues within the sentence or passage that suggest

the word's meaning. These could include synonyms, antonyms, examples, or definitions.

3. **USE YOUR BACKGROUND KNOWLEDGE:** Combine the clues from the passage with your own background knowledge and vocabulary to determine the most appropriate meaning of the word.

4. **SUBSTITUTE THE WORD:** Once you've determined the word's meaning, substitute it back into the sentence to ensure it makes sense in context.

Analyzing Text Structure and Author's Purpose

The structure of a passage refers to how the author organizes and presents the information. Different text structures serve different purposes, such as chronological order for narrating events, compare and contrast for highlighting similarities and differences, or cause and effect for explaining relationships between events.

The author's purpose is the reason or intent behind writing the passage. It could be to inform, persuade, entertain, or express an opinion. Understanding the author's purpose can help you better comprehend the passage and answer questions effectively.

To analyze text structure and author's purpose, follow these steps:

1. **IDENTIFY THE TEXT STRUCTURE:** Determine how the author organizes the information. Is it chronological, compare and contrast, cause and effect, or another structure?

2. **CONSIDER THE AUTHOR'S TONE AND STYLE:** Pay attention to the author's tone, style, and the overall message they want to convey.

3. **LOOK FOR CLUES:** Identify clues within the passage that suggest the author's purpose. These could include the use of persuasive language, emotional appeals, or informative details.

4. **ASK YOURSELF WHY THE AUTHOR WROTE THE PASSAGE:** What was the author's intent or goal in writing the passage?

3.2 TACKLING LITERATURE PASSAGES

Literature passages on the PSAT 8/9 present unique challenges and require a different approach compared to informational texts. This section delves into the strategies and techniques to effectively comprehend and analyze literature passages. It covers analyzing characters, setting, and plot, interpreting figurative language and literary devices, and understanding themes and central ideas.

Analyzing Characters, Setting, and Plot

Characters, setting, and plot are the fundamental elements of any narrative. Characters are the individuals who drive the story, the setting is the time and place where the story unfolds, and the plot is the sequence of events that make up the narrative.

To effectively analyze characters, setting, and plot, follow these steps:

1. **IDENTIFY THE MAIN CHARACTERS:** Determine the central figures in the story and their roles in the narrative.

2. **ANALYZE CHARACTER TRAITS:** Pay attention to the characters' personalities, motivations, and relationships with other characters. How do their actions and interactions contribute to the story's development?

3. **ESTABLISH THE SETTING:** Determine the time and place where the story takes place. How does the setting influence the characters and events in the story?

4. **TRACE THE PLOT:** Identify the key events in the story and their sequence. How does the plot unfold, and what are the conflicts and resolutions that drive the narrative?

5. **CONSIDER THE POINT OF VIEW:** From whose perspective is the story told? How does the point of view affect your understanding of the characters and events?

Interpreting Figurative Language and Literary Devices

Figurative language and literary devices are tools that authors use to enhance their writing and convey meaning beyond the literal words. These devices can include metaphors, similes, personification, imagery, symbolism, and irony.

To effectively interpret figurative language and literary devices, follow these steps:

1. **IDENTIFY THE DEVICE:** Determine the specific literary device used in the passage.

2. **ANALYZE ITS MEANING:** Consider the deeper meaning or message the author conveys through the device. How does it contribute to the overall theme or message of the passage?

3. **CONSIDER THE CONTEXT:** Pay attention to the surrounding words and sentences to understand how the device functions in context.

4. **LOOK FOR PATTERNS:** Identify any patterns or recurring themes associated with the device. How do these patterns contribute to the passage's overall meaning?

Understanding Themes and Central Ideas

The theme of a literary passage is the underlying message or idea that the author wants to convey. It's the universal truth or observation about human nature or the world that the passage explores. The central idea is the main point or argument that the passage makes about the theme.

To *effectively understand themes and central ideas, follow these steps:*

1. **IDENTIFY THE THEME:** Determine the overarching message or idea that the passage conveys. What is the author trying to say about human nature or the world?

2. **ANALYZE THE CENTRAL IDEA:** Identify the main point or argument that the passage makes about the theme. How does the author support this central idea?

3. **CONSIDER THE CHARACTERS AND EVENTS:** How do the characters and events in the passage contribute to the development of the theme and central idea?

4. **LOOK FOR SYMBOLISM AND IMAGERY:** How does the author use symbolism and imagery to convey the theme and central idea?

5. **CONNECT TO YOUR OWN EXPERIENCES:** How does the theme and central idea resonate with your own experiences and understanding of the world?

3.3 CONQUERING INFORMATIONAL TEXTS

Informational texts form a significant portion of the reading material you'll encounter on the PSAT 8/9. These texts aim to convey factual information and often present complex data and arguments. This section equips you with the strategies and techniques to effectively comprehend and analyze informational texts. It covers identifying key facts and data, understanding graphics and visual information, and evaluating evidence and arguments.

Identifying Key Facts and Data

Key facts and data are the core building blocks of informational texts. They provide the evidence and support for the author's arguments and conclusions. Identifying these key elements is crucial for understanding the passage and answering questions accurately.

To effectively identify key facts and data, follow these steps:

1. **SCAN THE PASSAGE:** Before diving into a detailed reading, scan the passage to get an overview of the topic and the structure of the information.

2. **PAY ATTENTION TO HEADINGS AND SUBHEADINGS:** Headings and subheadings provide valuable clues about the organization of the information and the key topics covered in each section.

3. **LOOK FOR KEYWORDS AND PHRASES:** Identify keywords and phrases that signal important information, such as dates, numbers, statistics, names, and definitions.

4. **HIGHLIGHT OR UNDERLINE KEY FACTS:** As you read, highlight or underline the key facts and data that support the author's arguments.

5. **SUMMARIZE EACH SECTION:** After reading each section, try to summarize the key facts and data in your own words.

Understanding Graphics and Visual Information

Informational texts often incorporate graphics and visual elements, such as charts, graphs, maps, and diagrams, to present data and illustrate complex concepts. Understanding these visual elements is crucial for comprehending the passage and answering related questions.

To understand graphics and visual information, follow these steps:

1. **READ THE TITLE AND LABELS:** Start by reading the title, axis labels, and any other accompanying text to understand what the graphic represents.

2. **IDENTIFY THE TYPE OF GRAPHIC:** Determine the type of graphic, such as a bar graph, line graph, pie chart, or table. Each type presents data in a specific way.

3. **ANALYZE THE DATA:** Examine the data presented in the graphic. What trends, patterns, or relationships does it reveal?

4. **CONNECT TO THE PASSAGE:** Relate the information in the graphic to the main ideas and arguments presented in the passage. How does the graphic support or illustrate the author's points?

5. **DRAW CONCLUSIONS:** Based on your analysis of the graphic and its connection to the passage, draw conclusions about the information presented.

Evaluating Evidence and Arguments

Informational texts often present arguments and support them with evidence. Evaluating the strength and validity of these arguments is crucial for critical thinking and forming your own informed opinions.

To evaluate evidence and arguments, follow these steps:

1. **IDENTIFY THE AUTHOR'S CLAIMS:** Determine the main arguments or claims that the author is making.
2. **ANALYZE THE SUPPORTING EVIDENCE:** Examine the evidence that the author uses to support their claims. Is the evidence relevant, credible, and sufficient?
3. **CONSIDER THE AUTHOR'S PERSPECTIVE:** Pay attention to the author's tone, style, and potential biases. How might their perspective influence their arguments?
4. **LOOK FOR COUNTERARGUMENTS:** Does the author acknowledge or address any counter arguments or opposing viewpoints?
5. **FORM YOUR OWN CONCLUSIONS:** Based on your evaluation of the evidence and arguments, form your own conclusions about the validity of the author's claims.

3.4 WORKING WITH PAIRED PASSAGES

Paired passages, a unique challenge on the PSAT 8/9, require you to analyze and synthesize information from two distinct texts. This section delves into the strategies and techniques to effectively tackle paired passages. It covers comparing and contrasting different perspectives, synthesizing information from multiple sources, and analyzing the relationships between texts.

Comparing and Contrasting Different Perspectives

Paired passages often present contrasting viewpoints or perspectives on a shared topic. Your task is to identify the main points of each passage and analyze how they relate to each other.

To compare and contrast different perspectives, follow these steps:

1. **READ THE FIRST PASSAGE CAREFULLY:** Start by reading the first passage attentively, paying attention to the author's main idea, supporting details, and tone.
2. **IDENTIFY THE AUTHOR'S PERSPECTIVE:** Determine the author's

stance or viewpoint on the topic. What are their key arguments and supporting evidence?

3. **READ THE SECOND PASSAGE WITH A CRITICAL EYE:** As you read the second passage, compare and contrast the author's perspective with that of the first passage. How do their viewpoints differ, and where do they agree?

4. **HIGHLIGHT KEY SIMILARITIES AND DIFFERENCES:** Mark the key similarities and differences in the authors' perspectives. How do these contrasting viewpoints contribute to a deeper understanding of the topic?

5. **SUMMARIZE THE PERSPECTIVES:** After reading both passages, summarize the main points of each perspective and their relationship to each other.

Synthesizing Information from Multiple Sources

Synthesizing information involves combining and integrating ideas from multiple sources to form a comprehensive understanding of the topic. Paired passages require you to synthesize information from two distinct texts, identifying common themes and connecting the ideas presented.

To synthesize information from multiple sources, follow these steps:

1. **IDENTIFY COMMON THEMES:** Determine the overarching themes or topics that both passages address.

2. **CONNECT THE IDEAS:** Analyze how the ideas presented in each passage relate to each other. Do they support, contradict, or complement each other?

3. **CREATE A UNIFIED UNDERSTANDING:** Combine the information from both passages to form a comprehensive understanding of the topic. How do the different perspectives contribute to a broader view of the subject matter?

4. **SUMMARIZE THE KEY TAKEAWAYS:** After synthesizing the information, summarize the key takeaways from both passages. What are the most important points to remember?

Analyzing Relationships Between Texts

Paired passages often have a specific relationship, such as agreement, disagreement, complementarity, or one text expanding on the other. Analyzing this relationship is crucial for understanding the passages and answering related questions.

To effectively analyze relationships between texts, follow these steps:

1. **IDENTIFY THE CONNECTION:** Determine the primary connection or relationship between the two passages. How do they relate to each other?

2. **ANALYZE THE PURPOSE:** Consider the purpose of each passage and how it contributes to the overall relationship between the texts.

3. **LOOK FOR CLUES:** Identify clues within the passages that signal the relationship between them. These could include contrasting viewpoints, supporting evidence, or one text referring to the other.

4. **SUMMARIZE THE RELATIONSHIP:** After analyzing the passages, summarize the relationship between them in your own words.

3.5 READING PRACTICE QUESTIONS

Practice is essential for mastering reading comprehension skills and achieving your desired score on the PSAT 8/9 Reading section. This segment provides a collection of practice questions designed to reinforce the concepts and strategies covered in the previous sections. It includes multiple-choice questions with detailed explanations and passage-based reading drills to hone your skills.

Multiple-Choice Questions with Detailed Explanations

PASSAGE 1:

The sun was setting, casting long shadows across the dusty field. A lone figure emerged from the horizon, his silhouette stark against the fiery sky. He walked with a determined stride, his eyes fixed on the distant farmhouse. As he drew closer, the details of his weathered face became visible

– the lines etched by years of toil under the relentless sun, the eyes that held both weariness and a glimmer of hope.

1. **Question:** The author's primary purpose in the passage is to...
   Answer Choices:

   o (A) Describe a picturesque landscape.

   o (B) Introduce a character and setting.

   o (C) Convey a sense of foreboding.

   o (D) Explain the effects of harsh weather.

2. **Explanation:** The passage focuses on describing the setting and introducing a character, highlighting his physical appearance and demeanor. Therefore, the answer is (B).

PASSAGE 2:

The old library was a treasure trove of forgotten stories, its shelves lined with books bound in worn leather and faded cloth. The air was thick with the scent of aged paper and dust motes danced in the shafts of sunlight that streamed through the arched windows. Each book held a universe waiting to be discovered, a portal to worlds both real and imagined.

2. **Question:** The word "portal" in line 4 most nearly means...
   Answer Choices:

   o (A) Doorway

   o (B) Barrier

   o (C) Window

   o (D) Obstacle

   Explanation: In this context, "portal" refers to a means of access or entry to another world or dimension. The closest synonym among the answer choices is "doorway," so the answer is (A).

PASSAGE 3:

The scientist peered into the microscope, her brow furrowed in concentration. The intricate dance of cells unfolded before her eyes, a symphony of life and death played out on a microscopic stage. She was captivated by the complexity of this hidden world, a world teeming with unseen wonders and endless possibilities.

3. **Question:** The author's attitude towards the subject can best be described as...

   Answer Choices:

   o (A) Indifferent

   o (B) Apprehensive

   o (C) Fascinated

   o (D) Skeptical

Explanation: The author portrays the scientist as being captivated and intrigued by the microscopic world, suggesting a sense of fascination. Therefore, the answer is (C).

PASSAGE 4:

The city was a cacophony of noise – the rumble of traffic, the chatter of pedestrians, the distant wail of sirens. Buildings stretched towards the sky, their glass facades reflecting the harsh glare of the sun. Amidst this urban jungle, a lone musician played his saxophone, his melancholic melody a counterpoint to the city's frenetic energy.

4. **Question:** The main idea of the passage is...

   Answer Choices:

   o (A) The city is a place of overwhelming noise and activity.

   o (B) Music provides a soothing contrast to the chaos of city life.

   o (C) The architecture of the city is imposing and impersonal.

   o (D) The passage describes a typical day in the life of a city musician.

Explanation: The passage contrasts the city's noise and activity with the musician's soothing melody, highlighting the role of music in providing a sense of calm amidst the chaos. Therefore, the answer is (B).

PASSAGE 5:

The ancient ruins stood silent and still, their crumbling walls bearing witness to the passage of time. Once a bustling metropolis, now a ghost town, its streets deserted and its buildings reclaimed by nature. The wind whispered through the empty windows, carrying with it the echoes of a forgotten civilization.

5. **Question:** — Which of the following best summarizes the passage?
   Answer Choices:

o (A) The passage describes the decline of a once-great city.

o (B) The passage explores the destructive power of nature.

o (C) The passage celebrates the resilience of ancient civilizations.

o (D) The passage warns against the dangers of neglecting historical sites.

Explanation: The passage focuses on the contrast between the city's former glory and its current state of ruin, highlighting its decline over time. Therefore, the answer is (A).

Passage-Based Reading Drills

Passage-based reading drills provide an opportunity to apply your reading comprehension skills to a specific passage. These drills typically include a passage followed by several multiple-choice questions that assess your understanding of the passage's main idea, supporting details, vocabulary, inferences, and author's purpose.

To tackle passage-based reading drills, follow these steps:

1. **READ THE PASSAGE CAREFULLY:** Start by reading the passage attentively, paying attention to the author's tone, style, and the overall flow of ideas.

2. **IDENTIFY THE MAIN IDEA:** Determine the central point or message the author wants to convey.

3. **PAY ATTENTION TO SUPPORTING DETAILS:** As you read, identify the details that support the main idea.

4. **ANSWER THE QUESTIONS:** Answer the multiple-choice questions based on your understanding of the passage. Refer back to the passage to support your answers.

5. **REVIEW YOUR ANSWERS:** After answering all the questions, review your answers and ensure they are supported by evidence from the passage.

CHAPTER 4: WRITING AND LANGUAGE

4.1 GRAMMAR FUNDAMENTALS

Grammar fundamentals form the bedrock of effective writing, ensuring clarity, precision, and adherence to the rules of Standard English. This section delves into the essential grammar concepts that are frequently tested on the PSAT 8/9 Writing and Language section. It covers subject-verb agreement, pronoun usage, verb tense and mood, and modifiers and parallelism.

Subject-Verb Agreement

Subject-verb agreement is a fundamental grammar rule that ensures the verb in a sentence matches the number of the subject. In simpler terms, if the subject is singular, the verb must be singular; if the subject is plural, the verb must be plural.

To master subject-verb agreement, keep these points in mind:

- **Identify the subject:** The subject is the noun or pronoun that performs the action of the verb. It's who or what the sentence is about.
- **Determine the number of the subject:** Is the subject singular or plural? Singular subjects refer to one person, place, or thing, while plural subjects refer to more than one.

- **Match the verb to the subject:** Once you've identified the subject and its number, ensure that the verb agrees in number. Singular subjects take singular verbs, and plural subjects take plural verbs.

Examples:

- **Singular:** The **dog** barks loudly.
- **Plural:** The **dogs** bark loudly.

Pronoun Usage

Pronouns are words that replace nouns, helping to avoid repetition and improve sentence flow. However, using pronouns correctly can be tricky, especially when ensuring they agree with their antecedents (the nouns they refer to).

To master pronoun usage, keep these points in mind:

- **PRONOUN-ANTECEDENT AGREEMENT:** Pronouns must agree with their antecedents in number, gender, and case.
1. **Number:** Singular antecedents take singular pronouns, and plural antecedents take plural pronouns.
2. **Gender:** Use pronouns that match the gender of their antecedents (he/him/his for masculine nouns, she/her/hers for feminine nouns, it/it's for neuter nouns).
3. **Case:** Use the correct pronoun case depending on its function in the sentence (subject pronouns like I, you, he, she, it, we, they; object pronouns like me, you, him, her, it, us, them; possessive pronouns like my/mine, your/yours, his, her/hers, its, our/ours, their/theirs).

- **CLEAR PRONOUN REFERENCE:** Ensure that each pronoun has a clear and unambiguous antecedent. Avoid using pronouns that could refer to multiple nouns, causing confusion for the reader.

EXAMPLES:

- **Agreement:** The **students** finished **their** project.
- **Clear reference: Sarah** went to the store, and **she** bought some milk.

Verb Tense and Mood

Verb tense indicates the time of an action or state of being. The main tenses are past, present, and future. Verb mood expresses the attitude or intention of the speaker or writer. The main moods are indicative (for statements of fact), imperative (for commands), and subjunctive (for hypothetical situations or wishes).

To master verb tense and mood, keep these points in mind:

- **MAINTAIN CONSISTENT TENSE:** Use the same verb tense throughout a sentence or paragraph, unless a shift in time is necessary.
- **CHOOSE THE APPROPRIATE MOOD:** Use the indicative mood for statements of fact, the imperative mood for commands, and the subjunctive mood for hypothetical situations or wishes.
- **PAY ATTENTION TO IRREGULAR VERBS:** Irregular verbs don't follow the standard rules for forming tenses. Memorize the common irregular verbs and their various forms.

EXAMPLES:

- **Consistent tense:** The cat sat on the mat and licked its paw.
- **Appropriate mood:**
  1. Indicative: The sun is shining.
  2. Imperative: Close the door.
  3. Subjunctive: If I were you, I would study for the test.

Modifiers and Parallelism

Modifiers are words or phrases that describe or qualify other words in a sentence. Parallelism is the use of similar grammatical structures to express related ideas.

To master modifiers and parallelism, keep these points in mind:

- **PLACE MODIFIERS CORRECTLY:** Modifiers should be placed as close as possible to the words they modify to avoid ambiguity or confusion.
- **USE PARALLEL STRUCTURE:** When listing or comparing items, use parallel grammatical structures to ensure clarity and balance.

EXAMPLES:

- **Correct modifier placement:** The dog barked loudly at the mailman.
- **Parallel structure:** The students were asked to read the chapter, take notes, and answer the questions.

4.2 SENTENCE STRUCTURE

Sentence structure is the backbone of clear and effective writing. It dictates how words and phrases are arranged to form grammatically sound and coherent sentences. This section delves into the intricacies of sentence structure, focusing on common errors that are frequently tested on the PSAT 8/9 Writing and Language section. It covers sentence fragments, run-on sentences, comma usage, punctuation, and techniques for combining sentences to enhance clarity and style.

Sentence Fragments and Run-on Sentences

A sentence fragment is an incomplete sentence that lacks a subject, a verb, or a complete thought. It leaves the reader hanging, as it doesn't express a full idea.

Examples:

- Running down the street. (No subject)
- The dog with the wagging tail. (No verb)
- Because it was raining. (Incomplete thought)

A run-on sentence, on the other hand, combines two or more independent clauses (complete sentences) without proper punctuation or conjunctions. It crams too many ideas into a single sentence, making it difficult to follow.

Examples:

- The cat sat on the mat the dog chased its tail. (No punctuation or conjunction)
- The students finished their project they were exhausted but happy. (No punctuation or conjunction)

Comma Usage and Punctuation

Commas are essential punctuation marks that help to clarify meaning and improve sentence flow. However, their usage can be nuanced and often trips up even experienced writers.

- **COMMAS IN LISTS:** Use commas to separate items in a list of three or more.
  - Example: The recipe called for flour, sugar, eggs, and milk.
- **COMMAS WITH COORDINATING CONJUNCTIONS:** Use a comma before a coordinating conjunction (FANBOYS: for, and, nor, but, or, yet, so) when it joins two independent clauses.
  - Example: The students finished their homework, but they still had time to watch a movie.
- **COMMAS WITH INTRODUCTORY ELEMENTS:** Use a comma after an introductory phrase or clause.
  - Example: After finishing her work, Sarah went for a walk.
- **COMMAS WITH NONESSENTIAL ELEMENTS:** Use commas to set off nonessential phrases or clauses (information that can be removed without changing the sentence's core meaning).
  - Example: The dog, a golden retriever, wagged its tail excitedly.
- **COMMAS WITH INTERRUPTERS:** Use commas to set off interrupters, such as direct addresses, parenthetical expressions, or appositives.
  - Example: The teacher, Mr. Smith, explained the lesson clearly.

Combining Sentences for Clarity and Style

Combining sentences can help to improve the flow and sophistication of your writing. It allows you to connect related ideas and create more complex sentence structures.

- **COORDINATION:** Use coordinating conjunctions (FANBOYS) to combine independent clauses of equal importance.
  - Example: The students finished their project, and they presented it to the class.
- **SUBORDINATION:** Use subordinating conjunctions (because, although, since,

while, etc.) to combine independent clauses where one clause is dependent on the other.

○ Example: Although it was raining, the team decided to play the game.

- **RELATIVE PRONOUNS:** Use relative pronouns (who, whom, whose, which, that) to introduce adjective clauses that provide additional information about a noun.

○ Example: The book, which was written by a famous author, was a bestseller.

- **PARTICIPIAL PHRASES:** Use participial phrases (verb forms ending in -ing or -ed that function as adjectives) to combine sentences concisely.

○ Example: The dog, barking loudly, chased the squirrel up the tree.

4.3 EFFECTIVE LANGUAGE USE

Effective language use is the art of choosing and arranging words to convey meaning with clarity, precision, and impact. This section delves into the nuances of effective language use, focusing on elements that are frequently tested on the PSAT 8/9 Writing and Language section. It covers word choice and diction, tone and style, and conciseness and precision.

Word Choice and Diction

Word choice refers to the selection of specific words to convey meaning, while diction encompasses the overall style and tone of language used in a piece of writing. Choosing the right words can significantly impact the clarity, tone, and effectiveness of your writing.

- **DENOTATION AND CONNOTATION:** Words have both denotative and connotative meanings. Denotation is the literal dictionary definition of a word, while connotation is the emotional or cultural association it carries. Consider both the denotation and connotation of words to ensure they convey the intended meaning and tone.

- o **Example:** The words "slim" and "skinny" have similar denotations (thin), but "skinny" carries a more negative connotation.

- **FORMAL AND INFORMAL LANGUAGE:** The level of formality in your writing should match the context and audience. Formal language is characterized by precise grammar, complex sentence structures, and avoidance of slang or colloquialisms. Informal language is more relaxed and conversational, often using contractions and simpler vocabulary.

- o **Example:** "The aforementioned incident" is formal, while "the thing I mentioned earlier" is informal.

- **FIGURATIVE LANGUAGE:** Figurative language, such as metaphors, similes, and personification, can add depth and creativity to your writing. However, use it sparingly and ensure it aligns with the overall tone and purpose of your writing.

- o **Example:** "The sun was a ball of fire in the sky" is a metaphor.

- **JARGON AND CLICHÉS:** Avoid using jargon (specialized language specific to a particular field) unless your audience is familiar with it. Similarly, avoid clichés (overused phrases that have lost their originality).

- o **Example:** "Think outside the box" is a cliché.

Tone and Style

Tone refers to the author's attitude or feeling towards the subject matter, while style encompasses the author's unique voice and writing choices. Tone and style work together to create the overall impression and impact of a piece of writing.

- **TONE:** Tone can be formal, informal, humorous, serious, sarcastic, objective, or subjective, among others. It's conveyed through word choice, sentence structure, and punctuation.
  - **Example:** A news report typically has an objective tone, while a personal essay might have a subjective tone.
- **STYLE:** Style encompasses various elements, including sentence structure, word choice, imagery, and figurative language. It's what makes an author's writing distinctive and recognizable.
  - **Example:** Ernest Hemingway is known for his concise and direct style, while Virginia Woolf is known for her lyrical and stream-of-consciousness style.
- **AUDIENCE AND PURPOSE:** Consider your audience and purpose when determining the appropriate tone and style for your writing. A formal research paper requires a different tone and style than a casual email to a friend.

Conciseness and Precision

Conciseness is the ability to express ideas clearly and effectively using as few words as possible. Precision involves choosing the most accurate and specific words to convey your meaning.

- **REDUNDANCY:** Avoid redundant words or phrases that repeat information unnecessarily.
  - **Example:** "The final outcome" is redundant; "outcome" implies finality.
- **WORDINESS:** Eliminate unnecessary words or phrases that clutter your writing and obscure your meaning.
  - **Example:** "Due to the fact that" can be replaced with "because."
- **AMBIGUITY:** Avoid ambiguous language that could be interpreted in multiple ways. Use precise words and clear sentence structures to ensure your meaning is unambiguous.
  - **Example:** "The dog chased the cat with the long tail" is ambiguous; it's unclear whether the dog or the cat has the long tail.
- **ACTIVE VOICE:** Use the active voice whenever possible to make your writing more direct and engaging. In the active voice, the subject performs the action; in the passive voice, the subject receives the action.

o **Example:** "The dog chased the cat" is active; "The cat was chased by the dog" is passive.

4.4 REVISION AND EDITING STRATEGIES

Revision and editing are essential steps in the writing process, ensuring your work is polished, clear, and effective. This section delves into the strategies and techniques for revising and editing your writing, focusing on elements that are frequently tested on the PSAT 8/9 Writing and Language section. It covers identifying and correcting errors, improving sentence flow and clarity, and strengthening arguments and supporting evidence.

Identifying and Correcting Errors

Identifying and correcting errors is crucial for ensuring your writing adheres to the rules of Standard English and effectively conveys your ideas. This involves recognizing and rectifying grammatical errors, punctuation mistakes, and stylistic inconsistencies.

- **GRAMMAR ERRORS:** Grammar errors can include subject-verb disagreement, incorrect pronoun usage, faulty verb tense or mood, misplaced modifiers, and lack of parallelism.
  - o **Example:** Subject-verb disagreement: The **group of students is** excited about the field trip. (The verb should be "are" to agree with the plural subject "group of students.")

- **PUNCTUATION ERRORS:** Punctuation errors can include missing or misplaced commas, semicolons, colons, apostrophes, and quotation marks.
  - o **Example:** Missing comma: After finishing her homework Sarah went for a walk. (A comma is needed after the introductory phrase "After finishing her homework.")

- **STYLISTIC INCONSISTENCIES:** Stylistic inconsistencies can include shifts in tone, inconsistent verb tense, and variations in sentence structure.

  o **Example:** Inconsistent verb tense: The dog barked loudly and then **chases** the squirrel. (The verb "chases" should be "chased" to maintain consistency with the past tense verb "barked.")

Improving Sentence Flow and Clarity

Sentence flow and clarity are essential for ensuring your writing is easy to read and understand. This involves using varied sentence structures, transitions, and precise language to create a smooth and coherent flow of ideas.

- **SENTENCE VARIETY:** Varying your sentence structure can make your writing more engaging and dynamic. Use a mix of simple, compound, and complex sentences to create rhythm and flow.

  o **Example:** Simple sentence: The dog barked. Compound sentence: The dog barked, and the cat ran away. Complex sentence: Because the dog barked, the cat ran away.

- **TRANSITIONS:** Transitions are words or phrases that connect ideas and create a smooth flow between sentences and paragraphs. Use transitions to signal relationships between ideas, such as addition, contrast, or cause and effect.

  o **Example:** Addition: furthermore, moreover. Contrast: however, nevertheless. Cause and effect: therefore, consequently.

- **PRECISE LANGUAGE:** Choose words that accurately and specifically convey your meaning. Avoid vague or ambiguous language that could confuse the reader.

o **Example:** Instead of "The thing happened," use "The experiment yielded unexpected results."

Strengthening Arguments and Supporting Evidence

Strengthening arguments and supporting evidence involves ensuring your claims are well-supported, logical, and persuasive. This involves using relevant evidence, addressing counterarguments, and maintaining a clear and consistent line of reasoning.

- **RELEVANT EVIDENCE:** Use evidence that directly supports your claims. This could include facts, statistics, examples, anecdotes, or expert opinions.
- o **Example:** Claim: Regular exercise improves cardiovascular health. Evidence: Studies have shown that people who exercise regularly have lower blood pressure and cholesterol levels.

- **COUNTERARGUMENTS:** Acknowledge and address potential counterarguments to strengthen your position. This shows that you've considered opposing viewpoints and reinforces the validity of your claims.
- o **Example:** Counterargument: Some people argue that exercise is time-consuming and inconvenient. Response: While it's true that exercise requires time and effort, the health benefits far outweigh the inconvenience.

- **LOGICAL REASONING:** Ensure your arguments follow a clear and logical progression. Use transitions and logical connectors to guide the reader through your line of reasoning.
- o **Example:** First, exercise strengthens the heart muscle. Second, it improves blood circulation. Therefore, regular exercise contributes to a healthier cardiovascular system.

CHAPTER 5: MATH

5.1 NUMBER SYSTEMS AND OPERATIONS

Number systems and operations form the foundation of mathematical understanding, providing the tools and concepts to work with various types of numbers. This section delves into the intricacies of number systems and operations, focusing on elements frequently tested on the PSAT 8/9 Math section. It covers integers, fractions, decimals, ratios, proportions, percentages, exponents, and roots.

Integers, Fractions, and Decimals

Integers are whole numbers (without fractions or decimals) that can be positive, negative, or zero. Fractions represent a part of a whole, expressed as a numerator (the top number) over a denominator (the bottom number). Decimals are another way to represent fractions, using a decimal point to indicate the fractional part.

- **INTEGERS:**
  - Examples: -3, 0, 5, 100
  - Operations: Addition, subtraction, multiplication, and division
- **FRACTIONS:**
  - Examples: 1/2, 3/4, 7/8
  - Operations: Addition, subtraction (requires common denominators), multiplication, division (invert and multiply), simplification (divide numerator and denominator by common factors)
- **DECIMALS:**
  - Examples: 0.5, 0.75, 0.875
  - Operations: Addition, subtraction, multiplication, division (align decimal points), conversion to fractions (place the decimal over the appropriate power of 10 and simplify)

EXAMPLE:

Convert the fraction 3/4 to a decimal.

Solution:

Divide the numerator (3) by the denominator (4) to get 0.75.

PROBLEM QUESTION:

A recipe calls for 1/4 cup of sugar and 1/3 cup of flour. If you want to double the recipe, how much sugar will you need?

SOLUTION:

Doubling the recipe means multiplying the amount of sugar by 2.

1/4 x 2 = 2/4 = 1/2 cup of sugar

Ratios, Proportions, and Percentages

Ratios compare two or more quantities, expressed as a:b or a/b. Proportions are equations that state two ratios are equal. Percentages represent a part of a whole out of one hundred, expressed as a%.

- **RATIOS:**

o Examples: 2:3, 4/5, 1 out of 10

o Applications: Comparing quantities, scaling recipes or measurements

- **PROPORTIONS:**

o Examples: a/b = c/d

o Applications: Solving for unknown quantities, scaling maps or models

- **PERCENTAGES:**

o Examples: 25%, 50%, 75%

o Operations: Conversion to decimals (divide by 100), calculating percentages of quantities (multiply the decimal equivalent by the quantity), percentage increase or decrease (calculate the difference, divide

by the original amount, and multiply by 100)

EXAMPLE:

A map has a scale of 1:100,000. If the distance between two cities on the map is 2 cm, what is the actual distance between the cities?

SOLUTION:

Set up a proportion: 1/100,000 = 2/x

Cross-multiply and solve for x: x = 200,000 cm = 2 km

PROBLEM QUESTION:

The price of a shirt is $20. If the price is increased by 10%, what is the new price?

SOLUTION:

Calculate the increase: $20 x 10/100 = $2

Add the increase to the original price: $20 + $2 = $22

Exponents and Roots

Exponents indicate repeated multiplication of a base number. Roots are the inverse operation of exponents, finding the base number that, when raised to a certain power, equals a given value.

- **EXPONENTS:**
  - Examples: $2^3 = 2 \times 2 \times 2 = 8$
  - Rules:
    1. Multiplication: $x^m \, x^n = x^{(m+n)}$
    2. Division: $x^m / x^n = x^{(m-n)}$
    3. Power of a power: $(x^m)^n = x^{(m*n)}$
    4. Negative exponent: $x^{-n} = 1/x^n$
    5. Fractional exponent: $x^{(m/n)} = $ nth root of x^m
- **ROOTS:**
  - Examples: $\sqrt{16} = 4$ (because $4^2 = 16$)
  - Types: Square root ($\sqrt{}$), cube root ($3\sqrt{}$), etc.

  EXAMPLE:

Simplify the expression $2^4 / 2^2$.

SOLUTION:

Using the division rule: $2^4 / 2^2 = 2^{(4-2)} = 2^2 = 4$

PROBLEM QUESTION:

Solve the equation $x^3 = 27$.

SOLUTION:

Take the cube root of both sides: $3\sqrt{x^3} = 3\sqrt{27}$

Simplify: $x = 3$

5.2 ALGEBRA

Algebra is a powerful branch of mathematics that uses symbols and equations to represent and solve problems. This section delves into the core concepts of algebra that are frequently tested on the PSAT 8/9 Math section. It covers linear equations and inequalities, systems of equations, functions, and graphs.

Linear Equations and Inequalities

Linear equations are equations where the highest power of the variable is 1. They represent straight lines when graphed. Linear inequalities involve inequality symbols ($<, >, \leq, \geq$) and represent a range of values that satisfy the inequality.

- **LINEAR EQUATIONS:**

  o Standard form: $ax + by = c$

  o Slope-intercept form: $y = mx + b$ ($m =$ slope, $b =$ y-intercept)

  o Point-slope form: $y - y1 = m(x - x1)$ ($m =$ slope, $(x1, y1) =$ a point on the line)

  o Solving: Isolate the variable by performing inverse operations on both sides of the equation.

- **LINEAR INEQUALITIES:**

  o Solving: Similar to solving equations, but remember to flip the inequality symbol when multiplying or dividing both sides by a negative number.

  o Graphing: Represent the solution set on a number line or coordinate plane by shading the region that satisfies the inequality.

EXAMPLE:

Solve the linear equation $2x + 5 = 11$.

SOLUTION:

Subtract 5 from both sides: $2x = 6$

Divide both sides by 2: $x = 3$

PROBLEM QUESTION:

Solve the linear inequality $3x - 7 < 5$.

SOLUTION:

Add 7 to both sides: $3x < 12$

Divide both sides by 3: $x < 4$

Systems of Equations

Systems of equations involve two or more equations with multiple variables. Solving a system of equations means finding the values of the variables that satisfy all the equations simultaneously.

- **METHODS FOR SOLVING:**

  o Substitution: Solve one equation for one variable and substitute it into the other equation(s).

  o Elimination: Multiply one or both equations by constants to make the coefficients of one variable match, then add or subtract the equations to eliminate that variable.

  o Graphing: Graph the equations and find the point(s) of intersection.

- **TYPES OF SOLUTIONS:**

  o One solution: The lines intersect at a single point.

  o No solution: The lines are parallel and never intersect.

  o Infinitely many solutions: The lines are the same and overlap.

  EXAMPLE:

  Solve the system of equations:

  $x + y = 5 \quad 2x - y = 1$

  SOLUTION:

Using elimination, add the two equations together:

$3x = 6$

Divide both sides by 3: $x = 2$

Substitute $x = 2$ into either equation to solve for y:

$2 + y = 5$

Subtract 2 from both sides: $y = 3$

PROBLEM QUESTION:

Solve the system of equations:

$y = 2x + 1 \quad y = -x + 4$

SOLUTION:

Using substitution, since both equations are solved for y, set them equal to each other:

$2x + 1 = -x + 4$

Add x to both sides: $3x + 1 = 4$

Subtract 1 from both sides: $3x = 3$

Divide both sides by 3: $x = 1$

Substitute $x = 1$ into either equation to solve for y:

$y = 2(1) + 1 =$

Functions and Graphs

Functions are mathematical relationships where each input (x-value) has exactly one output (y-value). Graphs visually represent functions, plotting the input-output pairs on a coordinate plane.

- **FUNCTION NOTATION:** $f(x) = y$ (read as "f of x equals y")

- **TYPES OF FUNCTIONS:**

  o Linear: $f(x) = mx + b$ (graph is a straight line)

  o Quadratic: $f(x) = ax^2 + bx + c$ (graph is a parabola)

  o Exponential: $f(x) = a^x$ (graph shows exponential growth or decay)

- **KEY FEATURES OF GRAPHS:**

  o x-intercept: where the graph crosses the x-axis ($y = 0$)

  o y-intercept: where the graph crosses the y-axis ($x = 0$)

  o Slope: the steepness of a line (rise/run)

  o Vertex: the highest or lowest point on a parabola

EXAMPLE:

Evaluate the function $f(x) = 2x + 3$ for $x = 4$.

SOLUTION:

Substitute $x = 4$ into the function: $f(4) = 2(4) + 3 = 8 + 3 = 11$

PROBLEM QUESTION:

Find the x-intercept of the linear function $f(x) = 3x - 6$.

SOLUTION:

Set $f(x) = 0$ and solve for x:

$0 = 3x - 6$

Add 6 to both sides: $6 = 3x$

Divide both sides by 3: $x = 2$

5.3 GEOMETRY

Geometry is the study of shapes, sizes, positions, and dimensions of objects in space. This section delves into the core concepts of geometry that are frequently tested on the PSAT 8/9 Math section. It covers lines, angles, triangles, circles, quadrilaterals, area, perimeter, and volume.

Lines, Angles, and Triangles

- **LINES:** A line is a straight path that extends infinitely in both directions.
  - Parallel lines: Two lines that never intersect.
  - Perpendicular lines: Two lines that intersect at a 90-degree angle.
- **ANGLES:** An angle is formed by two rays that share a common endpoint (vertex).
  - Types of angles: Acute (<90°), right (90°), obtuse (>90°), straight (180°)
  - Complementary angles: Two angles that add up to 90°.
  - Supplementary angles: Two angles that add up to 180°.
  - Vertical angles: Angles opposite each other when two lines intersect; they are always equal.

- **TRIANGLES:** A triangle is a three-sided polygon.
  - Types of triangles: Scalene (no equal sides), isosceles (two equal sides), equilateral (three equal sides), right (one right angle)
  - Angle sum property: The angles in a triangle add up to 180°.
  - Pythagorean theorem: In a right triangle, $a^2 + b^2 = c^2$, where a and b are the legs and c is the hypotenuse.

PROBLEM QUESTION:

A right triangle has legs of length 6 cm and 8 cm. What is the length of the hypotenuse?

SOLUTION:

Using the Pythagorean theorem:

$$a^2 + b^2 = c^2$$

$$6^2 + 8^2 = c^2$$

$$36 + 64 = c^2$$

$$100 = c^2$$

$$c = 10 \text{ cm}$$

Circles and Quadrilaterals

- **CIRCLES:** A circle is a set of points equidistant from a central point (center).
  - Radius: The distance from the center to any point on the circle.
  - Diameter: The distance across the circle through the center (twice the radius).
  - Circumference: The distance around the circle ($C = \pi d$ or $C = 2\pi r$).
  - Area: The space enclosed by the circle ($A = \pi r^2$).
- **QUADRILATERALS:** A quadrilateral is a four-sided polygon.
  - Types of quadrilaterals: Parallelogram (opposite sides parallel), rectangle (all angles 90°), square (all sides equal, all angles 90°), rhombus (all sides equal), trapezoid (one pair of parallel sides)
  - Angle sum property: The angles in a quadrilateral add up to 360°.

EXAMPLE:

A circle has a diameter of 10 cm. What is its circumference?

SOLUTION:

Using the circumference formula:

$$C = \pi d = \pi (10 \text{ cm}) = 10\pi \text{ cm}$$

PROBLEM QUESTION:

A rectangle has a length of 12 cm and a width of 8 cm. What is its area?

SOLUTION:

Using the area formula:

$A = lw = (12 \text{ cm})(8 \text{ cm}) = 96 \text{ cm}^2$

Area, Perimeter, and Volume

- **AREA:** The amount of space inside a two-dimensional shape.
  - Formulas:
    - Triangle: $A = (1/2) bh$ (b = base, h = height)
    - Square: $A = s^2$ (s = side length)
    - Rectangle: $A = lw$ (l = length, w = width)
    - Parallelogram: $A = bh$ (b = base, h = height)
    - Trapezoid: $A = (1/2) h (b1 + b2)$ (h = height, $b1$ and $b2$ = bases)
    - Circle: $A = \pi r^2$ (r = radius)
- **PERIMETER:** The total distance around the outside of a two-dimensional shape.
  - Formulas: Sum of the lengths of all sides
- **VOLUME:** The amount of space inside a three-dimensional object.
  - Formulas:
    - Cube: $V = s^3$ (s = side length)
    - Rectangular prism: $V = lwh$ (l = length, w = width, h = height)
    - Cylinder: $V = \pi r^2 h$ (r = radius, h = height)
    - Cone: $V = (1/3) \pi r^2 h$ (r = radius, h = height)
    - Sphere: $V = (4/3) \pi r^3$ (r = radius)

EXAMPLE:

A triangle has a base of 10 cm and a height of 6 cm. What is its area?

SOLUTION:

Using the area formula:

$A = (1/2)bh = (1/2)(10 \text{ cm})(6 \text{ cm}) = 30 \text{ cm}^2$

PROBLEM QUESTION:

A rectangular prism has a length of 8 cm, a width of 5 cm, and a height of 4 cm. What is its volume?

SOLUTION:

Using the volume formula:

$V = lwh = (8 \text{ cm})(5 \text{ cm})(4 \text{ cm}) = 160 \text{ cm}^3$

5.4 DATA ANALYSIS AND STATISTICS

Data analysis and statistics involve collecting, organizing, analyzing, and interpreting data to draw meaningful conclusions and make informed decisions. This section delves into the core concepts of data analysis and statistics that are frequently tested on the PSAT 8/9 Math section. It covers mean, median, mode, range, interpreting data from tables and graphs, probability, and data representation.

Mean, Median, Mode, and Range

These are basic measures used to describe a set of data:

- **MEAN:** The average of all the numbers in a data set. Calculated by adding all the numbers and dividing by the total number of values.

- **MEDIAN:** The middle value when the data set is arranged in order. If there are two middle values, the median is their average.

- **MODE:** The value that appears most frequently in a data set. A data set can have one mode, more than one mode, or no mode at all.

- **RANGE:** The difference between the largest and smallest values in a data set.

EXAMPLE:

Consider the following data set: 2, 4, 4, 6, 8, 10

- Mean: $(2 + 4 + 4 + 6 + 8 + 10) / 6 = 34 / 6 = 5.67$

- Median: The middle values are 4 and 6, so the median is (4 + 6) / 2 = 5

- Mode: The value 4 appears most frequently, so the mode is 4

- Range: 10 - 2 = 8

PROBLEM QUESTION:

The scores on a quiz are: 70, 75, 80, 85, 90, 90, 95. Find the mean, median, mode, and range of the scores.

SOLUTION:

- Mean: (70 + 75 + 80 + 85 + 90 + 90 + 95) / 7 = 685 / 7 = 97.86

- Median: The middle value is 85, so the median is 85.

- Mode: The value 90 appears most frequently, so the mode is 90.

- Range: 95 - 70 = 25

Interpreting Data from Tables and Graphs

Data is often presented in tables and graphs to make it easier to understand and analyze. Common types of graphs include:

- **BAR GRAPHS:** Use bars to represent data values.

- **LINE GRAPHS:** Use lines to show trends over time.

- **PIE CHARTS:** Use slices to represent proportions of a whole.

- **SCATTER PLOTS:** Use points to show the relationship between two variables.

Interpreting data from tables and graphs involves understanding the type of graph, reading the labels and scales, and identifying trends, patterns, and relationships in the data.

PROBLEM QUESTION:

A pie chart shows that 30% of students prefer pizza, 25% prefer burgers, and 45% prefer pasta. If there are 200 students in total, how many prefer pasta?

SOLUTION:

Calculate the number of students who prefer pasta: 200 x 45/100 = 90 students

Probability and Data Representation

Probability is the likelihood of an event occurring. It is expressed as a number between 0 and 1, where 0 indicates impossibility and 1 indicates certainty.

- **CALCULATING PROBABILITY:**
  - Probability = (Number of favorable outcomes) / (Total number of possible outcomes)
- **DATA REPRESENTATION:**
  - Data can be represented in various ways, including tables, graphs, and charts. The choice of representation depends on the type of data and the purpose of the analysis.

EXAMPLE:

A bag contains 5 red balls and 3 blue balls. What is the probability of drawing a red ball?

SOLUTION:

- Number of favorable outcomes: 5 (red balls)
- Total number of possible outcomes: 8 (total balls)
- Probability = 5/8

PROBLEM QUESTION:

A coin is flipped twice. What is the probability of getting heads both times?

SOLUTION:

- Possible outcomes: HH, HT, TH, TT (4 total)
- Favorable outcome: HH (1)
- Probability = 1/4

5.5 PROBLEM-SOLVING STRATEGIES

Solving math problems often requires more than just knowing formulas and procedures. It involves strategic thinking, logical reasoning, and effective problem-solving techniques. This section delves into essential problem-solving strategies that are crucial for success on the PSAT 8/9 Math section. It covers breaking down complex problems, using diagrams and visual aids, and checking your work.

Breaking Down Complex Problems

Complex math problems can seem daunting at first glance. However, by breaking them down into smaller, more manageable steps, you can make them easier to tackle.

- **READ THE PROBLEM CAREFULLY:** Start by reading the problem carefully, paying attention to the keywords, given information, and what you're asked to find.

- **IDENTIFY THE KEY INFORMATION:** Highlight or underline the key information and any relevant formulas or concepts.

- **DEVISE A PLAN:** Determine a strategy for solving the problem. This might involve using a formula, drawing a diagram, or working backward.

- **SOLVE STEP-BY-STEP:** Break the problem down into smaller steps and solve each step systematically.

- **CHECK FOR REASONABLENESS:** Once you have an answer, check if it makes sense in the context of the problem.

EXAMPLE:

A train travels 200 miles at an average speed of 50 miles per hour. How long does it take the train to complete the journey?

SOLUTION:

1. Identify the key information: distance = 200 miles, speed = 50 miles per hour, time =?

2. Formula: time = distance / speed

3. Solve: time = 200 miles / 50 miles per hour = 4 hours

4. Check: Does 4 hours seem like a reasonable time for a train to travel 200 miles at 50 miles per hour? Yes, it does.

Using Diagrams and Visual Aids

Diagrams and visual aids can be powerful tools for understanding and solving math problems. They help to visualize the problem, organize information, and identify relationships between different elements.

- **TYPES OF DIAGRAMS:**
  o Geometric diagrams: For problems involving shapes and figures.
  o Number lines: For problems involving integers and inequalities.
  o Graphs and charts: For problems involving data analysis and statistics.
  o Tree diagrams: For problems involving probability and combinations.

- **BENEFITS OF USING DIAGRAMS:**
  o Clarify the problem
  o Organize information
  o Identify patterns and relationships
  o Reduce errors

Checking Your Work

Checking your work is crucial for ensuring accuracy and avoiding careless mistakes. It helps to identify errors and build confidence in your solutions.

- **METHODS FOR CHECKING:**

- Re-read the problem and check if you answered the question asked.
- Substitute your answer back into the original equation or problem to see if it works.
- Use estimation to check if your answer is reasonable.
- Try a different method to solve the problem and see if you get the same answer.
- If time permits, redo the problem from scratch.

EXAMPLE:

Solve the equation $3x + 5 = 14$.

SOLUTION:

1. Subtract 5 from both sides: $3x = 9$
2. Divide both sides by 3: $x = 3$
3. Check: Substitute $x = 3$ back into the original equation: $3(3) + 5 = 9 + 5 = 14$. The answer checks out.

5.6 CALCULATOR TIPS AND STRATEGIES

Calculators are invaluable tools for solving math problems, especially on standardized tests like the PSAT 8/9. This section delves into essential calculator tips and strategies to help you maximize your efficiency and accuracy on the Math section. It covers understanding calculator functions and using your calculator effectively on the test.

Understanding Calculator Functions

Familiarizing yourself with your calculator's functions is crucial for utilizing it effectively. While basic operations like addition, subtraction, multiplication, and division are straightforward, many calculators offer advanced functions that can save you time and effort.

- **BASIC OPERATIONS:** Ensure you know how to perform basic arithmetic operations, including using parentheses to control the order of operations.

  - Example: $(3 + 5) \times 2 = 16$, whereas $3 + 5 \times 2 = 13$

- **FRACTIONS:** Learn how to input, simplify, and perform operations with fractions on your calculator.

o Example: To enter 1/2, use the fraction key or divide 1 by 2.

- **DECIMALS:** Understand how to input and perform operations with decimals, including converting between fractions and decimals.

- **EXPONENTS AND ROOTS:** Utilize the exponent key (^ or y^x) for calculations involving exponents and the root key (√ or x√y) for finding roots.

- **TRIGONOMETRIC FUNCTIONS:** If your calculator has trigonometric functions (sin, cos, tan), learn how to use them for problems involving angles and triangles.

- **LOGARITHMIC AND EXPONENTIAL FUNCTIONS:** Familiarize yourself with logarithmic (log) and exponential (e^x) functions if your calculator supports them.

- **MEMORY FUNCTIONS:** Utilize memory functions (M+, M-, MR, MC) to store and recall values, especially in multi-step problems.

- **GRAPHING FUNCTIONS:** If you have a graphing calculator, learn how to graph equations, find intercepts, and analyze functions visually.

EXAMPLE:

Calculate the value of 5^3 - √64 using your calculator.

SOLUTION:

Enter 5^3 - √64 into your calculator, ensuring you use the correct keys for exponents and square roots. The answer is 117.

Using Your Calculator Effectively on the Test

While calculators can be helpful, it's essential to use them strategically and avoid over-reliance. Here are some tips for using your calculator effectively on the PSAT 8/9 Math section:

- **KNOW WHEN TO USE IT:** Don't reach for your calculator for every problem. Some problems can be solved more quickly using mental math or estimation.

- **ESTIMATE FIRST:** Before using your calculator, estimate the answer to get a sense of the expected magnitude. This can help you catch errors.

- **INPUT CAREFULLY:** Double-check your inputs to avoid making mistakes. A single incorrect keystroke can lead to a wrong answer.

- **UNDERSTAND THE PROBLEM:** Don't blindly rely on your calculator. Ensure you understand the problem and the concepts involved before using your calculator.

- **USE APPROPRIATE FUNCTIONS:** Utilize the appropriate calculator functions for the task at hand. Don't waste time trying to solve a problem manually when your calculator has a built-in function for it.

- **CHECK YOUR WORK:** Even with a calculator, it's crucial to check your work. Re-read the problem, check your inputs, and ensure your answer makes sense in the context of the problem.

- **PRACTICE WITH YOUR CALCULATOR:** Familiarize yourself with your calculator's functions and practice using it for various types of problems before the test.

EXAMPLE:

A store offers a 20% discount on a shirt originally priced at $25. What is the sale price of the shirt?

SOLUTION:

While you could calculate this manually, using your calculator can be quicker and more efficient.

1. Calculate the discount: 25 x 20 / 100 = 5

2. Subtract the discount from the original price: 25 - 5 = 20

The sale price of the shirt is $20.

CHAPTER 6: ESSENTIAL TEST-TAKING STRATEGIES

6.1 TIME MANAGEMENT

Time management is a critical skill for success on standardized tests, especially the PSAT 8/9, where you have limited time to answer a significant number of questions. This section delves into essential time management strategies to help you maximize your efficiency and performance on the test. It covers pacing yourself for each section, skipping and returning to difficult questions, and making the most of your break time.

Pacing Yourself for Each Section

Each section of the PSAT 8/9 has a specific time limit. To ensure you have enough time to answer all the questions, it's crucial to pace yourself effectively.

- **KNOW THE TIME LIMITS:** Familiarize yourself with the time allotted for each section:
  - Reading Test: 60 minutes for 47 questions
  - Writing and Language Test: 35 minutes for 44 questions
  - Math Test: 70 minutes for 48 questions (No Calculator: 25 minutes for 17 questions; Calculator: 45 minutes for 31 questions)
- **Allocate time per question:** Divide the total time for each section by the number of questions to get an approximate time per question. However, remember that some questions might take longer than others.

- **Practice pacing:** During your practice tests, simulate the actual test conditions and practice pacing yourself to get a feel for how much time you can spend on each question.
- **Don't get bogged down:** If you find yourself spending too much time on a question, skip it and move on. You can always return to it later if you have time.
- **Use a watch or timer:** Keep track of time using a watch or timer to avoid losing track of your pace.

EXAMPLE:

In the Reading Test, you have 60 minutes to answer 47 questions. This gives you approximately 1 minute and 17 seconds per question. However, some passages might be longer or more complex, requiring more time. Therefore, it's crucial to pace yourself accordingly and not spend too much time on any single question.

Skipping and Returning to Difficult Questions

Encountering difficult questions is inevitable on the PSAT 8/9. Knowing when to skip a question and return to it later is a valuable time management strategy.

- **DON'T DWELL ON DIFFICULT QUESTIONS:** If you're struggling with a question, don't spend too much time on it. Mark it for review and move on to the next question.

- **PRIORITIZE EASIER QUESTIONS:** Focus on answering the easier questions first to maximize your score. You can always return to the more challenging questions later if you have time.

- **USE THE "MARK FOR REVIEW" FEATURE:** The digital PSAT 8/9 allows you to mark questions for review. This feature lets you easily return to skipped questions later.

- **DON'T LEAVE QUESTIONS BLANK:** If you have time at the end of a section, revisit the skipped questions. Even if you're unsure of the answer, make an educated guess. There's no penalty for wrong answers on the PSAT 8/9.

EXAMPLE:

If you encounter a challenging math problem that you're unsure how to solve, mark it for review and move on to the next question. Once you've answered all the easier questions, return to the marked question and try to solve it. If you're still stuck, make an educated guess and move on to the next marked question.

Making the Most of Your Break Time

The PSAT 8/9 includes breaks between sections. Utilize these breaks effectively to refresh yourself and prepare for the next section.

- **TAKE SHORT BREAKS:** Get up and stretch, move around, or go to the restroom to avoid getting stiff or fatigued.
- **STAY HYDRATED:** Drink water to stay hydrated and maintain focus.
- **AVOID DISTRACTIONS:** Don't engage in activities that might distract you or drain your mental energy, such as checking your phone or engaging in intense conversations.
- **REFOCUS YOUR MIND:** Take a few deep breaths and mentally prepare yourself for the next section.

- **REVIEW STRATEGIES:** IF needed, quickly review any strategies or formulas relevant to the upcoming section.

EXAMPLE:

During the break between the Reading Test and the Writing and Language Test, get up and stretch your legs, drink some water, and take a few deep breaths to refocus your mind. You can also quickly review any grammar or punctuation rules that you might have struggled with in your practice tests.

6.2 GUESSING STRATEGIES

Guessing strategically can be a valuable tool on standardized tests like the PSAT 8/9, where every point counts. This section delves into essential guessing strategies to help you maximize your score. It covers understanding the scoring system, knowing when to guess and when to leave a question blank, and effectively using the process of elimination.

Understanding the Scoring System

The PSAT 8/9 employs a unique scoring system that rewards correct answers and does not penalize incorrect answers. This means there's no reason to leave any question unanswered.

- **NO PENALTY FOR WRONG ANSWERS:** Unlike some standardized tests that deduct points for incorrect answers, the PSAT 8/9 only awards points for correct answers. This eliminates the risk of losing points for guessing.

- **RAW SCORE:** Your raw score is calculated by simply adding up the number of correct answers in each section.

- **SCALED SCORE:** Your raw score is then converted to a scaled score, which takes into account the difficulty of the test. Scaled scores allow for comparison across different test administrations.

- **SECTION SCORES:** You receive a scaled score for each section (Reading, Writing and Language, and Math), ranging from 120 to 720.

- **TOTAL SCORE:** Your total score is the sum of your three section scores, ranging from 360 to 2160.

EXAMPLE:

If you answer 30 questions correctly on the Reading Test, your raw score for that section would be 30. This raw score is then converted to a scaled score, which might be, for example, 600.

When to Guess and When to Leave a Question Blank

While there's no penalty for wrong answers on the PSAT 8/9, it's still essential to guess strategically.

- **GUESS WHEN YOU CAN ELIMINATE AT LEAST ONE ANSWER CHOICE:** If you can eliminate at least one answer choice, your chances of guessing correctly increase significantly. The more choices you can eliminate, the higher your probability of guessing the right answer.

- **DON'T GUESS RANDOMLY:** Avoid random guessing if you have no idea about the answer. Instead, try to use logic, common sense, or any clues from the question or passage to make an educated guess.

- **DON'T LEAVE ANY QUESTION BLANK:** Since there's no penalty for wrong answers, it's always better to guess than to leave a question blank. Even a random guess gives you a chance of getting it right.

EXAMPLE:

If you're unsure of the answer to a multiple-choice question with four answer choices, but you can eliminate two of them, your chances of guessing correctly increase from 25% to 50%.

Using the Process of Elimination

The process of elimination is a powerful guessing strategy that involves eliminating answer choices that are clearly incorrect or unlikely. This narrows down your options and increases your chances of selecting the correct answer.

- **IDENTIFY OBVIOUSLY WRONG ANSWERS:** Start by eliminating answer choices that are clearly wrong based on your knowledge or understanding of the question.
- **LOOK FOR CLUES IN THE QUESTION OR PASSAGE:** Use any clues from the question or passage to eliminate answer choices that don't fit the context or information provided.
- **CONSIDER THE ANSWER CHOICES THEMSELVES:** Sometimes, the answer choices themselves can provide clues. Look for patterns, contradictions, or inconsistencies that might help you eliminate some options.

- **DON'T OVERTHINK IT:** If you've eliminated all the answer choices you can, don't overthink it. Trust your instincts and make your best guess from the remaining options.

EXAMPLE:

Consider the following question:

What is the capital of France?

(A) London (B) Paris (C) Rome (D) Berlin

You can immediately eliminate options (A), (C), and (D) because you know they are the capitals of other countries. This leaves you with the correct answer, (B) Paris.

6.3 MANAGING TEST ANXIETY

Test anxiety is a common experience for many students, and it can significantly impact your performance on standardized tests like the PSAT 8/9. This section delves into effective strategies for managing test anxiety, helping you approach the exam with confidence and composure. It covers relaxation techniques and stress management, building confidence through practice, and positive self-talk and visualization.

Relaxation Techniques and Stress Management

Test anxiety often manifests as physical and emotional symptoms, such as racing heartbeat, sweaty palms, difficulty concentrating, and negative thoughts. Relaxation techniques and stress management practices can help you calm your nerves and regain control.

- **DEEP BREATHING:** Deep breathing exercises can help slow your heart rate and reduce feelings of anxiety. Inhale slowly and deeply through your nose, hold for a few seconds, and exhale slowly through your mouth. Repeat several times until you feel more relaxed.

- **PROGRESSIVE MUSCLE RELAXATION:** This technique involves tensing and relaxing different muscle groups in your body to release tension and promote relaxation. Start with your toes, tense the muscles for a few seconds, then release. Move up to your calves, thighs, abdomen, arms, shoulders, and face, tensing and relaxing each muscle group.

- **MINDFULNESS MEDITATION:** Mindfulness meditation involves focusing on the present moment and accepting your thoughts and feelings without judgment. This can help you reduce anxiety and improve focus. Find a quiet place, close your eyes, and focus on your breath or a calming image.

- **PHYSICAL ACTIVITY:** Regular exercise can help reduce stress and improve your mood. Engage in activities you enjoy, such as walking, running, swimming, or yoga.

- **HEALTHY SLEEP HABITS:** Getting enough sleep is crucial for managing stress and performing your best on the test. Aim for 7-9 hours of quality sleep each night leading up to the exam.

- **HEALTHY DIET:** Eating a balanced diet can help regulate your mood and energy levels. Avoid sugary foods and caffeine, which can exacerbate anxiety.

EXAMPLE:

If you feel anxious before or during the test, take a few minutes to practice deep breathing. Inhale slowly and deeply, hold for a few seconds, and exhale slowly. Repeat this several times until you feel your heart rate slowing down and your anxiety subsiding.

Building Confidence Through Practice

One of the best ways to manage test anxiety is to build confidence through practice. The more familiar you are with the test format, content, and your own abilities, the less anxious you'll feel.

- **TAKE PRACTICE TESTS:** Simulate the actual test conditions by taking practice tests under timed conditions. This will help you get used to the format, pace yourself, and identify areas where you need to improve.
- **REVIEW YOUR MISTAKES:** After taking a practice test, carefully review your mistakes and understand why you got certain questions wrong. This will help you learn from your errors and avoid making the same mistakes on the actual test.
- **FOCUS ON YOUR STRENGTHS:** Identify your strengths in each section and focus on building upon them. This will boost your confidence and help you approach the test with a positive mindset.
- **SEEK HELP IF NEEDED:** If you're struggling with specific concepts or question types, don't hesitate to seek help from your teachers, tutors, or classmates. Understanding the material will increase your confidence and reduce anxiety.

EXAMPLE:

If you're feeling anxious about the Math section, take several practice math tests and focus on reviewing your mistakes. Identify the types of questions you tend to get wrong and seek help from your math teacher or a tutor to understand those concepts better.

Positive Self-Talk and Visualization

Positive self-talk and visualization can be powerful tools for managing test anxiety and boosting your confidence.

- **CHALLENGE NEGATIVE THOUGHTS:** When you experience negative thoughts about the test or your abilities, challenge them with positive affirmations. Replace thoughts like "I'm going to fail" with "I've prepared well and I'm capable of doing well."

- **VISUALIZE SUCCESS:** Imagine yourself taking the test with confidence and calmness, answering questions accurately, and achieving your desired score. Visualization can help you program your mind for success.

- **FOCUS ON YOUR PAST SUCCESSES:** Remind yourself of your past academic achievements and successes. This will help you build confidence in your abilities and approach the test with a positive attitude.

- **STAY POSITIVE:** Maintain a positive attitude throughout your preparation and on the test day. Believe in yourself and your ability to succeed.

EXAMPLE:

Before the test, take a few minutes to visualize yourself sitting in the testing room, feeling calm and focused, answering questions with confidence, and completing the test successfully. This visualization can help you reduce anxiety and approach the test with a positive mindset.

CHAPTER 7: ANALYZING YOUR PRACTICE TESTS

Practice tests are invaluable tools in your PSAT 8/9 preparation journey. However, their value extends beyond simply providing a simulated test experience. Analyzing your performance on practice tests is crucial for identifying your strengths and weaknesses, tracking your progress, developing a personalized study plan, and learning from your mistakes. This chapter delves into the strategies and techniques for effectively analyzing your practice tests to maximize your learning and improvement.

Identifying Your Strengths and Weaknesses

After completing a practice test, the first step is to identify your areas of strength and weakness. This involves a thorough analysis of your performance in each section and question type.

- **REVIEW EACH SECTION CAREFULLY:** Go through each section of the practice test and analyze your performance on each question. Pay attention to the types of questions you answered correctly and those you missed.

- **IDENTIFY PATTERNS:** Look for patterns in your mistakes. Are you consistently missing questions on a particular topic or concept? Are there specific question types that you struggle with?

- **CATEGORIZE YOUR WEAKNESSES:** Categorize your weaknesses based on the specific skills or knowledge gaps they reveal. This could include grammar rules, reading comprehension strategies, mathematical concepts, or test-taking techniques.

- **ACKNOWLEDGE YOUR STRENGTHS:** Don't just focus on your weaknesses. Identify your strengths in each section and acknowledge the areas where you excel. This can boost your confidence and motivation.

EXAMPLE:

After reviewing your practice test, you might notice that you consistently miss questions on punctuation in the Writing and Language section. This indicates a weakness in your understanding of punctuation rules, which you can address through targeted study and practice.

Developing a Personalized Study Plan

Based on your analysis of your strengths and weaknesses, and your progress tracking, you can develop a personalized study plan that targets your specific needs and goals.

- **PRIORITIZE YOUR WEAKNESSES:** Focus your study efforts on the areas where you identified weaknesses. Allocate more time and resources to those topics or question types.
- **BUILD ON YOUR STRENGTHS:** Don't neglect your strengths. Continue to practice and reinforce those areas to maintain your proficiency.
- **UTILIZE VARIOUS RESOURCES:** Use a variety of study materials, such as textbooks, online resources, practice questions, and flashcards, to cater to your learning style and preferences.
- **CREATE A SCHEDULE:** Create a realistic study schedule that allows for consistent and focused study sessions. Be mindful of your other commitments and allocate time accordingly.
- **REVIEW AND ADAPT:** Regularly review your study plan and make adjustments as needed. Your plan should be flexible and adaptable to your changing needs and progress.

EXAMPLE:

If you identified weaknesses in grammar and punctuation, your study plan might include reviewing grammar rules, practicing with punctuation exercises, and seeking help from your English teacher or a tutor.

Learning from Your Mistakes

Mistakes are inevitable in the learning process, but they offer valuable opportunities for growth and improvement. Analyzing your mistakes on practice tests can help you identify patterns, understand your misconceptions, and avoid repeating those errors on the actual test.

- **DON'T JUST LOOK AT THE CORRECT ANSWER:** When reviewing your mistakes, don't just focus on the correct answer. Try to understand why you chose the wrong answer and what led to your misconception.

- **IDENTIFY THE UNDERLYING CONCEPT:** Determine the underlying concept or skill that the question was testing. Review that concept and ensure you understand it thoroughly.

- **SEEK CLARIFICATION IF NEEDED:** If you're unsure why you got a question wrong, don't hesitate to seek clarification from your teachers, tutors, or classmates.

- **PRACTICE SIMILAR QUESTIONS:** Once you understand your mistake, practice similar questions to reinforce your understanding and avoid making the same error again.

EXAMPLE:

If you missed a math question involving fractions, review the rules for adding and subtracting fractions, practice with similar problems, and seek clarification from your math teacher if needed.

CHAPTER 8: PRACTICE MAKES PERFECT

PRACTICE TEST 1

1. **PASSAGE:**

In 1901, the dermatological community was abuzz with the publication of Alfred Blaschko's observations on the lines of the human body. While the lines don't relate to any known anatomical or biological systems, they are still acknowledged today as delineating the cell groups in the human body. Later research would show that Blaschko's lines are a form of mosaicism, wherein a single organism has two or more sets of cells with different genotypes.

QUESTION: Which choice best describes the overall structure of the text?

ANSWER CHOICES:

- (A) It presents a hypothesis and then explains how it was disproved.
- (B) It describes a discovery and then explains its significance.
- (C) It contrasts two different scientific methods.
- (D) It argues for a change in a research area.

Correct Answer: (B)

Explanation: The passage describes Blaschko's discovery of the lines of the human body and then explains the significance of this discovery, particularly that later research would show the lines are a form of mosaicism.

2. **PASSAGE:**

The radish-like root vegetable maca (Lepidium meyenii) is cultivated in the high altitudes of the Andes Mountains. It is an important part of the diet of many Andean people, who harvest it for its nutritional and medicinal properties. Maca is rich in carbohydrates and protein and contains various vitamins and minerals. It is also believed to have medicinal properties, such as boosting energy and improving mood.

QUESTION: In the first paragraph, the author discusses the fact that many Andean people harvest maca primarily to

ANSWER CHOICES:

- (A) highlight the nutritional benefits of a plant.
- (B) explain why a plant is in danger of extinction.

- (C) provide an example of a plant with medicinal properties.
- (D) detail the cultural significance of a plant.

Correct Answer: (A)

Explanation: The passage states that Andean people harvest maca for its nutritional and medicinal properties. Then, the passage goes on to highlight the nutritional benefits of maca, particularly that it is rich in carbohydrates and protein and contains various vitamins and minerals.

3. **PASSAGE:**

The 1960 musical Camelot was written by Alan Jay Lerner and Frederick Loewe. It is based on T.H. White's novel The Once and Future King and reaches a diverse audience through its exploration of multiple themes, including love, duty, and betrayal.

QUESTION: As used in the second sentence of the passage, what does the word "reaches" most nearly mean?

ANSWER CHOICES:

- (A) Accomplishes
- (B) Arrives at
- (C) Stretches to
- (D) Interacts with

Correct Answer: (A)

Explanation: The passage states that Camelot reaches a diverse audience through its

exploration of multiple themes. This means that the musical accomplishes reaching a diverse audience.

4. **PASSAGE:**

The phenomenon of a "phantom limb" occurs when an individual continues to feel sensations in a limb that has been amputated. While the biological mechanism by which this occurs is not fully understood, it is believed to be related to the brain's reorganization of sensory inputs. When a limb is amputated, the brain's corresponding sensory areas may become rewired to receive input from other body parts, leading to the perception of sensations in the missing limb.

QUESTION: Which choice best describes the overall structure of the text?

ANSWER CHOICES:

- (A) It describes a scientific phenomenon and then explains its cause.
- (B) It argues for a change in a scientific theory.
- (C) It contrasts two different scientific phenomena.
- (D) It explains how scientists arrived at a conclusion.

Correct Answer: (A)

Explanation: The passage describes the scientific phenomenon of a "phantom limb" and then explains its cause, particularly that it is related to the brain's reorganization of sensory inputs.

5. **PASSAGE:**

The term "Cambrian explosion" refers to the sudden appearance of complex life forms in the fossil record approximately 540 million years ago. This period marks a significant turning point in the history of life on Earth, as it witnessed the rapid diversification of animal life, including the evolution of many of the major animal groups we know today. The Cambrian explosion is a testament to the remarkable adaptive capacity of life and the profound impact of environmental change on evolutionary processes.

QUESTION: Which choice best describes the function of the first sentence in the overall structure of the text?

ANSWER CHOICES:

o (A) It describes a scientific phenomenon that is later shown to be a myth.

o (B) It presents a hypothesis that is later supported by the text.

o (C) It introduces a concept that is central to the rest of the discussion.

o (D) It makes an argument that is contradicted by the text.

Correct Answer: (C)

Explanation: The first sentence introduces the concept of the "Cambrian explosion,"

which is central to the rest of the discussion in the passage. The passage goes on to describe the significance of this period and its impact on the evolution of life on Earth.

6. **PASSAGE:**

The Chauvet Cave in France is home to some of the oldest and most well-preserved cave paintings in the world, dating back to the Aurignacian period, approximately 30,000 to 32,000 years ago. The paintings depict a variety of animals, including horses, lions, bears, and rhinoceroses, as well as human handprints and abstract symbols. The remarkable artistry and detail of these paintings provide a glimpse into the minds and lives of our early human ancestors.

QUESTION: Which choice best describes the function of the underlined sentence in the text as a whole?

ANSWER CHOICES:

o (A) It explains how scientists were able to determine the age of the cave paintings.

o (B) It highlights the cultural significance of the cave paintings.

o (C) It describes the technique used to create the cave paintings.

o (D) It details certain notable aspects of the cave paintings.

Correct Answer: (D)

Explanation: The underlined sentence details

certain notable aspects of the cave paintings, particularly that they depict a variety of animals, human handprints, and abstract symbols.

7. **PASSAGE:**

The Higgs boson, a fundamental particle that gives mass to other particles, was discovered in 2012 at the Large Hadron Collider (LHC). This discovery was a major milestone in particle physics, confirming a long-held theoretical prediction and providing a deeper understanding of the fundamental building blocks of the universe.

QUESTION: Which choice best states the main idea of the text?

ANSWER CHOICES:

o (A) The discovery of the Higgs boson confirmed a long-held scientific theory.

o (B) The Higgs boson is a fundamental particle that gives mass to other particles.

o (C) The Large Hadron Collider is a powerful tool for scientific discovery.

o (D) The search for the Higgs boson was a challenging but ultimately successful endeavor.

Correct Answer: (A)

Explanation: The main idea of the text is that the discovery of the Higgs boson confirmed a long-held scientific theory. The passage highlights the significance of this discovery in

the field of particle physics and its contribution to our understanding of the universe.

8. **PASSAGE:**

Mae C. Jemison, an American engineer, physician, and former NASA astronaut, made history in 1992 as the first African American woman to travel to space. Jemison's remarkable career exemplifies the power of pursuing one's dreams and breaking barriers in science and technology.

QUESTION: Which choice best states the main purpose of the text?

ANSWER CHOICES:

o (A) To describe the challenges of space exploration.

o (B) To highlight the contributions of women in science.

o (C) To detail the accomplishments of a notable scientist.

o (D) To explain the significance of a scientific discovery.

Correct Answer: (C)

Explanation: The main purpose of the text is to detail the accomplishments of Mae C. Jemison, a notable scientist and the first African American woman to travel to space. The passage highlights her remarkable career and its significance as an inspiration for pursuing dreams and breaking barriers.

9. **PASSAGE:**

The concept of "herd immunity" suggests that when a sufficiently high percentage of a population is immune to a contagious disease, the spread of the disease is effectively contained, protecting even those who are not immune. This occurs because the chain of transmission is broken, preventing the disease from spreading further. Herd immunity is a crucial factor in controlling outbreaks of infectious diseases and is often achieved through vaccination.

QUESTION: Which choice best describes the function of the underlined portion in the text as a whole?

ANSWER CHOICES:

o (A) It provides a definition of a key term.

o (B) It introduces a concept that is later refuted.

o (C) It states a claim that is supported by the text.

o (D) It presents an argument that is countered by the text.

Correct Answer: (A)

Explanation: The underlined portion provides a definition of the key term "herd immunity," explaining how it works and its significance in controlling infectious diseases.

10. **PASSAGE:**

The term "meme," coined by Richard Dawkins in his 1976 book The Selfish Gene, refers to a unit of cultural information that spreads from person to person through imitation or replication. Memes can take various forms, including ideas, behaviors, tunes, or any other cultural artifact that can be transmitted. The concept of memes has been influential in understanding how cultural information evolves and spreads within a society.

QUESTION: Which choice best states the main purpose of the text?

ANSWER CHOICES:

o (A) To explain the origins of a scientific term.

o (B) To argue for the importance of cultural transmission.

o (C) To describe the different forms that memes can take.

o (D) To highlight the influence of memes on social behavior.

Correct Answer: (A)

Explanation: The main purpose of the text is to explain the origins of the scientific term "meme," coined by Richard Dawkins in his book The Selfish Gene. The passage defines the term and briefly explains its significance in understanding cultural evolution.

11. In the early 20th century, the American artist Georgia O'Keeffe was a pioneering

figure in the modernist art movement, known for her bold and innovative depictions of flowers, landscapes, and New York City skyscrapers.

Question: Which choice completes the text so that it conforms to the conventions of Standard English?

Answer Choices:

o (A) NO CHANGE

o (B) movement, she was

o (C) movement being

o (D) movement, having been

Correct Answer: (A)

Explanation: The original sentence is grammatically correct and effectively conveys the information. The phrase "known for her bold and innovative depictions of flowers, landscapes, and New York City skyscrapers" is a participial phrase that correctly modifies the noun "figure."

12. The term "biomimicry," which combines the Greek words bios (life) and mimesis (imitation), refers to the practice of designing and developing technologies and materials inspired by nature.

Question: Which choice completes the text so that it conforms to the conventions of Standard English?

Answer Choices:

o (A) NO CHANGE

o (B) (life) and, mimesis

o (C) life) and mimesis,

o (D) life), and (imitation)

Correct Answer: (A)

Explanation: The original sentence is grammatically correct and effectively uses punctuation. The commas after "biomimicry" and "bios (life)" are correctly placed to set off the nonessential phrase.

13. The concept of "flow state," a term coined by psychologist Mihaly Csikszentmihalyi, describes a state of deep focus and immersion in an activity, characterized by a loss of self-consciousness and a sense of effortless action.

Question: Which choice completes the text so that it conforms to the conventions of Standard English?

Answer Choices:

o (A) NO CHANGE

o (B) activity. It is

o (C) activity being

o (D) activity, and is

Correct Answer: (A)

Explanation: The original sentence is grammatically correct and effectively conveys the information. The phrase "characterized by a loss of self-consciousness and a sense of effortless action" is a participial phrase that correctly modifies the noun "activity."

14. The Great Pacific Garbage Patch, a massive collection of marine debris in the

North Pacific Ocean, is a stark reminder of the environmental impact of human activities.

Question: Which choice completes the text so that it conforms to the conventions of Standard English?

Answer Choices:

- (A) NO CHANGE
- (B) Ocean, it is
- (C) Ocean being
- (D) Ocean, is

Correct Answer: (A)

Explanation: The original sentence is grammatically correct and effectively conveys the information. The phrase "a massive collection of marine debris in the North Pacific Ocean" is an appositive phrase that correctly renames the noun phrase "The Great Pacific Garbage Patch."

15. What is the value of x in the equation $3x + 7 = 22$?

16. (A) 3

(B) 5

(C) 7

(D) 9

Correct Answer: (B)

Explanation:

1. Subtract 7 from both sides: $3x = 15$
2. Divide both sides by 3: $x = 5$

16. What is the solution to the inequality $2x - 5 > 9$?

Answer Choices:

- (A) $x > 2$
- (B) $x > 4$
- (C) $x > 7$
- (D) $x > 9$

Correct Answer: (C)

Explanation:

- Add 5 to both sides: $2x > 14$
- Divide both sides by 2: $x > 7$

17. If $3x + 2y = 10$ and $x - y = 1$, what is the value of x?

Answer Choices:

- (A) 2
- (B) 3
- (C) 4
- (D) 5

Correct Answer: (C)

Explanation:

- Solve the second equation for x: $x = y + 1$
- Substitute this value of x into the first equation: $3(y + 1) + 2y = 10$
- Simplify and solve for y: $3y + 3 + 2y = 10$
  $5y = 7$ $y = 7/5$
- Substitute the value of y back into the equation $x = y + 1$: $x = 7/5 + 1 = 12/5 = 2.4$

18. If $f(x) = 2x - 5$, what is the value of $f(3)$?

Answer Choices:

- (A) 1

- (B) 3
- (C) 6
- (D) 11
- **Correct Answer:** (A)

  Explanation:

  Substitute x = 3 into the function: f(3) = 2(3) - 5 = 6 - 5 = 1

19. **Question:** What is the slope of the line that passes through the points (2, 5) and (4, 9)?

    Answer Choices:

    - (A) 1/2
    - (B) 1
    - (C) 2
    - (D) 4
    - **Correct Answer:** (C)

      Explanation:

      Use the slope formula: m = (y2 - y1) / (x2 - x1) = (9 - 5) / (4 - 2) = 4 / 2 = 2

20. **Question:** A triangle has angles measuring 30 degrees, 60 degrees, and x degrees. What is the value of x?

    Answer Choices:

    - (A) 30
    - (B) 60
    - (C) 90
    - (D) 120
    - **Correct Answer:** (C)

      Explanation:

      The angles in a triangle add up to 180 degrees. Therefore: 30 + 60 + x = 180 90 + x = 180 x = 90

21. **Question:** What is the product of the solutions to the equation x² - 5x + 6 = 0?

    Answer Choices:

    - (A) -6
    - (B) -5
    - (C) 5
    - (D) 6
    - **Correct Answer:** (D)

      Explanation:

      - Factor the quadratic equation: (x - 2) (x - 3) = 0
      - The solutions are x = 2 and x = 3.
      - The product of the solutions is 2 x 3 = 6.

22. **Question:** If 2^(x+1) = 16, what is the value of x?

    Answer Choices:

    - (A) 2
    - (B) 3
    - (C) 4
    - (D) 5
    - **Correct Answer:** (B)

      Explanation:

      - Express 16 as a power of 2: 16 = 2^4
      - Set the exponents equal to each other: x + 1 = 4
      - Solve for x: x = 3

23. **Question:** A rectangle has a length of 12 cm and a width of 8 cm. What is its

perimeter?

Answer Choices:

o (A) 20 cm

o (B) 40 cm

o (C) 96 cm

o (D) 192 cm

o **Correct Answer:** (B)

Explanation:

Perimeter of a rectangle = 2(length + width) = 2(12 + 8) = 2(20) = 40 cm

24. **Question:** A circle has a radius of 5 cm. What is its area?

Answer Choices:

o (A) 10π cm²

o (B) 25π cm²

o (C) 50π cm²

o (D) 100π cm²

o **Correct Answer:** (B)

Explanation:

Area of a circle = $\pi r^2 = \pi(5)^2 = 25\pi$ cm²

25. **Question:** The mean of the numbers 4, 8, 12, and x is 10. What is the value of x?

Answer Choices:

o (A) 10

o (B) 16

o (C) 20

o (D) 24

o **Correct Answer:** (B)

Explanation:

o Sum of the numbers = 4 + 8 + 12 + x = 24 + x

o Mean = (Sum of the numbers) / (Number of numbers) = (24 + x) / 4 = 10

o Solve for x: 24 + x = 40 x = 16

26. **Question:** What is the median of the following data set: 2, 5, 7, 9, 11, 12?

Answer Choices:

o (A) 7

o (B) 8

o (C) 9

o (D) 10

o **Correct Answer:** (B)

Explanation:

The median is the average of the two middle numbers when the data set is arranged in order. In this case, the middle numbers are 7 and 9, so the median is (7 + 9) / 2 = 8.

27. **Sentence:** The term "déjà vu," which is French for "already seen," refers to the eerie feeling of having experienced a situation before, even though you know you haven't.

Question: Which choice completes the text so that it conforms to the conventions of Standard English?

Answer Choices:

o (A) NO CHANGE

o (B) before even

o (C) before, but

o (D) before, although

- **Correct Answer:** (A)

Explanation: The original sentence is grammatically correct and effectively uses punctuation. The comma after "déjà vu" and the comma after "before" are correctly placed to set off the nonessential phrase.

28. **Sentence:** The concept of "sunk cost fallacy" describes the tendency for people to continue investing in something that has already cost them time, money, or effort, even if it's no longer rational to do so.

Question: Which choice completes the text so that it conforms to the conventions of Standard English?

Answer Choices:

- (A) NO CHANGE
- (B) effort even
- (C) effort, even,
- (D) effort; even
- **Correct Answer:** (A)

Explanation: The original sentence is grammatically correct and effectively conveys the information. The phrase "even if it's no longer rational to do so" is a subordinate clause that correctly modifies the verb phrase "continue investing."

29. **Sentence:** The term "cognitive dissonance" refers to the mental discomfort experienced when holding two

or more contradictory beliefs, ideas, or values.

Question: Which choice completes the text so that it conforms to the conventions of Standard English?

Answer Choices:

- (A) NO CHANGE
- (B) beliefs, ideas or,
- (C) beliefs ideas, or
- (D) beliefs, ideas, or,
- **Correct Answer:** (A)

Explanation: The original sentence is grammatically correct and effectively uses punctuation. The commas after "beliefs" and "ideas" are correctly placed to separate the items in the list.

30. **Sentence:** The phenomenon of "confirmation bias" occurs when people tend to favor information that confirms their existing beliefs or hypotheses.

Question: Which choice completes the text so that it conforms to the conventions of Standard English?

Answer Choices:

- (A) NO CHANGE
- (B) when people, tend
- (C) when people tend,
- (D) when, people, tend
- **Correct Answer:** (A)

Explanation: The original sentence is grammatically correct and effectively conveys the information. The adverbial clause "when people tend to favor information that confirms their existing beliefs or hypotheses" correctly modifies the verb "occurs."

31. **Sentence:** The "mere-exposure effect" suggests that people tend to develop a preference for things merely because they are familiar with them.

    Question: Which choice completes the text so that it conforms to the conventions of Standard English?

    Answer Choices:

    o (A) NO CHANGE

    o (B) for things, merely,

    o (C) for things merely,

    o (D) for, things, merely

    o **Correct Answer:** (A)

    Explanation: The original sentence is grammatically correct and clearly conveys the meaning. The adverb "merely" modifies the adverbial phrase "because they are familiar with them," and no additional punctuation is needed.

32. **Question:** If 5x - 3 = 12, what is the value of x?

    Answer Choices:

    o (A) 1.8

    o (B) 2.4

    o (C) 3

    o (D) 3.6

o **Correct Answer:** (C)

Explanation:

o Add 3 to both sides: $5x = 15$

o Divide both sides by 5: $x = 3$

33. **Question:** What is the solution to the inequality $4x + 6 \leq 22$?

    Answer Choices:

    o (A) $x \leq 2$

    o (B) $x \leq 4$

    o (C) $x \leq 6$

    o (D) $x \leq 8$

    o **Correct Answer:** (B)

    Explanation:

    o Subtract 6 from both sides: $4x \leq 16$

    o Divide both sides by 4: $x \leq 4$

34. **Question:** If $2x + y = 7$ and $x - 2y = -4$, what is the value of y?

    Answer Choices:

    o (A) 1

    o (B) 2

    o (C) 3

    o (D) 4

    o **Correct Answer:** (C)

    Explanation:

    o Multiply the first equation by 2: $4x + 2y = 14$

    o Add this equation to the second equation: $5x = 10$

    o Solve for x: $x = 2$

○ Substitute the value of x into either original equation to solve for y. Using the first equation: $2(2) + y = 7\ 4 + y = 7\ y = 3$

35. **Question:** If $f(x) = 3x^2 - 2x + 1$, what is the value of $f(-1)$?

Answer Choices:

○ (A) -4

○ (B) 0

○ (C) 2

○ (D) 6

○ **Correct Answer:** (D)

Explanation:

Substitute $x = -1$ into the function: $f(-1) = 3(-1)^2 - 2(-1) + 1 = 3 + 2 + 1 = 6$

36. **Question:** What is the slope of the line represented by the equation $2x - 3y = 6$?

Answer Choices:

○ (A) -2/3

○ (B) -1/3

○ (C) 2/3

○ (D) 3/2

○ **Correct Answer:** (C)

Explanation:

○ Rewrite the equation in slope-intercept form $(y = mx + b)$: $-3y = -2x + 6\ y = (2/3)x - 2$

○ The slope (m) is 2/3.

37. **Question:** A triangle has sides of length 5 cm, 12 cm, and 13 cm. Is it a right triangle?

Answer Choices:

○ (A) Yes, because $5^2 + 12^2 = 13^2$

○ (B) No, because $5^2 + 12^2 \neq 13^2$

○ (C) Yes, because it is a scalene triangle.

○ (D) No, because it is an isosceles triangle.

○ **Correct Answer:** (A)

Explanation:

A triangle is a right triangle if it satisfies the Pythagorean theorem $(a^2 + b^2 = c^2)$, where c is the hypotenuse (the longest side). In this case, $5^2 + 12^2 = 25 + 144 = 169 = 13^2$, so it is a right triangle.

38. **Question:** What is the circumference of a circle with a diameter of 14 cm?

Answer Choices:

○ (A) 7π cm

○ (B) 14π cm

○ (C) 28π cm

○ (D) 49π cm

○ **Correct Answer:** (B)

Explanation:

Circumference of a circle = $\pi d = \pi(14\ cm) = 14\pi$ cm

39. **Question:** The data set 2, 4, 6, 8, 10, and x has a mean of 7. What is the value of x?

Answer Choices:

○ (A) 7

○ (B) 12

○ (C) 14

○ (D) 16

o Correct Answer: (B)

Explanation:

o Sum of the numbers = 2 + 4 + 6 + 8 + 10 + x = 30 + x

o Mean = (Sum of the numbers) / (Number of numbers) = (30 + x) / 6 = 7

o Solve for x: 30 + x = 42 x = 12

40. Question: What is the mode of the following data set: 3, 5, 5, 7, 8, 8, 8, 9?

Answer Choices:

o (A) 5

o (B) 7

o (C) 8

o (D) 9

o Correct Answer: (C)

Explanation:

The mode is the value that appears most frequently in the data set. In this case, the value 8 appears three times, which is more than any other value.

41. Passage:

The rise of social media platforms has significantly transformed the way people communicate and interact. These platforms have facilitated the creation of online communities and fostered connections across geographical boundaries. However, the pervasive nature of social media has also raised concerns about its impact on mental health, social interactions, and the spread of misinformation.

Question: Which choice best reflects the author's perspective on social media?

Answer Choices:

• (A) Social media has had a uniformly positive impact on society.

• (B) Social media has had a uniformly negative impact on society.

• (C) Social media has had both positive and negative impacts on society.

• (D) Social media's impact on society is negligible.

Correct Answer: (C)

Explanation: The author acknowledges both the positive and negative aspects of social media, highlighting its role in facilitating connections and creating online communities, while also expressing concerns about its impact on mental health and the spread of misinformation.

42. Passage:

The term "neuroplasticity" refers to the brain's ability to reorganize itself by forming new neural connections throughout life. This remarkable capacity allows the brain to adapt to new experiences, learn new skills, and even recover from injuries. Neuroplasticity is a testament to the brain's dynamic nature and its ability to change and evolve in response to its environment.

Question: Which choice best describes the function of the underlined sentence in the text as a whole?

Answer Choices:

- (A) It provides a definition of a key term.
- (B) It introduces a concept that is later refuted.
- (C) It states a claim that is supported by the text.
- (D) It presents an argument that is countered by the text.

Correct Answer: (C)

Explanation: The underlined sentence states a claim about the brain's ability to adapt and recover, which is supported by the explanation of neuroplasticity and its role in forming new neural connections.

43. **Passage:**

The discovery of penicillin, the first antibiotic, revolutionized medicine and led to the development of numerous life-saving treatments for bacterial infections.

However, the overuse and misuse of antibiotics have contributed to the emergence of antibiotic-resistant bacteria, posing a significant threat to public health.

Question: Which choice best reflects the author's perspective on antibiotics?

Answer Choices:

- (A) Antibiotics are a universally beneficial medical advancement.
- (B) Antibiotics should be avoided entirely due to the risk of resistance.
- (C) Antibiotics are valuable but should be used responsibly to mitigate resistance.
- (D) The benefits of antibiotics outweigh the risks of resistance.

Correct Answer: (C)

Explanation: The author acknowledges the revolutionary impact of antibiotics but also expresses concern about the consequences of their overuse and misuse, suggesting a need for responsible use to mitigate the risk of antibiotic resistance.

44. **Sentence:** The term "imposter syndrome" describes the psychological phenomenon in which individuals doubt their accomplishments and fear being exposed as a fraud, despite evidence of their competence.

Question: Which choice completes the text so that it conforms to the conventions of Standard English?

Answer Choices:

- (A) NO CHANGE
- (B) fraud. Despite
- (C) fraud despite,
- (D) fraud, despite,

Correct Answer: (A)

Explanation: The original sentence is grammatically correct and effectively conveys the information. The phrase "despite evidence of their competence" is a prepositional phrase that correctly modifies the verb "fear."

45. **Sentence:** The concept of "growth mindset," developed by psychologist Carol Dweck, emphasizes the belief that abilities and intelligence can be developed through dedication and hard work.

Question: Which choice completes the text so that it conforms to the conventions of Standard English?

Answer Choices:

- (A) NO CHANGE
- (B) developed, through
- (C) developed. Through
- (D) developed through,

Correct Answer: (A)

Explanation: The original sentence is grammatically correct and effectively conveys the information. The phrase "through dedication and hard work" is a prepositional phrase that correctly modifies the verb "developed."

46. **Question:** If $4x + 5 = 21$, what is the value of x?

Answer Choices:

- (A) 2
- (B) 3
- (C) 4
- (D) 5
- **Correct Answer:** (C)
- **Explanation:**
- Subtract 5 from both sides: $4x = 16$
- Divide both sides by 4: $x = 4$

47. **Question:** What is the solution to the inequality $3x - 7 \geq 8$?

Answer Choices:

- (A) $x \geq 1$
- (B) $x \geq 3$
- (C) $x \geq 5$
- (D) $x \geq 7$
- **Correct Answer:** (C)
- **Explanation:**
- Add 7 to both sides: $3x \geq 15$

- Divide both sides by 3: $x \geq 5$

48. **Question:** If $x + 2y = 11$ and $2x - y = 7$, what is the value of x?

    Answer Choices:

    - (A) 3
    - (B) 4
    - (C) 5
    - (D) 6
    - **Correct Answer:** (C)

    Explanation:

    - Multiply the second equation by 2: $4x - 2y = 14$
    - Add this equation to the first equation: $5x = 25$
    - Solve for x: $x = 5$

49. **Question:** If $f(x) = 2x^2 + 3x - 1$, what is the value of f(-2)?

    Answer Choices:

    - (A) -3
    - (B) 1
    - (C) 5
    - (D) 9
    - **Correct Answer:** (B)

    Explanation:

    Substitute $x = -2$ into the function: $f(-2) = 2(-2)^2 + 3(-2) - 1 = 8 - 6 - 1 = 1$

50. **Question:** What is the slope of the line represented by the equation $4x + 2y = 10$?

    Answer Choices:

    - (A) -4
    - (B) -2

- (C) 2
- (D) 4
- **Correct Answer:** (B)

Explanation:

- Rewrite the equation in slope-intercept form ($y = mx + b$): $2y = -4x + 10$ $y = -2x + 5$
- The slope (m) is -2.

51. **Question:** A triangle has sides of length 8 cm, 15 cm, and 17 cm. Is it a right triangle?

    Answer Choices:

    - (A) Yes, because $8^2 + 15^2 = 17^2$
    - (B) No, because $8^2 + 15^2 \neq 17^2$
    - (C) Yes, because it is a scalene triangle.
    - (D) No, because it is an isosceles triangle.
    - **Correct Answer:** (A)

    Explanation:

    A triangle is a right triangle if it satisfies the Pythagorean theorem ($a^2 + b^2 = c^2$), where c is the hypotenuse (the longest side). In this case, $8^2 + 15^2 = 64 + 225 = 289 = 17^2$, so it is a right triangle.

52. **Question:** What is the area of a circle with a radius of 7 cm?

    Answer Choices:

    - (A) 7π cm²
    - (B) 14π cm²
    - (C) 49π cm²
    - (D) 196π cm²

o **Correct Answer:** (C)

Explanation:

Area of a circle = $\pi r^2 = \pi(7)^2 = 49\pi$ cm²

53. **Question:** The data set 3, 6, 9, 12, 15, and x has a mean of 10. What is the value of x?

Answer Choices:

1. (A) 10
2. (B) 15
3. (C) 20
4. (D) 25
5. **Correct Answer:** (C)

Explanation:

6. Sum of the numbers = $3 + 6 + 9 + 12 + 15 + x = 45 + x$
7. Mean = (Sum of the numbers) / (Number of numbers) = $(45 + x) / 6 = 10$
8. Solve for x: $45 + x = 60$ $x = 15$

54. **Question:** What is the range of the following data set: 1, 3, 5, 7, 9, 11?

Answer Choices:

1. (A) 5
2. (B) 8
3. (C) 10
4. (D) 11
5. **Correct Answer:** (C)

Explanation:

The range is the difference between the largest and smallest values in the data set. In this case, the range is $11 - 1 = 10$.

55. **Passage:**

The term "cognitive bias" refers to a systematic pattern of deviation from norm or rationality in judgment. Individuals create their own "subjective reality" from their perception of the input. An individual's construction of reality, not the objective input, may dictate their behavior in the world.

Question: Which choice best describes the function of the underlined sentence in the text as a whole?

Answer Choices:

1. (A) It describes the "subjective reality" of a group of people.
2. (B) It explains how "cognitive bias" can be avoided.
3. (C) It provides a definition of the term "subjective reality."
4. (D) It explains how an individual's "subjective reality" may be the product of "cognitive bias."
5. **Correct Answer:** (D)

Explanation: The underlined sentence explains how individuals create their own "subjective reality" from their perception of the input, which is related to the concept of "cognitive bias" as a deviation from norm or rationality in judgment.

56. **Passage:**

The "bystander effect" is a social

psychological phenomenon in which individuals are less likely to offer help to a victim when other people are present. The greater the number of bystanders, the less likely it is that any one of them will help. This effect is believed to be driven by factors such as diffusion of responsibility, social influence, and fear of embarrassment.

Question: Which choice best states the main idea of the text?

Answer Choices:

1. (A) The "bystander effect" is a rare phenomenon that occurs only in extreme situations.

2. (B) The "bystander effect" is influenced by various psychological and social factors.

3. (C) The "bystander effect" is a well-understood phenomenon with clear solutions.

4. (D) The "bystander effect" describes the tendency for people to be less helpful when others are present.

Correct Answer: (D)

Explanation: The main idea of the text is that the "bystander effect" describes the tendency for people to be less likely to help a victim when others are present. The passage explains this effect and some of the factors that contribute to it.

57. **Passage:**

The term "Dunning-Kruger effect" describes a cognitive bias in which people with low ability at a task overestimate their ability. Without the self-awareness of metacognition, low-ability people cannot objectively evaluate their competence or incompetence. Their incompetence robs them of the metacognitive ability to realize their errors.

Question: Which choice best describes the function of the underlined sentence in the text as a whole?

Answer Choices:

1. (A) It explains why people with low ability overestimate their ability.

2. (B) It describes how the "Dunning-Kruger effect" can be overcome.

3. (C) It provides a definition of the term "metacognition."

4. (D) It contrasts the "Dunning-Kruger effect" with other cognitive biases.

Correct Answer: (A)

Explanation: The underlined sentence explains that people with low ability at a task overestimate their ability because they lack the self-awareness of metacognition, which is the ability to objectively evaluate their competence.

58. **Sentence:** The term "false consensus effect" refers to the tendency for people to overestimate the extent to which others share their beliefs and behaviors.

Question: Which choice completes the text so that it conforms to the conventions of Standard English?

Answer Choices:

1. (A) NO CHANGE
2. (B) for people, to
3. (C) for, people to
4. (D) for people to,

Correct Answer: (A)

Explanation: The original sentence is grammatically correct and clearly conveys the meaning. The prepositional phrase "to overestimate the extent..." correctly modifies the verb "refers."

59. **Sentence:** The "halo effect" is a cognitive bias in which our overall impression of a person influences how we feel and think about their character.

Question: Which choice completes the text so that it conforms to the conventions of Standard English?

Answer Choices:

1. (A) NO CHANGE
2. (B) person, influences
3. (C) person, influences,
4. (D) person influences,

Correct Answer: (A)

Explanation: The original sentence is grammatically correct and clearly conveys the meaning. The adverbial clause "in which our overall impression of a person influences how we feel and think about their character" correctly modifies the noun phrase "cognitive bias."

60. **Question:** If $2(x - 3) = 14$, what is the value of x?

Answer Choices:

1. (A) 5
2. (B) 8
3. (C) 10
4. (D) 11

Correct Answer: (C)

Explanation:

5. Distribute the 2: $2x - 6 = 14$
6. Add 6 to both sides: $2x = 20$
7. Divide both sides by 2: $x = 10$

61. **Question:** What is the solution to the inequality $-3(x + 2) < 15$?

Answer Choices:

1. (A) $x < -7$
2. (B) $x > -7$
3. (C) $x < -3$
4. (D) $x > -3$

Correct Answer: (B)

Explanation:

5. Distribute the -3: $-3x - 6 < 15$

6. Add 6 to both sides: $-3x < 21$

7. Divide both sides by -3 (and remember to flip the inequality sign): $x > -7$

62. **Question:** If $2x + 3y = 11$ and $x - y = 2$, what is the value of y?

Answer Choices:

1. (A) 1
2. (B) 1.4
3. (C) 2.2
4. (D) 3

Correct Answer: (A)

Explanation:

5. Solve the second equation for x: $x = y + 2$

6. Substitute this value of x into the first equation: $2(y + 2) + 3y = 11$

7. Simplify and solve for y: $2y + 4 + 3y = 11$ $5y = 7$ $y = 7/5 = 1.4$

63. **Question:** If $f(x) = 4x - 7$, what is the value of $f(5)$?

Answer Choices:

1. (A) 8
2. (B) 13
3. (C) 20
4. (D) 27

Correct Answer: (B)

Explanation:

Substitute $x = 5$ into the function: $f(5) = 4(5) - 7 = 20 - 7 = 13$

64. **Question:** What is the slope of the line that passes through the points (-3, 2) and (1, -4)?

Answer Choices:

1. (A) -3/2
2. (B) -2/3
3. (C) 2/3
4. (D) 3/2

Correct Answer: (A)

Explanation:

Use the slope formula: $m = (y_2 - y_1) / (x_2 - x_1) = (-4 - 2) / (1 - (-3)) = -6 / 4 = -3/2$

65. **Question:** A triangle has angles measuring 45 degrees, 45 degrees, and x degrees. What is the value of x?

Answer Choices:

1. (A) 45
2. (B) 60
3. (C) 90
4. (D) 135

Correct Answer: (C)

Explanation:

The angles in a triangle add up to 180 degrees. Therefore: $45 + 45 + x = 180$ $90 + x = 180$ $x = 90$

66. **Question:** What is the sum of the solutions to the equation $x^2 + 3x - 10 = 0$?

Answer Choices:

1. (A) -10
2. (B) -3
3. (C) 3
4. (D) 10

Correct Answer: (B)

Explanation:

5. For a quadratic equation in the standard form $ax^2 + bx + c = 0$, the sum of the solutions is $-b/a$.

6. In this case, $a = 1$ and $b = 3$, so the sum of the solutions is $-3/1 = -3$.

67. **Question:** If $5^{(x-2)} = 125$, what is the value of x?

Answer Choices:

1. (A) 1
2. (B) 3
3. (C) 5
4. (D) 7

Correct Answer: (C)

Explanation:

5. Express 125 as a power of 5: $125 = 5^3$

6. Set the exponents equal to each other: $x - 2 = 3$

7. Solve for x: $x = 5$

68. **Question:** A rectangle has a length of 10 cm and a width of 6 cm. What is its area?

Answer Choices:

1. (A) 16 cm²
2. (B) 32 cm²
3. (C) 60 cm²
4. (D) 120 cm²

Correct Answer: (C)

Explanation:

Area of a rectangle = length x width = 10 cm x 6 cm = 60 cm²

69. **Question:** A circle has a diameter of 20 cm. What is its circumference?

Answer Choices:

1. (A) 10π cm
2. (B) 20π cm
3. (C) 40π cm
4. (D) 100π cm

Correct Answer: (B)

Explanation:

Circumference of a circle = $\pi d = \pi(20$ cm$)$ = 20π cm

70. **Question:** The data set 5, 7, 9, 11, 13, and x has a mean of 10. What is the value of x?

Answer Choices:

1. (A) 10
2. (B) 15
3. (C) 20

4. (D) 25

Correct Answer: (B)
Explanation:

5. Sum of the numbers = 5 + 7 + 9 + 11 + 13 + x = 45 + x
6. Mean = (Sum of the numbers) / (Number of numbers) = (45 + x) / 6 = 10
7. Solve for x: 45 + x = 60 x = 15

71. Question: What is the range of the following data set: 2, 4, 6, 8, 10, 12?

Answer Choices:
○ (A) 6
○ (B) 8
○ (C) 10
○ (D) 12
○ Correct Answer: (C)
Explanation:
The range is the difference between the largest and smallest values in the data set. In this case, the range is 12 - 2 = 10.

72. Passage:
The term "groupthink" describes a psychological phenomenon that occurs within a group of people in which the desire for harmony or conformity in the group results in an irrational or dysfunctional decision-making outcome. Group members try to minimize conflict and reach a consensus decision without critical evaluation of alternative

viewpoints, by actively suppressing dissenting viewpoints, and by isolating themselves from outside influences.

Question: Which choice best describes the function of the underlined portion in the text as a whole?

Answer Choices:
○ (A) It explains why "groupthink" is a negative phenomenon.
○ (B) It describes how "groupthink" can be avoided.
○ (C) It provides a definition of the term "groupthink."
○ (D) It contrasts "groupthink" with other psychological phenomena.

Correct Answer: (C)
Explanation: The underlined portion provides a definition of the term "groupthink," explaining how it occurs and its potential negative consequences.

73. Passage:
The "IKEA effect" is a cognitive bias in which consumers place a disproportionately high value on products they partially created. The effect is named after the Swedish furniture company IKEA, which sells products that require assembly. The labor invested in assembling the furniture enhances the perceived value of the furniture for the

consumer.

Question: Which choice best states the main idea of the text?

Answer Choices:

o (A) The "IKEA effect" is a marketing strategy used by the IKEA company to increase sales.

o (B) The "IKEA effect" demonstrates that people value things more when they have invested effort in creating them.

o (C) The "IKEA effect" is a cognitive bias that affects only a small percentage of the population.

o (D) The "IKEA effect" is a psychological phenomenon that has no real-world applications.

Correct Answer: (B)

Explanation: The main idea of the text is that the "IKEA effect" demonstrates that people value things more when they have invested effort in creating them. The passage explains this effect using the example of IKEA furniture that requires assembly.

74. **Passage:**

The "loss aversion" bias describes people's tendency to prefer avoiding losses to acquiring equivalent gains. It is better to not lose $5 than to find $5. Some studies have suggested that losses are twice as powerful, psychologically, as gains.

Question: Which choice best describes the function of the underlined sentence in the text as a whole?

Answer Choices:

o (A) It explains why "loss aversion" is a common bias.

o (B) It provides an example of "loss aversion" in action.

o (C) It defines the term "loss aversion."

o (D) It contrasts "loss aversion" with other cognitive biases.

Correct Answer: (B)

Explanation: The underlined sentence provides a specific example of "loss aversion" in action, illustrating the concept that people feel the pain of a loss more strongly than the pleasure of an equivalent gain.

75. **Sentence:** The term "framing effect" refers to the cognitive bias in which people react to a particular choice in different ways depending on how it is presented.

Question: Which choice completes the text so that it conforms to the conventions of Standard English?

Answer Choices:

o (A) NO CHANGE

○ (B) which people, react

○ (C) which, people react

○ (D) which, people, react

Correct Answer: (A)

Explanation: The original sentence is grammatically correct and clearly conveys the meaning. The adverbial clause "in which people react to a particular choice in different ways depending on how it is presented" correctly modifies the noun phrase "cognitive bias."

76. **Sentence:** The "peak-end rule" is a psychological heuristic in which people judge an experience largely based on how they felt at its peak (i.e., its most intense point) and at its end, rather than based on the total sum or average of every moment of the experience.

Question: Which choice completes the text so that it conforms to the conventions of Standard English?

Answer Choices:

○ (A) NO CHANGE

○ (B) end. Rather

○ (C) end rather,

○ (D) end, rather,

Correct Answer: (A)

Explanation: The original sentence is grammatically correct and effectively uses

punctuation. The comma after "end" is correctly placed to separate the contrasted phrases "rather than based on the total sum or average of every moment of the experience."

77. **Question:** If $5(x + 2) = 35$, what is the value of x?

Answer Choices:

○ (A) 3

○ (B) 5

○ (C) 7

○ (D) 9

Correct Answer: (B)

Explanation:

○ Distribute the 5: $5x + 10 = 35$

○ Subtract 10 from both sides: $5x = 25$

○ Divide both sides by 5: $x = 5$

78. **Question:** What is the solution to the inequality $2(x - 4) \leq -6$?

Answer Choices:

○ (A) $x \leq -1$

○ (B) $x \leq 1$

○ (C) $x \leq 5$

○ (D) $x \leq 7$

Correct Answer: (B)

Explanation:

○ Distribute the 2: $2x - 8 \leq -6$

○ Add 8 to both sides: $2x \leq 2$

o   Divide both sides by 2: $x \leq 1$

79. **Question:** If $3x + y = 10$ and $x - 2y = -1$, what is the value of x?

Answer Choices:

o   (A) 1

o   (B) 2

o   (C) 3

o   (D) 4

Correct Answer: (C)

Explanation:

o   Multiply the second equation by 3: $3x - 6y = -3$

o   Subtract this equation from the first equation: $7y = 13$

o   Solve for y: $y = 13/7$

o   Substitute the value of y into either original equation to solve for x. Using the second equation: $x - 2(13/7) = -1$ $x - 26/7 = -1$ $x = 19/7 = 2.71$

80. **Question:** If $f(x) = -2x^2 + 5x - 3$, what is the value of $f(4)$?

Answer Choices:

o   (A) -15

o   (B) -9

o   (C) 9

o   (D) 15

Correct Answer: (A)

Explanation:

Substitute $x = 4$ into the function: $f(4) = -2(4)^2 + 5(4) - 3 = -32 + 20 - 3 = -15$

81. **Question:** What is the slope of the line that passes through the points (1, -3) and (5, 1)?

Answer Choices:

o   (A) -1

o   (B) 1

o   (C) 2

o   (D) 4

Correct Answer: (B)

Explanation:

Use the slope formula: $m = (y_2 - y_1) / (x_2 - x_1) = (1 - (-3)) / (5 - 1) = 4 / 4 = 1$

82. **Question:** A triangle has sides of length 3 cm, 4 cm, and 5 cm. Is it a right triangle?

Answer Choices:

o   (A) Yes, because $3^2 + 4^2 = 5^2$

o   (B) No, because $3^2 + 4^2 \neq 5^2$

o   (C) Yes, because it is a scalene triangle.

o   (D) No, because it is an isosceles triangle.

Correct Answer: (A)

Explanation:

A triangle is a right triangle if it satisfies the Pythagorean theorem ($a^2 + b^2 = c^2$), where c is the hypotenuse (the longest side). In this case, $3^2 + 4^2 = 9 + 16 = 25 = 5^2$, so it is a right triangle.

83. **Question:** What is the area of a triangle with a base of 10 cm and a height of 8 cm?

Answer Choices:

- (A) 80 cm²
- (B) 40 cm²
- (C) 20 cm²
- (D) 10 cm²

Correct Answer: (B)

Explanation:

Area of a triangle = (1/2) * base * height = (1/2) * 10 cm * 8 cm = 40 cm²

84. **Question:** What is the volume of a cube with a side length of 5 cm?

Answer Choices:

- (A) 125 cm³
- (B) 100 cm³
- (C) 75 cm³
- (D) 25 cm³

Correct Answer: (A)

Explanation:

Volume of a cube = side³ = 5 cm * 5 cm * 5 cm = 125 cm³

85. **Question:** The data set 1, 3, 5, 7, 9, and x has a median of 6. What is the value of x?

Answer Choices:

- (A) 6
- (B) 7
- (C) 8

- (D) 9

Correct Answer: (B)

Explanation:

The median is the middle value when the data set is arranged in order. Since the median is 6, and the data set is already in order, x must be 7 to make 6 the middle value.

86. **Passage:**

The "placebo effect" is a phenomenon in which a fake treatment, an inactive substance like sugar, distilled water, or saline solution, can sometimes improve a patient's condition simply because the person has the expectation that it will be helpful. The placebo effect is a testament to the power of the mind-body connection and the influence of expectations on health outcomes.

Question: Which choice best describes the function of the underlined portion in the text as a whole?

Answer Choices:

- (A) It provides a definition of a key term.
- (B) It introduces a concept that is later refuted.
- (C) It states a claim that is supported by the text.
- (D) It presents an argument that is countered by the text.

Correct Answer: (A)

Explanation: The underlined portion provides a definition of the key term "placebo effect," explaining what it is and its significance in demonstrating the mind-body connection.

87. **Passage:**

The term "self-fulfilling prophecy" refers to a prediction that directly or indirectly causes itself to become true, by the very terms of the prophecy itself, due to positive feedback between belief and behavior. A belief or expectation, positive or negative, about a subject, whether correct or not, affects the behavior of the subject in such a way that the belief or expectation becomes true.

Question: Which choice best states the main idea of the text?

Answer Choices:

○ (A) Self-fulfilling prophecies are always based on accurate information.

○ (B) Self-fulfilling prophecies can have both positive and negative effects.

○ (C) Self-fulfilling prophecies are a rare phenomenon with limited impact.

○ (D) Self-fulfilling prophecies demonstrate the power of beliefs and expectations to shape reality.

Correct Answer: (D)

Explanation: The main idea of the text is that self-fulfilling prophecies demonstrate the power of beliefs and expectations to shape reality. The passage explains how a belief or expectation can influence behavior in a way that makes the belief come true.

88. **Passage:**

The "anchoring bias" is a cognitive bias that describes the common human tendency to rely too heavily on the first piece of information offered (the "anchor") when making decisions. During decision making, anchoring occurs when individuals use an initial piece of information to make subsequent judgments.

Question: Which choice best describes the function of the underlined sentence in the text as a whole?

Answer Choices:

○ (A) It explains why "anchoring bias" is a common bias.

○ (B) It provides an example of "anchoring bias" in action.

○ (C) It defines the term "anchoring bias."

○ (D) It contrasts "anchoring bias" with other cognitive biases.

Correct Answer: (C)

Explanation: The underlined sentence provides a definition of the term "anchoring bias," explaining how it influences decision-making by causing people to over-rely on the first piece of information they receive.

89. **Sentence:** The term "availability heuristic" refers to a mental shortcut that relies on immediate examples that come to a given person's mind when evaluating a specific topic, concept, method, or decision.

Question: Which choice completes the text so that it conforms to the conventions of Standard English?

Answer Choices:
- (A) NO CHANGE
- (B) mind, when
- (C) mind. When
- (D) mind when,

Correct Answer: (A)

Explanation: The original sentence is grammatically correct and clearly conveys the meaning. The adverbial clause "when evaluating a specific topic, concept, method, or decision" correctly modifies the verb phrase "come to a given person's mind."

90. **Sentence:** The "bandwagon effect" is a psychological phenomenon in which people do something primarily because they believe many other people are doing it, regardless of their own beliefs, which they may ignore or override.

Question: Which choice completes the text so that it conforms to the conventions of Standard English?

Answer Choices:
- (A) NO CHANGE
- (B) it regardless
- (C) it, regardless
- (D) it. Regardless

Correct Answer: (A)

Explanation: The original sentence is grammatically correct and effectively conveys the information. The phrase "regardless of their own beliefs" is a prepositional phrase that correctly modifies the verb "do."

91. **Question:** If $3(x - 5) = 9$, what is the value of x?

Answer Choices:
- (A) 2
- (B) 4
- (C) 6
- (D) 8

Correct Answer: (D)

Explanation:

o Distribute the 3: $3x - 15 = 9$

o Add 15 to both sides: $3x = 24$

o Divide both sides by 3: $x = 8$

92. **Question:** What is the solution to the inequality $-2(x + 3) \geq 10$?

Answer Choices:

o (A) $x \leq -8$

o (B) $x \geq -8$

o (C) $x \leq -2$

o (D) $x \geq -2$

Correct Answer: (A)

Explanation:

o Distribute the -2: $-2x - 6 \geq 10$

o Add 6 to both sides: $-2x \geq 16$

o Divide both sides by -2 (and remember to flip the inequality sign): $x \leq -8$

93. **Question:** If $x + 4y = 14$ and $2x - y = 5$, what is the value of y?

Answer Choices:

o (A) 2

o (B) 3

o (C) 4

o (D) 5

Correct Answer: (A)

Explanation:

o Multiply the second equation by 4: $8x - 4y = 20$

o Add this equation to the first equation: $9x = 34$

o Solve for x: $x = 34/9$

o Substitute the value of x into either original equation to solve for y. Using the first equation: $34/9 + 4y = 14$ $4y = 92/9$ $y = 23/9 = 2.56$

94. **Question:** If $f(x) = 3x^2 - 7x + 2$, what is the value of $f(-1)$?

Answer Choices:

o (A) -8

o (B) 2

o (C) 12

o (D) 18

Correct Answer: (C)

Explanation:

Substitute $x = -1$ into the function: $f(-1) = 3(-1)^2 - 7(-1) + 2 = 3 + 7 + 2 = 12$

95. **Question:** What is the y-intercept of the line represented by the equation $5x + 2y = 8$?

Answer Choices:

o (A) -8/5

o (B) -5/2

o (C) 4

o (D) 8

Correct Answer: (C)

Explanation:

o Rewrite the equation in slope-intercept form ($y = mx + b$): $2y = -5x + 8$ $y = (-5/2)$ $x + 4$

o The y-intercept (b) is 4.

96. **Question:** A triangle has sides of length 7 cm, 24 cm, and 25 cm. Is it a right triangle?

Answer Choices:

o (A) Yes, because $7^2 + 24^2 = 25^2$

o (B) No, because $7^2 + 24^2 \neq 25^2$

o (C) Yes, because it is a scalene triangle.

o (D) No, because it is an isosceles triangle.

Correct Answer: (A)

Explanation:

A triangle is a right triangle if it satisfies the Pythagorean theorem ($a^2 + b^2 = c^2$), where c is the hypotenuse (the longest side). In this case, $7^2 + 24^2 = 49 + 576 = 625 = 25^2$, so it is a right triangle.

97. **Question:** What is the area of a rectangle with a length of 9 cm and a width of 5 cm?

Answer Choices:

o (A) 14 cm²

o (B) 28 cm²

o (C) 45 cm²

o (D) 90 cm²

Correct Answer: (C)

Explanation:

Area of a rectangle = length x width = 9 cm x 5 cm = 45 cm²

98. **Question:** What is the volume of a rectangular prism with a length of 6 cm, a width of 4 cm, and a height of 3 cm?

Answer Choices:

o (A) 13 cm³

o (B) 24 cm³

o (C) 36 cm³

o (D) 72 cm³

Correct Answer: (D)

Explanation:

Volume of a rectangular prism = length x width x height = 6 cm x 4 cm x 3 cm = 72 cm³

99. **Question:** The data set 2, 3, 4, 5, 6, and x has a median of 4.5. What is the value of x?

Answer Choices:

o (A) 4

o (B) 5

o (C) 6

o (D) 7

Correct Answer: (B)

Explanation:

The median is the average of the two middle numbers when the data set is arranged in order. Since the median is 4.5, and the data set is already in order, x must be 5 to make the average of 4 and 5 equal to 4.5.

100.   **Passage:**

The term "in-group bias" refers to the tendency for humans to give preferential treatment to others they perceive to be members of their own groups. These groups can be based on various factors, such as race, gender, religion, or even shared interests. In-group bias is a deeply ingrained social phenomenon that can have significant implications for fairness and equality.

Question: Which choice best describes the function of the underlined portion in the text as a whole?

(A) It provides a definition of a key term.

(B) It introduces a concept that is later refuted.

(C) It states a claim that is supported by the text.

(D) It presents an argument that is countered by the text.

Correct Answer: (A)

Explanation: The underlined portion provides a definition of the key term "in-group bias," explaining what it is and its potential implications for social interactions.

101.   **Passage:**

The "fundamental attribution error" is a cognitive bias that describes the tendency to overemphasize dispositional or personality-based explanations for an individual's observed behavior while underemphasizing situational explanations. In other words, people tend to overemphasize internal characteristics, such as personality traits, in an individual's behavior and underemphasize external factors that may have contributed to their behavior.

Question: Which choice best states the main idea of the text?

Answer Choices:

o   (A) The "fundamental attribution error" is a rare cognitive bias that affects only a small percentage of the population.

o   (B) The "fundamental attribution error" can be easily overcome with increased awareness and education.

o   (C) The "fundamental attribution error" highlights the importance of considering both internal and external factors when explaining behavior.

(D) The "fundamental attribution error" describes the tendency to overemphasize personality-based explanations for behavior while underemphasizing situational factors.

Correct Answer: (D)

Explanation: The main idea of the text is that the "fundamental attribution error" describes the tendency to overemphasize personality-based explanations for behavior while underemphasizing situational factors. The passage explains this bias and provides a clear definition of the concept.

102.   **Passage:**

The "Google effect," also known as "digital amnesia," is the tendency for people to forget information that can be easily found online using search engines such as Google. This effect is believed to be driven by the easy accessibility of information online, leading people to rely less on their memory and more on external sources.

Question: Which choice best describes the function of the underlined sentence in the text as a whole?

Answer Choices:

o (A) It explains why the "Google effect" is a growing concern in the digital age.

o (B) It provides an example of the "Google effect" in action.

o (C) It defines the term "Google effect" and its alternative name.

o (D) It contrasts the "Google effect" with other cognitive biases.

Correct Answer: (C)

Explanation: The underlined sentence provides a definition of the term "Google effect" and its alternative name "digital amnesia," explaining the phenomenon of forgetting information that can be easily found online.

103.   **Sentence:** The term "misinformation effect" refers to the tendency for post-event information to interfere with the memory of the original event.

Question: Which choice completes the text so that it conforms to the conventions of Standard English?

Answer Choices:

o (A) NO CHANGE

o (B) for, post-event, information

o (C) for post-event information,

o (D) for, post-event information,

Correct Answer: (A)

Explanation: The original sentence is grammatically correct and clearly conveys the meaning. The prepositional phrase "for post-event information" correctly modifies the verb "interfere."

104.   The "framing effect" is a cognitive bias in which people decide on options based on whether the options are presented with positive or negative connotations; e.g. as a loss or as a gain.
Question: Which choice completes the text so that it conforms to the conventions of Standard English?
Answer Choices:

o   (A) NO CHANGE

o   (B) connotations, e.g.,

o   (C) connotations: e.g.,

o   (D) connotations, e.g.

Correct Answer: (B)

Explanation: The original sentence is grammatically correct, but the punctuation can be improved. The abbreviation "e.g." (for example) should be set off with commas.

105.   **Question:** If $4(x - 3) = 8$, what is the value of x?

Answer Choices:

(A) 2

(B) 3

(C) 5

(D) 6

Correct Answer: (C)

Explanation:

1. Distribute the 4: $4x - 12 = 8$

2. Add 12 to both sides: $4x = 20$

3. Divide both sides by 4: $x = 5$

106.   **Question:** What is the solution to the inequality $-5(x + 1) < 20$?

Answer Choices:

(A) $x < -5$

(B) $x > -5$

(C) $x < -3$

(D) $x > -3$

Correct Answer: (B)

Explanation:

1. Distribute the -5: $-5x - 5 < 20$

2. Add 5 to both sides: $-5x < 25$

3. Divide both sides by -5 (and remember to flip the inequality sign): $x > -5$

107. **Question:** If $2x + y = 9$ and $x - 3y = -8$, what is the value of y?

Answer Choices:

(A) 1

(B) 2

(C) 3

(D) 4

Correct Answer: (C)

Explanation:

1. Multiply the first equation by 3: $6x + 3y = 27$

2. Add this equation to the second equation: $7x = 19$

3. Solve for x: $x = 19/7$

4. Substitute the value of x into either original equation to solve for y. Using the first equation: $2(19/7) + y = 9$

   $38/7 + y = 9$

   $y = 25/7 = 3.57$

108. **Question:** If $f(x) = -x^2 + 4x - 1$, what is the value of $f(2)$?

Answer Choices:

(A) -5

(B) -1

(C) 3

(D) 7

Correct Answer: (C)

Explanation:

Substitute x = 2 into the function: $f(2) = -(2)^2 + 4(2) - 1 = -4 + 8 - 1 = 3$

109. **Question:** What is the x-intercept of the line represented by the equation $3x - 2y = 6$?

Answer Choices:

(A) -3

(B) -2

(C) 2

(D) 3

Correct Answer: (C)

Explanation:

1. To find the x -intercept, set y = 0: 3 x - 2(0) = 6

2. Solve for x: 3 x = 6

x = 2

110.   **Question:** A triangle has sides of length 9 cm, 40 cm, and 41 cm. Is it a right triangle?

Answer Choices:

(A) Yes, because $9^2 + 40^2 = 41^2$

(B) No, because $9^2 + 40^2 \neq 41^2$

(C) Yes, because it is a scalene triangle.

(D) No, because it is an isosceles triangle.

Correct Answer: (A)

Explanation: A triangle is a right triangle if it satisfies the Pythagorean theorem ($a^2 + b^2 = c^2$), where c is the hypotenuse (the longest side). In this case, $9^2 + 40^2 = 81 + 1600 = 1681 = 41^2$, so it is a right triangle.

111.   **Question:** What is the volume of a cylinder with a radius of 4 cm and a height of 7 cm?

Answer Choices:

(A) 28π cm³

(B) 56π cm³

(C) 112π cm³

(D) 196π cm³

Correct Answer: (C)

Explanation:

Volume of a cylinder = $\pi r^2 h = \pi$ (4 cm) ²(7 cm) = 112π cm³

112.   **Question:** A bag contains 3 red marbles, 5 blue marbles, and 2 green marbles. What is the probability of randomly selecting a blue marble?

Answer Choices:

(A) 1/2

(B) 1/5

(C) 3/10

(D) 1/10

Correct Answer: (A)

Explanation:

Number of favorable outcomes (blue marbles): 5

Total number of possible outcomes: 3 + 5 + 2 = 10

Probability = 5/10 = 1/2

113. **Passage:**

The "Pygmalion effect," also known as the "Rosenthal effect," is a psychological phenomenon in which high expectations lead to improved performance in a given area. The effect is named after the Greek myth of Pygmalion, a sculptor who fell in love with a statue he had carved. His love for the statue brought it to life.

Question: Which choice best describes the function of the underlined sentence in the text as a whole?

Answer Choices:

- (A) It provides an example of the "Pygmalion effect" in action.
- (B) It explains the origins of the term "Pygmalion effect."
- (C) It defines the term "Pygmalion effect."
- (D) It contrasts the "Pygmalion effect" with other psychological phenomena.

Correct Answer: (B)

Explanation: The underlined sentence explains the origins of the term "Pygmalion effect" by referencing the Greek myth of Pygmalion, providing context for the psychological phenomenon.

114. **Passage:**

The recency illusion" is a cognitive bias in which people believe that things they have noticed recently have only just appeared, when in fact they have been around for some time. This illusion is driven by the availability heuristic, which causes people to overestimate the importance of information that is readily available to them.

Question: Which choice best states the main idea of the text?

Answer Choices:

- (A) The "recency illusion" is a rare phenomenon that affects only a small percentage of the population.
- (B) The "recency illusion" can be easily overcome with increased awareness and education.
- (C) The "recency illusion" highlights the importance of considering historical context when evaluating new trends.
- (D) The "recency illusion" describes the tendency to believe that recently noticed things are new, even if they have existed for a while.

Correct Answer: (D)

Explanation: The main idea of the text is that the "recency illusion" describes the tendency to believe that recently noticed things are new, even if they have existed for a while. The passage explains this illusion and its connection to the availability heuristic.

115.   **Passage:**

The "serial position effect" is the tendency of a person to recall the first and last items in a series best, and the middle items worst. The term was coined by Hermann Ebbinghaus through studies he performed on himself, and refers to the finding that recall accuracy varies as a function of an item's position within a study list.

Question: Which choice best describes the function of the underlined sentence in the text as a whole?

Answer Choices:

o   (A) It explains why the "serial position effect" is a common phenomenon.

o   (B) It provides an example of the "serial position effect" in action.

o   (C) It defines the term "serial position effect."

o   (D) It contrasts the "serial position effect" with other memory-related phenomena.

Correct Answer: (C)

   Explanation: The underlined sentence provides a definition of the term "serial position effect," explaining how it affects memory recall based on the position of items in a list.

116.   **Sentence:** The term "social proof" refers to a psychological and social phenomenon wherein people copy the actions of others in an attempt to undertake behavior in a given situation.

Question: Which choice completes the text so that it conforms to the conventions of Standard English?

Answer Choices:

(A) NO CHANGE

(B) situation,

(C) situation;

(D) situation:

Correct Answer: (A)

Explanation: The original sentence is grammatically correct and clearly conveys the meaning. The prepositional phrase "in a given situation" correctly modifies the verb "undertake."

117.   **Sentence:** The "spotlight effect" is a cognitive bias that causes people to overestimate the degree to which others notice their actions or appearance.

Question: Which choice completes the text so that it conforms to the conventions of Standard English?

Answer Choices:

(A) NO CHANGE

(B) which causes people,

(C) which, causes people

(D) which causes, people

Correct Answer: (A)

Explanation: The original sentence is grammatically correct and effectively conveys the information. The relative clause "that causes people to overestimate the degree to which others notice their actions or appearance" correctly modifies the noun phrase "cognitive bias."

118. **Question:** If $3(x + 4) = 21$, what is the value of x?

Answer Choices:

(A) 1

(B) 3

(C) 5

(D) 7

Correct Answer: (A)

Explanation:

1. Distribute the 3: $3x + 12 = 21$

2. Subtract 12 from both sides: $3x = 9$

3. Divide both sides by 3: $x = 3$

119.   **Question:** What is the solution to the inequality $-4(x - 2) \leq 12$?

Answer Choices:

(A) $x \leq -1$

(B) $x \geq -1$

(C) $x \leq 5$

(D) $x \geq 5$

Correct Answer: (B)

Explanation:

1. Distribute the -4: $-4x + 8 \leq 12$

2. Subtract 8 from both sides: $-4x \leq 4$

3. Divide both sides by -4 (and remember to flip the inequality sign): $x \geq -1$

120. **Question:** If $x + 3y = 10$ and $2x - y = 5$, what is the value of x?

(A) 2

(B) 3

(C) 4

(D) 5

Correct Answer: (D)

Explanation:

1. Multiply the second equation by 3: 6x - 3y = 15

2. Add this equation to the first equation: 7x = 25

3. Solve for x: x = 25/7 = 3.57

121. **Question:** If $f(x) = 2x - 3$ and $g(x) = x + 1$, what is the value of $f(g(2))$?

(A) 1

(B) 3

(C) 5

(D) 7

Correct Answer: (C)

Explanation:

1. Find the value of g (2): g (2) = 2 + 1 = 3

2. Substitute this value into f(x): f (g (2)) = f (3) = 2(3) - 3 = 6 - 3 = 3

122. **Question:** What is the slope of a line that is perpendicular to the line represented by the equation $y = (1/3)\, x + 2$?

(A) -3

(B) -1/3

(C) 1/3

(D) 3

Correct Answer: (A)

Explanation:

1. The slope of the given line is 1/3.

2. The slopes of perpendicular lines are negative reciprocals of each other.

3. The negative reciprocal of 1/3 is -3.

123. **Question:** A triangle has sides of length 5 cm, 5 cm, and 7 cm. What type of triangle is it?

(A) Scalene

(B) Isosceles

(C) Equilateral

(D) Right

Correct Answer: (B)

Explanation: An isosceles triangle has two sides of equal length.

124.   **Question:** What is the area of a triangle with a base of 6 cm and a height of 4 cm?

(A) 24 cm²

(B) 12 cm²

(C) 10 cm²

(D) 5 cm²

Correct Answer: (B)

Explanation:

Area of a triangle = (1/2) * base * height = (1/2) * 6 cm * 4 cm = 12 cm²

125.   **Question:** What is the volume of a rectangular prism with a length of 4 cm, a width of 3 cm, and a height of 2 cm?

(A) 9 cm³

(B) 12 cm³

(C) 14 cm³

(D) 24 cm³

Correct Answer: (D)

Explanation:

Volume of a rectangular prism = length x width x height = 4 cm x 3 cm x 2 cm = 24 cm³

126. **Question:** A bag contains 4 red marbles, 3 blue marbles, and 2 green marbles. What is the probability of randomly selecting a red or a green marble?

(A) 2/3

(B) 1/3

(C) 1/2

(D) 5/9

Correct Answer: (A)

Explanation:

Number of favorable outcomes (red or green marbles): 4 + 2 = 6

Total number of possible outcomes: 4 + 3 + 2 = 9

Probability = 6/9 = 2/3

127. **Passage:**

The "straw man fallacy" is a form of argument and an informal fallacy of having the impression of refuting an argument, whereas the real subject of the argument was not addressed or refuted, but instead replaced with a false one. One who engages in this fallacy is said to be "attacking a straw man."

Question: Which choice best describes the function of the underlined portion in the text as a whole?

Answer Choices:

○ (A) It provides an example of the "straw man fallacy" in action.

○ (B) It explains the origins of the term "straw man fallacy."

○ (C) It defines the term "straw man fallacy."

○ (D) It contrasts the "straw man fallacy" with other logical fallacies.

Correct Answer: (C)

Explanation: The underlined portion provides a definition of the term "straw man fallacy," explaining how it

misrepresents an opponent's argument to make it easier to attack.

128. **Passage:**

The term "Texas sharpshooter fallacy" is an informal fallacy which is committed when differences in data are ignored, but similarities are stressed. From this reasoning, a false conclusion is inferred. This fallacy is the philosophical or rhetorical equivalent of the metaphor of a Texan firing gunshots at the side of a barn, then painting a target centered on the tightest cluster of hits and claiming to be a sharpshooter.

Question: Which choice best states the main idea of the text?

Answer Choices:

○ (A) The "Texas sharpshooter fallacy" is a common error in statistical reasoning.

○ (B) The "Texas sharpshooter fallacy" is often used to mislead or deceive people.

○ (C) The "Texas sharpshooter fallacy" highlights the importance of considering all data, not just selective portions.

○ (D) The "Texas sharpshooter fallacy" describes the tendency to focus on similarities while ignoring differences.

Correct Answer: (D)

Explanation: The main idea of the text is that the "Texas sharpshooter fallacy" describes the tendency to focus on similarities while ignoring differences in data to draw a false conclusion. The passage explains this fallacy using the metaphor of a Texan sharpshooter.

129.   **Passage:**

The "third-person effect" hypothesis predicts that people tend to perceive that mass media messages have a greater effect on others than on themselves. The effect is prominent in the field of media studies and communication studies. The phenomenon was first identified by W. Phillips Davison in 1983.

Question: Which choice best describes the function of the underlined sentence in the text as a whole?

Answer Choices:

- (A) It explains why the "third-person effect" is a common bias.
- (B) It provides an example of the "third-person effect" in action.
- (C) It defines the term "third-person effect."
- (D) It contrasts the "third-person effect" with other cognitive biases.

Correct Answer: (C)

Explanation: The underlined sentence provides a definition of the term "third-person effect," explaining how people

perceive media messages to have a greater influence on others than on themselves.

130.   **Sentence:** The term "ultimate attribution error" refers to the tendency for people to attribute negative behaviors by members of an outgroup to dispositional qualities and positive behaviors to situational, circumstantial, or chance factors.

Question: Which choice completes the text so that it conforms to the conventions of Standard English?

(A) NO CHANGE

(B) outgroup, to

(C) outgroup to,

(D) outgroup. To

Correct Answer: (A)

Explanation: The original sentence is grammatically correct and clearly conveys the meaning. The prepositional phrase "to dispositional qualities" correctly modifies the verb "attribute."

131. **Sentence:** The "unit bias" is the tendency for individuals to want to complete a unit of a given item or task, regardless of the appropriateness of the size of the unit.

Question: Which choice completes the text so that it conforms to the conventions of Standard English?

Answer Choices:

- (A) NO CHANGE
- (B) task. Regardless
- (C) task regardless
- (D) task, regardless,

Correct Answer: (A)

Explanation: The original sentence is grammatically correct and clearly conveys the meaning. The prepositional phrase "regardless of the appropriateness of the size of the unit" correctly modifies the verb "complete."

132. **Question:** If $2(x + 3) = 10$, what is the value of x?

(A) 2

(B) 3

(C) 4

(D) 5

Correct Answer: (A)

Explanation:

1. Distribute the 2: $2*x* + 6 = 10$

2. Subtract 6 from both sides: $2*x* = 4$

3. Divide both sides by 2: $*x* = 2$

133. **Question:** What is the solution to the inequality $-3(x - 1) \leq 6$?

(A) $x \leq -1$

(B) $x \geq -1$

(C) $x \leq 3$

(D) $x \geq 3$

Correct Answer: (B)

Explanation:

1. Distribute the -3: $-3 x + 3 \leq 6$

2. Subtract 3 from both sides: $-3 x \leq 3$

3. Divide both sides by -3 (and remember to flip the inequality sign): $x \geq -1$

134. **Question:** If $x + 2y = 7$ and $3x - y = 8$, what is the value of y?

(A) 1

(B) 2

(C) 3

(D) 4

Correct Answer: (A)

Explanation:

1. Multiply the second equation by 2: 6 x - 2 y = 16

2. Add this equation to the first equation: 7 x = 23

3. Solve for x: x = 23/7

4. Substitute the value of x into either original equation to solve for y. Using the first equation: 23/7 + 2 y = 7

   2y = 26/7

   y = 13/7 = 1.86

135. **Question:** If $f(x) = x^2 - 2x + 3$, what is the value of $f(-3)$?

(A) -12

(B) 0

(C) 6

(D) 18

Correct Answer: (D)

Explanation:

Substitute x = -3 into the function: f (-3) = (-3) ^{2} - 2(-3) + 3 = 9 + 6 + 3 = 18

136. **Question:** What is the equation of a line that passes through the point (2, 5) and has a slope of 3?

(A) y = 3x - 1

(B) y = 3x + 1

(C) y = 3x - 11

(D) y = 3x + 11

Correct Answer: (A)

Explanation:

1. Use the point-slope form of a linear equation: $y - y_1 = m (x - x_1)$

2. Substitute the given values: y - 5 = 3(x - 2)

3. Simplify to get the equation in slope-intercept form: y - 5 = 3x - 6

   y = 3x - 1

137. **Question:** A triangle has sides of length 6 cm, 8 cm, and 10 cm. What type of triangle is it?

(A) Scalene

(B) Isosceles

(C) Equilateral

(D) Right

Correct Answer: (D)

Explanation:

The side lengths satisfy the Pythagorean theorem ($6^2 + 8^2 = 10^2$), so it is a right triangle.

138. **Question:** What is the circumference of a circle with a radius of 3 cm?

(A) 3π cm

(B) 6π cm

(C) 9π cm

(D) 12π cm

Correct Answer: (B)

Explanation:

Circumference of a circle = $2\pi r = 2\pi$ (3 cm) = 6π cm

139. **Question:** What is the volume of a cone with a radius of 3 cm and a height of 4 cm?

(A) 12π cm^3

(B) 36π cm^3

(C) 48π cm^3

(D) 144π cm^3

Correct Answer: (A)

Explanation:

Volume of a cone = (1/3) $\pi r^2 h$ = (1/3) π (3 cm)^2 (4 cm) = 12π cm^3

140. **Question:** A die is rolled. What is the probability of rolling a number greater than 4?

(A) 1/6

(B) 1/3

(C) 1/2

(D) 2/3

Correct Answer: (B)

Explanation:

Number of favorable outcomes (numbers greater than 4): 2 (5 and 6)

Total number of possible outcomes: 6

Probability = 2/6 = 1/3

141. **Passage:** The "veil of ignorance" is a philosophical concept that proposes a hypothetical situation in which individuals are unaware of their own social status, abilities, and other personal characteristics when making decisions about a just society. This thought experiment

encourages people to consider the principles of fairness and equality without bias or self-interest.

Question: Which choice best states the main idea of the text?

Answer Choices:

- (A) The "veil of ignorance" is a practical tool for resolving social conflicts.
- (B) The "veil of ignorance" is a philosophical concept that encourages impartial decision-making about a just society.
- (C) The "veil of ignorance" is a psychological phenomenon that explains why people make biased decisions.
- (D) The "veil of ignorance" is a social experiment that has been successfully implemented in various communities.

Correct Answer: (B)

Explanation: The main idea of the text is that the "veil of ignorance" is a philosophical concept that encourages impartial decision-making about a just society. The passage explains this concept and its purpose in promoting fairness and equality.

142. **Passage:**

The "zero-sum bias" is a cognitive bias that describes the tendency to incorrectly perceive a situation as zero-sum, even when it is not. A zero-sum situation occurs when one person's gain is equivalent to another person's loss, so the net change in wealth or benefit is zero.

Question: Which choice best describes the function of the underlined sentence in the text as a whole?

Answer Choices:

- (A) It explains why the "zero-sum bias" is a common bias.
- (B) It provides an example of the "zero-sum bias" in action.
- (C) It defines the term "zero-sum situation."
- (D) It contrasts the "zero-sum bias" with other cognitive biases.

Correct Answer: (C)

Explanation: The underlined sentence provides a definition of the term "zero-sum situation," explaining the concept of one person's gain being equivalent to another person's loss.

143. **Sentence:** The term "actor-observer bias" refers to a type of attributional bias in which people tend to attribute their own actions to situational factors and the actions of others to dispositional factors.

Question: Which choice completes the text so that it conforms to the conventions of Standard English?

(A) NO CHANGE

(B) which, people

(C) which people,

(D) which people;

Correct Answer: (A)

Explanation: The original sentence is grammatically correct and clearly conveys the meaning. The relative clause "in which people tend to attribute their own actions to situational factors and the actions of others to dispositional factors" correctly modifies the noun phrase "attributional bias."

144. **Sentence:** The "availability cascade" is a self-reinforcing process in which a collective belief gains more and more plausibility through its increasing repetition in public discourse (or "repeat something long enough and it will become true").

Question: Which choice completes the text so that it conforms to the conventions of Standard English?

(A) NO CHANGE

(B) discourse: ("repeat

(C) discourse ("repeat

(D) discourse. ("repeat

Correct Answer: (B)

Explanation: The original sentence is grammatically correct, but the punctuation can be improved. The parenthetical phrase "repeat something long enough and it will become true" should be introduced with a colon to indicate that it is an explanation or elaboration of the preceding phrase.

145. **Question:** If $7(x - 2) = 21$, what is the value of x?

(A) 1

(B) 3

(C) 5

(D) 7

Correct Answer: (C)

Explanation:

1. Distribute the 7: $7x - 14 = 21$

2. Add 14 to both sides: $7x = 35$

3. Divide both sides by 7: x = 5

146. **Question:** What is the solution to the inequality $-2(x + 5) \leq -14$?

(A) $x \leq -2$

(B) $x \geq -2$

(C) $x \leq 2$

(D) $x \geq 2$

Correct Answer: (D)

Explanation:

1. Distribute the -2: $-2x - 10 \leq -14$

2. Add 10 to both sides: $-2x \leq -4$

3. Divide both sides by -2 (and remember to flip the inequality sign): $x \geq 2$

147. **Question:** If $4x + y = 13$ and $x - 2y = -1$, what is the value of x?

(A) 2

(B) 3

(C) 4

(D) 5

Correct Answer: (B)

Explanation:

1. Multiply the second equation by 4: $4x - 8y = -4$

2. Subtract this equation from the first equation: $9y = 17$

3. Solve for y: $y = 17/9$

4. Substitute the value of y into either original equation to solve for x. Using the second equation: $x - 2(17/9) = -1$

$x - 34/9 = -1$

$x = 25/9 = 2.78$

148. **Question:** If $f(x) = -3x^2 + 2x + 5$, what is the value of $f(-2)$?

(A) -15

(B) -5

(C) 5

(D) 15

Correct Answer: (B)

Explanation:

Substitute x = -2 into the function: $f(-2) = -3(-2)^2 + 2(-2) + 5 = -12 - 4 + 5 = -11$

149. **Question:** What is the equation of a line that passes through the point (-1, 3) and has a slope of -2?

(A) y = -2x + 1

(B) y = -2x - 1

(C) y = -2x + 5

(D) y = -2x - 5

Correct Answer: (A)

Explanation:

1. Use the point-slope form of a linear equation: y - y₁ = m (x - x₁)

2. Substitute the given values: y - 3 = -2(x - (-1))

3. Simplify to get the equation in slope-intercept form: y - 3 = -2x - 2

    y = -2x + 1

150. **Question:** A triangle has sides of length 5 cm, 12 cm, and 13 cm. What type of triangle is it?

(A) Scalene

(B) Isosceles

(C) Equilateral

(D) Right

Correct Answer: (D)

Explanation:

The side lengths satisfy the Pythagorean theorem ($5^2 + 12^2 = 13^2$), so it is a right triangle.

151. **Question:** What is the area of a parallelogram with a base of 12 cm and a height of 5 cm?

(A) 30 cm²

(B) 60 cm²

(C) 70 cm²

(D) 120 cm²

Correct Answer: (B)

Explanation:

Area of a parallelogram = base * height = 12 cm * 5 cm = 60 cm²

152. **Question:** A spinner has 8 equal sections, numbered 1 through 8. What is the probability of spinning a number less than 4?

(A) 1/8

(B) 1/4

(C) 3/8

(D) 1/2

Correct Answer: (C)

Explanation:

Number of favorable outcomes (numbers less than 4): 3 (1, 2, and 3)

Total number of possible outcomes: 8

Probability = 3/8

153. **Passage:**

The "worse-than-average effect" is a cognitive bias in which people believe that they are worse than average at tasks which are difficult. However, for simple tasks, they believe that they are better than average.

Question: Which choice best describes the overall structure of the text?

Answer Choices:

○ (A) It presents a hypothesis and then explains how it was disproved.

○ (B) It describes a phenomenon and then provides a possible explanation.

○ (C) It contrasts two different cognitive biases.

○ (D) It argues for a change in the way people perceive their abilities.

Correct Answer: (B)

Explanation: The passage describes the "worse-than-average effect" and then provides a possible explanation for why people perceive themselves differently for difficult versus simple tasks.

154. **Passage:**

The "Zeigarnik effect" is a psychological phenomenon describing a tendency to remember interrupted or incomplete tasks or events more easily than tasks that have been completed. The effect is named after Soviet psychologist Bluma Zeigarnik.

Question: Which choice best states the main idea of the text?

Answer Choices:

○ (A) The "Zeigarnik effect" is a rare phenomenon that affects only a small percentage of the population.

○ (B) The "Zeigarnik effect" can be used to improve memory and learning.

○ (C) The "Zeigarnik effect" describes the tendency to remember incomplete tasks more easily than completed ones.

○ (D) The "Zeigarnik effect" is a cognitive bias that has no real-world applications.

Correct Answer: (C)

Explanation: The main idea of the text is that the "Zeigarnik effect" describes the tendency to remember incomplete tasks more easily than completed ones. The passage defines this effect and its origins.

155. **Passage:**

The "anchoring and adjustment heuristic" is a psychological heuristic that influences the way people intuitively assess probabilities. According to this heuristic, people start with an implicitly suggested reference point (the "anchor") and make adjustments to it to reach their estimate.

Question: Which choice best describes the function of the underlined sentence in the text as a whole?

Answer Choices:

o (A) It explains why the "anchoring and adjustment heuristic" is a common heuristic.

o (B) It provides an example of the "anchoring and adjustment heuristic" in action.

o (C) It defines the term "anchoring and adjustment heuristic."

o (D) It contrasts the "anchoring and adjustment heuristic" with other heuristics.

Correct Answer: (C)

Explanation: The underlined sentence provides a definition of the term "anchoring and adjustment heuristic," explaining how it affects people's intuitive assessment of probabilities.

156. **Sentence:** The term "availability heuristic" refers to a mental shortcut that relies on immediate examples that come to a given person's mind when evaluating a specific topic, concept, method, or decision.

Question: Which choice completes the text so that it conforms to the conventions of Standard English?

(A) NO CHANGE

(B) mind, when

(C) mind. When

(D) mind—when

Correct Answer: (A)

Explanation: The original sentence is grammatically correct and clearly conveys the meaning. The adverbial clause "when evaluating a specific topic, concept, method, or decision" correctly modifies the verb phrase "come to a given person's mind."

157. **Sentence:** The "base rate fallacy" is a formal fallacy in which people tend to ignore general information and focus on specific information.

Question: Which choice completes the text so that it conforms to the conventions of Standard English?

(A) NO CHANGE

(B) information, and,

(C) information and,

(D) information. And

Correct Answer: (A)

Explanation: The original sentence is grammatically correct and effectively conveys the information. The coordinating conjunction "and" correctly joins the two verb phrases "ignore general information" and "focus on specific information."

158. **Question:** If $5(x - 4) = 10$, what is the value of x?

(A) 2

(B) 4

(C) 6

(D) 8

Correct Answer: (C)

Explanation:

1. Distribute the 5: $5x - 20 = 10$

2. Add 20 to both sides: $5x = 30$

3. Divide both sides by 5: $x = 6$

159. **Question:** What is the solution to the inequality $-2(x + 3) > -8$?

(A) $x < 1$

(B) $x > 1$

(C) $x < 5$

(D) $x > 5$

Correct Answer: (A)

Explanation:

1. Distribute the -2: $-2x - 6 > -8$

2. Add 6 to both sides: $-2x > -2$

3. Divide both sides by -2 (and remember to flip the inequality sign): $x < 1$

160. **Question:** If $3x + 2y = 14$ and $x - y = 1$, what is the value of y?

(A) 2

(B) 3

(C) 4

(D) 5

Correct Answer: (B)

Explanation:

1. Solve the second equation for x: x = y + 1

2. Substitute this value of x into the first equation: 3(y + 1) + 2y = 14

3. Simplify and solve for y: 3y + 3 + 2y = 14

   5y = 11

   y = 11/5 = 2.2

161. **Question:** If $f(x) = 5x - 2$ and $g(x) = x^2 + 1$, what is the value of $f(g(-1))$?

(A) -8

(B) 3

(C) 8

(D) 13

Correct Answer: (C)

Explanation:

1. Find the value of g (-1): $g(-1) = (-1)^2 + 1 = 1 + 1 = 2$

2. Substitute this value into f (x): $f(g(-1)) = f(2) = 5(2) - 2 = 10 - 2 = 8$

162. **Question:** What is the slope of a line that is parallel to the line represented by the equation $y = -2x + 5$?

(A) -2

(B) -1/2

(C) 1/2

(D) 2

Correct Answer: (A)

Explanation:

Parallel lines have the same slope. The slope of the given line is -2.

163. **Question:** A triangle has sides of length 10 cm, 10 cm, and 10 cm. What type of triangle is it?

(A) Scalene

(B) Isosceles

(C) Equilateral

(D) Right

Correct Answer: (C)

Explanation:

An equilateral triangle has all three sides of equal length.

164. **Question:** A recipe calls for 2 cups of flour and 1 cup of sugar. If you want to make half the recipe, how much flour will you need?

(A) 1/2 cup

(B) 1 cup

(C) 1 1/2 cups

(D) 2 cups

Correct Answer: (B)

Explanation:

To make half the recipe, divide the amount of flour by 2: 2 cups / 2 = 1 cup

165. **Question:** A train travels 300 miles at an average speed of 60 miles per hour. How long does it take the train to complete the journey?

(A) 3 hours

(B) 4 hours

(C) 5 hours

(D) 6 hours

Correct Answer: (C)

Explanation:

Time = Distance / Speed = 300 miles / 60 miles per hour = 5 hours

166. **Question:** A store is having a sale where all items are 25% off. If a shirt originally costs $20, how much will it cost during the sale?

(A) $5

(B) $10

(C) $15

(D) $17

Correct Answer: (C)

Explanation:

1. Calculate the discount: $20 * 25/100 = $5

2. Subtract the discount from the original price: $20 - $5 = $15

167. **Question:** If $3^x = 81$, what is the value of x?

(A) 3

(B) 4

(C) 5

(D) 6

Correct Answer: (B)

Explanation:

81 is the same as 3 x 3 x 3 x 3 or
3^4. Therefore, x = 4

168. **Question:** What is the value of $(-2)^3$?

(A) -8

(B) -6

(C) 6

(D) 8

Correct Answer: (A)

Explanation:

$(-2)^3 = -2 \times -2 \times -2 = -8$

169. **Question:** If $\sqrt{x} = 9$, what is the value of x?

(A) 3

(B) 18

(C) 81

(D) 729

Correct Answer: (C)

Explanation:

$\sqrt{x} = 9$ means $x = 9^2 = 81$

170. **Question:** What is the volume of a cube with a side length of 4 cm?

(A) 12 cm³

(B) 16 cm³

(C) 36 cm³

(D) 64 cm³

Correct Answer: (D)

Explanation:

Volume of a cube = side³ = 4 cm * 4 cm * 4 cm = 64 cm³

171. **Question:** A bag contains 5 red marbles, 4 blue marbles, and 3 green marbles. What is the probability of randomly selecting a red marble?

(A) 1/4

(B) 5/12

(C) 1/3

(D) 1/2

Correct Answer: (B)

Explanation:

Number of favorable outcomes (red marbles): 5

Total number of possible outcomes: $5 + 4 + 3 = 12$

Probability $= 5/12$

172. **Passage:**

The "availability heuristic" is a mental shortcut that relies on immediate examples that come to a given person's mind when evaluating a specific topic, concept, method, or decision.

Question: As used in the passage, what does the word "immediate" most nearly mean?

Answer Choices:

o (A) Urgent

o (B) Recent

o (C) Closest

o (D) Fastest

Correct Answer: (B)

Explanation:

In this context, "immediate" refers to examples that come to mind readily because they have been recently encountered or are easily accessible in memory.

173. **Passage:**

The "bandwagon effect" is a psychological phenomenon in which people do something primarily because they believe many other people are doing it, regardless of their own beliefs, which they may ignore or override.

Question: Which choice best states the main idea of the text?

Answer Choices:

o (A) The "bandwagon effect" is a form of peer pressure that can lead to conformity.

o (B) The "bandwagon effect" is a cognitive bias that affects only a small percentage of the population.

o (C) The "bandwagon effect" describes the tendency to follow the crowd, regardless of one's own beliefs.

o (D) The "bandwagon effect" is a social phenomenon that has no positive effects.

Correct Answer: (C)

Explanation:

The main idea of the text is that the "bandwagon effect" describes the tendency to follow the crowd, regardless of one's own beliefs. The passage explains this effect and how it can lead people to adopt behaviors or beliefs simply because they are popular.

174. **Passage:**

The "base rate fallacy" is a formal fallacy in which people tend to ignore general information and focus on specific information.

Question: Which choice best describes the function of the underlined sentence in the text as a whole?

Answer Choices:

o (A) It provides an example of the "base rate fallacy" in action.

o (B) It explains the origins of the term "base rate fallacy."

o (C) It defines the term "base rate fallacy."

o (D) It contrasts the "base rate fallacy" with other logical fallacies.

Correct Answer: (C)

Explanation:

The underlined sentence provides a definition of the term "base rate fallacy," explaining how it involves ignoring general information in favor of specific information.

175. **Sentence:** The term "bias blind spot" refers to the cognitive bias of recognizing the impact of biases on the judgment of others, while failing to see the impact of biases on one's own judgment.

Question: Which choice completes the text so that it conforms to the conventions of Standard English?

(A) NO CHANGE

(B) others while,

(C) others. While

(D) others; while

Correct Answer: (A)

Explanation: The original sentence is grammatically correct. The comma after "others" correctly separates the two parts of the sentence, which are joined by the conjunction "while."

176. **Question:** What is the slope of a line that is parallel to the line represented by the equation $y = -2x + 5$?

(A) -2

(B) -1/2

(C) 1/2

(D) 2

Correct Answer: (A)

Explanation:

Parallel lines have the same slope. The slope of the given line is -2.

177. **Passage:**

The "base rate fallacy" is a formal fallacy in which people tend to ignore general information and focus on specific information.

Question: Which choice best describes the function of the underlined sentence in the text as a whole?

Answer Choices:

○ (A) It provides an example of the "base rate fallacy" in action.

○ (B) It explains the origins of the term "base rate fallacy."

○ (C) It defines the term "base rate fallacy."

○ (D) It contrasts the "base rate fallacy" with other logical fallacies.

Correct Answer: (C)

Explanation:

The underlined sentence provides a definition of the term "base rate fallacy," explaining how it involves ignoring general information in favor of specific information.

178. **Sentence:** The term "bias blind spot" refers to the cognitive bias of recognizing the impact of biases on the judgment of others, while failing to see the impact of biases on one's own judgment.

Question: Which choice completes the text so that it conforms to the conventions of Standard English?

(A) NO CHANGE

(B) others while,

(C) others. While

(D) others; while

Correct Answer: (A)

Explanation: The original sentence is grammatically correct. The comma after "others" correctly separates the two parts of the sentence, which are joined by the conjunction "while."

179. **Sentence:** The "choice-supportive bias" is the tendency to retroactively ascribe positive attributes to an option one has selected and negative attributes to options not selected.

Question: Which choice completes the text so that it conforms to the conventions of Standard English?

(A) NO CHANGE

(B) selected, and

(C) selected: and

(D) selected. And

Correct Answer: (B)

Explanation: The original sentence contains a compound predicate (ascribe positive attributes AND negative attributes). To join these with a conjunction, a comma is needed before the "and."

180. **Sentence:** The "clustering illusion" is the tendency to erroneously consider the inevitable "streaks" or "clusters" arising in small samples from random distributions to be non-random.

Question: Which choice completes the text so that it conforms to the conventions of Standard English?

(A) NO CHANGE

(B) to be non-random.

(C) to be non-random,

(D) to be; non-random.

Correct Answer: (A)

Explanation: The original sentence is grammatically correct. "To be non-random" functions as an adjective phrase modifying "streaks" or "clusters."

181. **Question:** What is the value of x in the equation $2(x + 3) - 5 = 11$?

(A) 3

(B) 4

(C) 5

(D) 6

Correct Answer: (C)

Explanation:

1. Distribute the 2: $2x + 6 - 5 = 11$

2. Combine like terms: $2x + 1 = 11$

3. Subtract 1 from both sides: $2x = 10$

4. Divide both sides by 2: $x = 5$

182. **Question:** What is the solution to the inequality $4 - 3x < 13$?

(A) $x < -3$

(B) $x > -3$

(C) $x < 3$

(D) $x > 3$

Correct Answer: (B)

Explanation:

1. Subtract 4 from both sides: $-3x < 9$

2. Divide both sides by -3 (and remember to flip the inequality sign): $x > -3$

183. **Question:** If $x - 2y = 5$ and $2x + y = 7$, what is the value of y?

(A) -1

(B) 1

(C) 2

(D) 3

Correct Answer: (A)

Explanation:

1. Multiply the first equation by 2: $2x - 4y = 10$

2. Subtract the second equation from this new equation: $-5y = 3$

3. Solve for y: $y = -3/5$

4. Substitute the value of y into either original equation to solve for x. Using the first equation: $x - 2(-3/5) = 5$

   $x + 6/5 = 5$

   $x = 19/5 = 3.8$

184. **Question:** If $f(x) = 2x^2 - 3x + 1$, what is the value of $f(-2)$?

(A) -13

(B) -3

(C) 11

(D) 15

Correct Answer: (D)

Explanation:

Substitute x = -2 into the function: $f(-2) = 2(-2)^2 - 3(-2) + 1 = 8 + 6 + 1 = 15$

185. **Question:** What is the equation of the line that passes through the points (1, 2) and (3, 8)?

(A) $y = 3x - 1$

(B) $y = 3x + 1$

(C) $y = 2x + 4$

(D) $y = 2x - 4$

Correct Answer: (A)

Explanation:

1. Find the slope: $m = (y_2 - y_1) / (x_2 - x_1) = (8 - 2) / (3 - 1) = 6 / 2 = 3$

2. Use the point-slope form of a linear equation: $y - y_1 = m (x - x_1)$

3. Substitute one of the points and the slope: $y - 2 = 3(x - 1)$

4. Simplify to get the equation in slope-intercept form: y - 2 = 3x - 3

   y = 3x - 1

186. **Question:** Which of the following is an equation of a line that is perpendicular to the line with equation y = (2/3) x - 5?

(A) y = (2/3) x + 2

(B) y = (-3/2) x + 2

(C) y = (3/2) x + 2

(D) y = (-2/3) x + 2

Correct Answer: (B)

Explanation:

Perpendicular lines have slopes that are negative reciprocals of each other. The slope of the given line is 2/3, and the negative reciprocal of 2/3 is -3/2.

187. **Question:** What is the length of the hypotenuse of a right triangle with legs of length 8 cm and 15 cm?

(A) 12 cm

(B) 17 cm

(C) 20 cm

(D) 23 cm

Correct Answer: (B)

Explanation:

Use the Pythagorean theorem: $a^2 + b^2 = c^2$

$8^2 + 15^2 = c^2$

$64 + 225 = c^2$

$289 = c^2$

$c = \sqrt{289} = 17$ cm

188. **Question:** A circle has a circumference of 20π cm. What is its diameter?

(A) 10 cm

(B) 20 cm

(C) 40 cm

(D) 100 cm

Correct Answer: (B)

Explanation:

Circumference of a circle = πd, where d is the diameter.

20π cm = πd

d = 20 cm

189. **Question:** A bag contains 6 red marbles, 4 blue marbles, and 2 green

marbles. If a marble is selected at random, what is the probability that it is NOT green?

(A) 1/6

(B) 1/3

(C) 5/6

(D) 2/3

Correct Answer: (C)

Explanation:

Number of favorable outcomes (not green marbles): 6 + 4 = 10

Total number of possible outcomes: 6 + 4 + 2 = 12

Probability (not green) = 10/12 = 5/6

190. **Question:** The average of five numbers is 12. If one of the numbers is removed, the average of the remaining four numbers is 10. What number was removed?

(A) 10

(B) 15

(C) 20

(D) 22

Correct Answer: (C)

Explanation:

1. Sum of the original five numbers: 5 numbers * 12 average = 60

2. Sum of the remaining four numbers: 4 numbers * 10 average = 40

3. The removed number is the difference: 60 - 40 = 20

191. **Passage:**

The "conjunction fallacy" is a formal fallacy that occurs when it is assumed that specific conditions are more probable than a single general one.

Question: Which choice provides the most accurate definition of the underlined word in the passage?

(A) A mistaken belief, especially one based on unsound argument

(B) A failure in reasoning that renders an argument invalid

(C) A statement or proposition that is regarded as being established, accepted, or self-evidently true

(D) A deceptive or misleading argument

Correct Answer: (B)

Explanation:

In this context, "fallacy" refers specifically to a flaw in the logical structure of an argument, rendering it invalid. While options (A) and (D) are related to the idea of a fallacy, they don't capture the precise meaning in this context. Option (C) is incorrect as it describes an axiom, not a fallacy.

192. **Passage:**

The "continued influence effect" is the tendency to believe previously learned misinformation even after it has been corrected. Misinformation can still influence inferences one generates after a correction has occurred.

Question: Which choice best states the main idea of the text?

(A) People are always able to identify and correct misinformation.

(B) Misinformation can have a lasting impact on beliefs even after being corrected.

(C) The "continued influence effect" is a rare phenomenon that affects only a small percentage of the population.

(D) The "continued influence effect" can be easily overcome with proper education.

Correct Answer: (B)

Explanation:

The passage highlights that even after misinformation has been corrected, it can still subtly influence people's beliefs and the conclusions they draw.

193. **Passage:**

The "correspondence bias" is the tendency to draw inferences about a person's unique and enduring dispositions from behaviors that can be entirely explained by the situations in which they occur.

Question: Which choice best describes the function of the underlined sentence in the text as a whole?

(A) It provides an example of the "correspondence bias" in action.

(B) It explains the origins of the term "correspondence bias."

(C) It defines the term "correspondence bias."

(D) It contrasts the "correspondence bias" with other cognitive biases.

Correct Answer: (C)

Explanation:

The underlined sentence provides a clear definition of the "correspondence bias," explaining how it involves incorrectly attributing behavior to a person's disposition rather than the situation.

194. **Sentence:** The term "curse of knowledge" refers to a cognitive bias that occurs when an individual, communicating with other individuals, unknowingly assumes that the others have the background to understand.

Question: Which choice completes the text so that it conforms to the conventions of Standard English?

(A) NO CHANGE

(B) individuals. Unknowingly

(C) individuals, unknowingly,

(D) individuals unknowingly,

Correct Answer: (A)

Explanation:

The original sentence is grammatically correct. The adverb "unknowingly" modifies the verb "assumes."

195. **Sentence:** The "decoy effect" is a phenomenon whereby consumers will tend to have a specific change in preference between two options when also presented with a third option that is asymmetrically dominated.

Question: Which choice completes the text so that it conforms to the conventions of Standard English?

(A) NO CHANGE

(B) preference, between

(C) preference between,

(D) preference. Between

Correct Answer: (A)

Explanation:

The original sentence is grammatically correct. The prepositional phrase "between two options" correctly modifies the noun "change."

196. **Question:** If $6(x - 3) = 18$, what is the value of x?

(A) 3

(B) 4

(C) 5

(D) 6

Correct Answer: (D)

Explanation:

1. Distribute the 6: 6x - 18 = 18

2. Add 18 to both sides: 6x = 36

3. Divide both sides by 6: x = 6

197. **Question:** What is the solution to the inequality $-3(x + 4) < -9$?

(A) x < -1

(B) x > -1

(C) x < 1

(D) x > 1

Correct Answer: (D)

Explanation:

1. Distribute the -3: -3*x* - 12 < -9

2. Add 12 to both sides: -3*x* < 3

3. Divide both sides by -3 (and remember to flip the inequality sign): x > 1

198. **Question:** If $2x + 3y = 11$ and $x - y = 2$, what is the value of x?

(A) 2

(B) 3

(C) 4

(D) 5

Correct Answer: (C)

Explanation:

1. Solve the second equation for x: x = y + 2

2. Substitute this value of x into the first equation: 2(y + 2) + 3y = 11

3. Simplify and solve for y: 2y + 4 + 3y = 11

5y = 7

y = 7/5 = 1.4

4. Substitute the value of y back into the equation x = y + 2: x = 7/5 + 2 = 17/5 = 3.4

199. **Question:** If $f(x) = 4x - 1$ and $g(x) = x^2 + 2$, what is the value of $g(f(1))$?

(A) 7

(B) 11

(C) 13

(D) 18

Correct Answer: (B)

Explanation:

1. Find the value of f (1): f (1) = 4(1) - 1 = 4 - 1 = 3

2. Substitute this value into g (x): g (f (1)) = g (3) = (3) ^{2} + 2 = 9 + 2 = 11

200. **Question:** What is the *y*-intercept of the line that passes through the points (2, 3) and (5, 9)?

(A) -3

(B) -1

(C) 1

(D) 3

Correct Answer: (B)

Explanation:

1. Find the slope: m = (y_2 - y_1) / (x_2 - x_1) = (9 - 3) / (5 - 2) = 6 / 3 = 2

2. Use the point-slope form of a linear equation: y - y_1 = m (x - x_1)

3. Substitute one of the points and the slope: y - 3 = 2(x - 2)

4. Simplify to get the equation in slope-intercept form: y - 3 = 2x - 4

   y = 2x - 1

5. The *y*-intercept is -1.

PRACTICE TEST 2

1. **PASSAGE 1:**

Herd immunity is a form of indirect protection from infectious disease that occurs when a large percentage of a population has become immune to an infection, thereby providing a measure of protection for individuals who are not immune. Herd immunity is a concept used for vaccination, in which a population can be protected from a certain virus if a threshold of vaccination is reached.

PASSAGE 2:

The precise herd immunity threshold for COVID-19 is not yet definitively known, and it may vary depending on factors such as the transmissibility of the virus and the effectiveness of vaccines. However, experts estimate that a vaccination rate of 70% to 85% may be needed to achieve herd immunity for COVID-19.

Question: Based on the texts, how would the author of Passage 1 most likely respond to the claim in Passage 2 that "the precise herd immunity threshold for COVID-19 is not yet definitively known"?

Answer Choices:

1. (A) By arguing that the herd immunity threshold for COVID-19 is well-established and does not vary.

2. (B) By acknowledging that the herd immunity threshold can vary depending on various factors.

3. (C) By suggesting that vaccination is not an effective way to achieve herd immunity for COVID-19.

4. (D) By proposing that further research is needed to determine the herd immunity threshold for other infectious diseases.

Correct Answer: (B)

Explanation: The author of Passage 1 would likely acknowledge that the herd immunity threshold can vary depending on various factors, as the passage states that herd immunity is a concept used for vaccination, in which a population can be protected from a certain virus if a threshold of vaccination is reached.

2. **PASSAGE 1:**

The term "tipping point" refers to the point at which a series of small changes or incidents becomes significant enough to cause a larger, more important change. The term was first used in the field of epidemiology to describe the point at which a disease outbreak becomes an epidemic.

PASSAGE 2:

The concept of a tipping point has been applied to various fields, including sociology, economics, and climate science. In climate science, the term is used to describe the point at which global warming becomes irreversible, leading to significant and potentially catastrophic changes in the Earth's climate system.

Question: Based on the texts, how would the author of Passage 1 most likely respond to the claim in Passage 2 that "the concept of a tipping point has been applied to various fields"?

Answer Choices:

1. (A) By arguing that the concept of a tipping point is only relevant to the field of epidemiology.

2. (B) By acknowledging that the concept of a tipping point has broad applicability across different disciplines.

3. (C) By suggesting that the term "tipping point" should not be used in fields other than epidemiology.

4. (D) By proposing that further research is needed to determine the specific tipping points for various phenomena.

Correct Answer: (B)

Explanation: The author of Passage 1 would likely acknowledge that the concept of a tipping point has broad applicability across different disciplines, as the passage states that the term was first used in the field of epidemiology but does not limit its relevance to that field alone.

3. **PASSAGE 1:**

The term "uncanny valley" refers to the unsettling feeling people experience when they encounter robots or other artificial entities that closely resemble humans but are not quite perfect. This eerie sensation is thought to arise from a mismatch between the entity's appearance and behavior, creating a sense of unease or even revulsion.

PASSAGE 2:

The concept of the uncanny valley has implications for the design and development of robots and other artificial intelligence systems. As these technologies become more sophisticated and lifelike, it's crucial to consider the potential psychological impact on users and ensure that these entities do not fall into the uncanny valley.

Question: Based on the texts, how would the author of Passage 1 most likely respond to the claim in Passage 2 that "the concept of the uncanny valley has implications for the design and development of robots"?

Answer Choices:

1. (A) By arguing that the uncanny valley is a purely theoretical concept with no practical implications.
2. (B) By acknowledging that the uncanny valley is an important consideration in the design of human-like robots.
3. (C) By suggesting that the uncanny valley is a phenomenon that only affects a small percentage of the population.
4. (D) By proposing that further research is needed to determine the specific factors that contribute to the uncanny valley.

Correct Answer: (B)

Explanation: The author of Passage 1 would likely acknowledge that the uncanny valley is an important consideration in the design of human-like robots, as the passage explains the unsettling feeling people experience when encountering artificial entities that closely resemble humans but are not quite perfect.

4. **Sentence:** The term "wisdom of crowds" refers to the phenomenon in which the collective knowledge of a group of people can often be more accurate than the knowledge of any single individual within the group.

Question: Which choice completes the text so that it conforms to the conventions of Standard English?

Answer Choices:

1. (A) NO CHANGE
2. (B) group, can
3. (C) group can,
4. (D) group. Can

Correct Answer: (A)

Explanation: The original sentence is grammatically correct and effectively conveys the information. The phrase "the collective knowledge of a group of people" is the subject of the sentence, and the verb "can be" agrees with the subject in number.

5. **Sentence:** The "halo effect" is a cognitive bias in which our overall impression of a person influences how we feel and think about their character.

Question: Which choice completes the text so that it conforms to the conventions of Standard English?

Answer Choices:

1. (A) NO CHANGE
2. (B) person, influences
3. (C) person influences,
4. (D) person; influences

Correct Answer: (A)

Explanation: The original sentence is grammatically correct and effectively conveys the information. The relative clause "in which our overall impression of a person influences how we feel and think about their character" correctly modifies the noun phrase "cognitive bias."

6. **Question:** If $2(x - 3)^2 = 32$, what is the value of x?

   Answer Choices:

   1. (A) 1
   2. (B) 5
   3. (C) 7
   4. (D) 9

Correct Answer: (C)

   Explanation:

5. Divide both sides by 2: $(x - 3)^2 = 16$
6. Take the square root of both sides: $x - 3 = \pm 4$
7. Solve for x: $x = 3 \pm 4$
8. The two possible solutions are $x = 7$ and $x = -1$. Since only 7 is an answer choice, the correct answer is (C).
7. **Question:** What is the solution to the inequality $x^2 - 4x - 5 < 0$?

   Answer Choices:

   1. (A) $x < -1$ or $x > 5$
   2. (B) $-1 < x < 5$
   3. (C) $x < -5$ or $x > 1$
   4. (D) $-5 < x < 1$

Correct Answer: (B)

   Explanation:

5. Factor the quadratic: $(x - 5)(x + 1) < 0$
6. The critical points are $x = 5$ and $x = -1$.
7. Create a sign chart or test values in each interval to determine where the inequality is true.
8. The solution is $-1 < x < 5$.
8. **Question:** If $f(x) = x^2 - 2x + 3$ and $g(x) = 2x - 1$, what is the value of $f(g(2))$?

   Answer Choices:

   1. (A) 3
   2. (B) 6
   3. (C) 9
   4. (D) 12

Correct Answer: (C)

   Explanation:

5. Find the value of g (2): $g(2) = 2(2) - 1 = 4 - 1 = 3$
6. Substitute this value into f(x): $f(g(2)) = f(3) = 3^2 - 2(3) + 3 = 9 - 6 + 3 = 6$

9. **Question:** What is the area of a regular hexagon with a side length of 6 cm?

   Answer Choices:

○ (A) 18√3 cm²

○ (B) 36√3 cm²

○ (C) 54√3 cm²

○ (D) 72√3 cm²

Correct Answer: (C)

Explanation:

○ A regular hexagon can be divided into 6 equilateral triangles.

○ The area of an equilateral triangle with side length s is $(\sqrt{3}/4)\, s^2$.

○ Area of one triangle: $(\sqrt{3}/4) *(6\text{ cm})^2 = 9\sqrt{3}$ cm²

○ Area of the hexagon: $6 * 9\sqrt{3}$ cm² $= 54\sqrt{3}$ cm²

10. **Question:** A rectangular prism has a volume of 120 cm³, a length of 6 cm, and a width of 4 cm. What is its height?

Answer Choices:

○ (A) 3 cm

○ (B) 5 cm

○ (C) 8 cm

○ (D) 10 cm

Correct Answer: (B)

Explanation:

Volume of a rectangular prism = length * width * height 120 cm³ = 6 cm * 4 cm * height 120 cm³ = 24 cm² * height = 120 cm³ / 24 cm² = 5 cm

11. **Question:** A bag contains 5 red marbles, 3 blue marbles, and 2 yellow marbles. If two marbles are drawn at random without replacement, what is the probability that both marbles are red?

Answer Choices:

○ (A) 1/5

○ (B) 2/9

○ (C) 1/4

○ (D) 5/18

Correct Answer: (B)

Explanation:

○ Probability of drawing one red marble: 5/10 = 1/2

○ After removing one red marble, there are 4 red marbles left and 9 total marbles.

○ Probability of drawing another red marble: 4/9

○ Probability of drawing two red marbles in a row: (1/2) * (4/9) = 2/9

12. **Passage 1:**

The term "confirmation bias" refers to the tendency to search for, interpret, favor, and recall information in a way that confirms or supports one's prior beliefs or values. People display this bias when they gather or remember information selectively, or when they interpret it in a biased way.

Passage 2:

Confirmation bias is a pervasive cognitive bias that can have significant implications for decision-making, problem-solving, and interpersonal interactions. It can lead people to make inaccurate judgments, hold onto false beliefs, and resist new information that challenges their existing views.

Question: Which choice best describes the relationship between the two passages?

Answer Choices:

- (A) Passage 2 provides a specific example of the concept described in Passage 1.
- (B) Passage 2 presents a contrasting perspective to the one presented in Passage 1.
- (C) Passage 2 expands on the definition provided in Passage 1 by discussing the implications of the concept.
- (D) Passage 2 challenges the validity of the concept introduced in Passage 1.

Correct Answer: (C)

Explanation: Passage 1 defines confirmation bias, while Passage 2 elaborates on this definition by discussing the potential consequences and implications of this bias.

13. **Passage 1:**

The term "cognitive dissonance" refers to the mental discomfort experienced by a person who simultaneously holds two or more contradictory beliefs, ideas, or values. This discomfort is triggered by a situation in which a person's belief clashes with new evidence perceived by that person.

Passage 2:

Cognitive dissonance can lead people to engage in various strategies to reduce this mental discomfort, such as changing their beliefs, seeking out information that supports their existing views, or avoiding information that challenges their beliefs.

Question: Which choice best describes the relationship between the two passages?

Answer Choices:

- (A) Passage 2 provides a specific example of the concept described in Passage 1.
- (B) Passage 2 presents a contrasting perspective to the one presented in Passage 1.
- (C) Passage 2 explains the consequences and potential responses to the concept described in Passage 1.
- (D) Passage 2 challenges the validity of the concept introduced in Passage 1.

Correct Answer: (C)

Explanation: Passage 1 defines cognitive dissonance, while Passage 2 explains the potential consequences of this discomfort and the strategies people use to reduce it.

14. **Passage 1:**

The term "Dunning-Kruger effect" describes a cognitive bias in which people with low ability at a task overestimate their ability.

Passage 2:

The Dunning-Kruger effect is often observed in situations where people lack the metacognitive skills to accurately assess their own competence. This can lead to overconfidence and a lack of awareness of one's own limitations.

Question: Which choice best describes the relationship between the two passages?

Answer Choices:

o (A) Passage 2 provides a specific example of the concept described in Passage 1.

o (B) Passage 2 presents a contrasting perspective to the one presented in Passage 1.

o (C) Passage 2 explains the underlying mechanisms and consequences of the concept described in Passage 1.

o (D) Passage 2 challenges the validity of the concept introduced in Passage 1.

Correct Answer: (C)

Explanation: Passage 1 provides a basic

definition of the Dunning-Kruger effect, while Passage 2 delves deeper into the underlying reasons for this bias and its potential consequences.

15. **Sentence:** The term "false consensus effect" refers to the tendency for people to overestimate the extent to which others share their beliefs and behaviors.

Question: Which choice completes the text so that it conforms to the conventions of Standard English?

Answer Choices:

o (A) NO CHANGE

o (B) for people, to

o (C) for, people to

o (D) for people to,

Correct Answer: (A)

Explanation: The original sentence is grammatically correct and clearly conveys the meaning. The prepositional phrase "to overestimate the extent..." correctly modifies the verb "refers."

16. **Sentence:** The "framing effect" is a cognitive bias in which people react to a particular choice in different ways depending on how it is presented; e.g. as a loss or as a gain.

Question: Which choice completes the text so that it conforms to the conventions of Standard English?

Answer Choices:

- (A) NO CHANGE
- (B) presented, e.g.,
- (C) presented: e.g.,
- (D) presented. E.g.,

Correct Answer: (B)

Explanation: The original sentence is grammatically correct, but the punctuation can be improved. The abbreviation "e.g." (for example) should be set off with commas.

17. **Question:** If $3(x + 2)^2 - 5 = 43$, what is the value of x?

Answer Choices:

- (A) -1
- (B) 1
- (C) 2
- (D) 4

Correct Answer: (B)

Explanation:

- Add 5 to both sides: $3(x + 2)^2 = 48$
- Divide both sides by 3: $(x + 2)^2 = 16$
- Take the square root of both sides: $x + 2 = \pm 4$
- Solve for x: $x = -2 \pm 4$
- The two possible solutions are $x = 2$ and $x = -6$. Since only 2 is an answer choice, the correct answer is (C).

18. **Question:** What is the solution to the system of inequalities: $y > x + 2$ and $y < -2x + 1$?

Answer Choices:

- (A) The solution is the region where the shaded areas of the two inequalities overlap.
- (B) There is no solution, as the lines are parallel.
- (C) The solution is the entire shaded area of both inequalities.
- (D) The solution is only the points on the lines.

Correct Answer: (A)

Explanation:

To find the solution to a system of inequalities, graph each inequality and shade the appropriate region. The solution to the system is the region where the shaded areas overlap.

19. **Question:** The graph of the equation $y = x^2 - 4x + 3$ is a parabola. What are the x-intercepts of the parabola?

Answer Choices:

- (A) 1 and 3
- (B) -1 and -3
- (C) 2 and -2
- (D) 0 and 4

Correct Answer: (A)

Explanation:

o To find the *x*-intercepts, set $y = 0$: $x^2 - 4x + 3 = 0$

o Factor the quadratic: $(x - 3)(x - 1) = 0$

o The solutions, which are the *x*-intercepts, are $x = 3$ and $x = 1$.

20. **Question:** The graph of the equation $y = -2x + 4$ is a line. What is the *y*-intercept of the line?

Answer Choices:

o (A) -2

o (B) 2

o (C) 4

o (D) -4

Correct Answer: (C)

Explanation:

The *y*-intercept is the point where the line crosses the *y*-axis. This occurs when $x = 0$. Substituting $x = 0$ into the equation, we get $y = -2(0) + 4 = 4$.

21. **Question:** A rectangular garden has a length of 10 meters and a width of 6 meters. A path 2 meters wide is built around the garden. What is the area of the path?

Answer Choices:

o (A) 40 m²

o (B) 60 m²

o (C) 88 m²

o (D) 144 m²

Correct Answer: (C)

Explanation:

o Draw a diagram to visualize the situation.

o Calculate the dimensions of the outer rectangle: length = $10 + 2 + 2 = 14$ meters, width = $6 + 2 + 2 = 10$ meters

o Calculate the area of the outer rectangle: 14 m * 10 m = 140 m²

o Calculate the area of the inner rectangle (garden): 10 m * 6 m = 60 m²

o Subtract the area of the garden from the area of the outer rectangle to find the area of the path: 140 m² - 60 m² = 80 m²

22. **Question:** A cylindrical can has a radius of 5 cm and a height of 10 cm. What is its volume?

Answer Choices:

o (A) 50π cm³

o (B) 100π cm³

o (C) 250π cm³

o (D) 500π cm³

Correct Answer: (C)

Explanation:

Volume of a cylinder = $\pi r^2 h = \pi(5 \text{ cm})^2(10 \text{ cm}) = 250\pi$ cm³

23. **Question:** A bag contains 4 red marbles, 3 blue marbles, and 2 green marbles. If

two marbles are drawn at random without replacement, what is the probability that the first marble is red and the second marble is blue?

Answer Choices:

- (A) 1/6
- (B) 2/9
- (C) 4/27
- (D) ⅓

Correct Answer: (C)

Explanation:

- Probability of drawing a red marble first: 4/9

- After removing one red marble, there are 3 blue marbles left and 8 total marbles.

- Probability of drawing a blue marble second: 3/8

- Probability of drawing a red marble then a blue marble: (4/9) * (3/8) = 12/72 = 1/6

24. **Passage 1:**

The term "anchoring bias" describes the common human tendency to rely too heavily on the first piece of information offered (the "anchor") when making decisions.

Passage 2:

Anchoring bias can be a significant factor in negotiations, pricing strategies, and other situations where individuals are making judgments or estimations based on

limited information.

Question: Which choice best describes the relationship between the two passages?

Answer Choices:

- (A) Passage 2 provides a specific example of the concept described in Passage 1.

- (B) Passage 2 presents a contrasting perspective to the one presented in Passage 1.

- (C) Passage 2 expands on the definition provided in Passage 1 by discussing the applications of the concept.

- (D) Passage 2 challenges the validity of the concept introduced in Passage 1.

Correct Answer: (C)

Explanation: Passage 1 defines anchoring bias, while Passage 2 expands on this definition by discussing the various applications and real-world implications of this bias.

25. **Passage 1:**

The "availability heuristic" is a mental shortcut that relies on immediate examples that come to a given person's mind when evaluating a specific topic, concept, method, or decision.

Passage 2:

The availability heuristic can lead to biased judgments, as people tend to overestimate the importance of information that is readily available to them, while neglecting information that is less accessible.

Question: Which choice best describes the relationship between the two passages?

Answer Choices:

o (A) Passage 2 provides a specific example of the concept described in Passage 1.

o (B) Passage 2 presents a contrasting perspective to the one presented in Passage 1.

o (C) Passage 2 explains the potential consequences and limitations of the concept described in Passage 1.

o (D) Passage 2 challenges the validity of the concept introduced in Passage 1.

Correct Answer: (C)

Explanation: Passage 1 defines the availability heuristic, while Passage 2 explains the potential consequences of this heuristic, such as biased judgments and overestimation of readily available information.

26. **Passage 1:**

The "bandwagon effect" is a psychological phenomenon in which people do something primarily because they believe many other people are doing

it, regardless of their own beliefs, which they may ignore or override.

Passage 2:
The bandwagon effect can be a powerful force in social dynamics, influencing trends, fashion, and even political opinions.

Question: Which choice best describes the relationship between the two passages?

Answer Choices:

o (A) Passage 2 provides a specific example of the concept described in Passage 1.

o (B) Passage 2 presents a contrasting perspective to the one presented in Passage 1.

o (C) Passage 2 expands on the definition provided in Passage 1 by discussing the influence of the concept.

o (D) Passage 2 challenges the validity of the concept introduced in Passage 1.

Correct Answer: (C)

Explanation: Passage 1 defines the bandwagon effect, while Passage 2 expands on this definition by discussing the influence and impact of this effect on various aspects of society.

27. **Sentence:** The term "belief bias" refers to the tendency for one's preexisting beliefs to distort logical reasoning, sometimes by

making invalid conclusions seem valid, or valid conclusions seem invalid.

Question: Which choice completes the text so that it conforms to the conventions of Standard English?

Answer Choices:

- (A) NO CHANGE
- (B) reasoning sometimes,
- (C) reasoning, sometimes
- (D) reasoning. Sometimes

Correct Answer: (C)

Explanation: The original sentence is grammatically correct, but the punctuation can be improved. The adverb "sometimes" should be set off with commas to show it modifies the entire verb phrase ("distort logical reasoning").

28. **Sentence:** The "conjunction fallacy" is a formal fallacy that occurs when it is assumed that specific conditions are more probable than a single general one.

Question: Which choice completes the text so that it conforms to the conventions of Standard English?

Answer Choices:

- (A) NO CHANGE
- (B) occurs, when
- (C) occurs. When
- (D) occurs when,

Correct Answer: (A)

Explanation: The original sentence is grammatically correct. The adverbial clause "when it is assumed..." correctly modifies the verb "occurs."

29. **Question:** If the function f is defined by $f(x) = 2x^2 - 5x + 3$, what is the value of $f(4)$?

Answer Choices:

- (A) 15
- (B) 18
- (C) 21
- (D) 27

Correct Answer: (A)

Explanation:

Substitute $x = 4$ into the function: $f(4) = 2(4)^2 - 5(4) + 3 = 32 - 20 + 3 = 15$

30. **Question:** What is the sum of the solutions to the quadratic equation $x^2 - 7x + 10 = 0$?

Answer Choices:

- (A) -7
- (B) -5
- (C) 5
- (D) 7

Correct Answer: (D)

Explanation:

- For a quadratic equation in the standard form $ax^2 + bx + c = 0$, the sum of the solutions is $-b/a$.
- In this case, $a = 1$ and $b = -7$, so the sum of the solutions is $-(-7)/1 = 7$.

31. **Question:** A line passes through the points $(2, 5)$ and $(6, 13)$. What is the equation of the line?

    Answer Choices:
    - (A) $y = 2x + 1$
    - (B) $y = 2x + 5$
    - (C) $y = (1/2)x + 4$
    - (D) $y = (1/2)x + 6$

Correct Answer: (A)

   Explanation:

- Find the slope: $m = (y_2 - y_1)/(x_2 - x_1) = (13 - 5)/(6 - 2) = 8/4 = 2$
- Use the point-slope form of a linear equation: $y - y_1 = m(x - x_1)$
- Substitute one of the points and the slope: $y - 5 = 2(x - 2)$
- Simplify to get the equation in slope-intercept form: $y - 5 = 2x - 4$ $y = 2x + 1$

32. **Question:** The circle shown below has a center at O and a radius of 5. If the length of arc AB is 2π, what is the measure of $\angle AOB$ in degrees?

    (Insert a diagram of a circle with center O, radius 5, and arc AB marked)

    Answer Choices:
    - (A) $36°$
    - (B) $72°$
    - (C) $144°$
    - (D) $288°$

Correct Answer: (B)

   Explanation:

- Circumference of the circle: $2\pi r = 2\pi(5) = 10\pi$
- Arc AB represents $(2\pi)/(10\pi) = 1/5$ of the circle's circumference.
- $\angle AOB$ represents $1/5$ of the circle's total degrees ($360°$).
- Measure of $\angle AOB$: $(1/5) * 360° = 72°$

33. **Question:** A box contains 5 red balls, 3 green balls, and 2 blue balls. If two balls are drawn at random without replacement, what is the probability that both balls are green?

    Answer Choices:
    - (A) $1/15$
    - (B) $3/50$
    - (C) $9/100$
    - (D) $1/10$

Correct Answer: (B)

   Explanation:

- Probability of drawing one green ball: $3/10$
- After removing one green ball, there are 2 green balls left and 9 total balls.

- Probability of drawing another green ball: 2/9
- Probability of drawing two green balls in a row: $(3/10) * (2/9) = 6/90 = 1/15$

34. **Passage 1:**

    The "endowment effect" is the finding that people are more likely to retain an object they own than acquire that same object when they do not own it.

    Passage 2:

    This is typically illustrated in two ways. First, people will tend to pay more to retain something they own than to obtain something they do not own—even when there is no cause for attachment, or even if the item was only obtained minutes ago. Second, people given a good are reluctant to trade it for another good of similar value.

    Question: Which choice best describes the relationship between the two passages?

    Answer Choices:

    - (A) Passage 2 provides specific examples to illustrate the concept described in Passage 1.
    - (B) Passage 2 presents a contrasting perspective to the one presented in Passage 1.
    - (C) Passage 2 explains the underlying causes of the phenomenon described in Passage 1.
    - (D) Passage 2 challenges the validity of the concept introduced in Passage 1.

    Correct Answer: (A)

    Explanation: Passage 1 defines the endowment effect, while Passage 2 provides specific examples to illustrate how this effect manifests in people's behavior.

35. **Sentence:** The "availability cascade" is a self-reinforcing process in which a collective belief gains more and more plausibility through its increasing repetition in public discourse (or "repeat something long enough and it will become true").

    Question: Which choice completes the text so that it conforms to the conventions of Standard English?

    Answer Choices:

    - (A) NO CHANGE
    - (B) plausibility, through
    - (C) plausibility through,
    - (D) plausibility. Through

    Correct Answer: (A)

    Explanation: The original sentence is grammatically correct. The prepositional phrase "through its increasing repetition..." correctly modifies the verb "gains."

36. **Sentence:** The "backfire effect" is the tendency to strengthen one's previous beliefs when presented with evidence contradicting those beliefs.

    Question: Which choice completes the text so that it conforms to the conventions of Standard English?

    Answer Choices:

    ○ (A) NO CHANGE

    ○ (B) beliefs, when

    ○ (C) beliefs when,

    ○ (D) beliefs. When

Correct Answer: (A)

    Explanation: The original sentence is grammatically correct. The adverbial clause "when presented with evidence..." correctly modifies the verb "strengthen."

37. **Question:** If the function f is defined by $f(x) = 3x^2 + 2x - 5$, what is the value of $f(-2)$?

    Answer Choices:

    ○ (A) -17

    ○ (B) -7

    ○ (C) 3

    ○ (D) 13

Correct Answer: (C)

    Explanation:

    Substitute $x = -2$ into the function: $f(-2) = 3(-2)^2 + 2(-2) - 5 = 12 - 4 - 5 = 3$

38. **Question:** What are the solutions to the quadratic equation $2x^2 - 5x - 3 = 0$?

    Answer Choices:

    ○ (A) x = -1/2 and x = 3

    ○ (B) x = 1/2 and x = -3

    ○ (C) x = -1 and x = 3/2

    ○ (D) x = 1 and x = -3/2

Correct Answer: (A)

    Explanation:

    ○ Factor the quadratic equation: $(2x + 1)(x - 3) = 0$

    ○ Set each factor equal to zero and solve: $2x + 1 = 0$ or $x - 3 = 0$

    ○ The solutions are x = -1/2 and x = 3.

39. **Question:** A line passes through the points (-1, 4) and (3, -4). What is the equation of the line?

    Answer Choices:

    ○ (A) $y = -2x + 2$

    ○ (B) $y = -2x + 4$

    ○ (C) $y = (1/2)x + 2$

    ○ (D) $y = (1/2)x + 4$

Correct Answer: (A)

    Explanation:

- Find the slope: m = (y₂ - y₁) / (x₂ - x₁) = (-4 - 4) / (3 - (-1)) = -8 / 4 = -2
- Use the point-slope form of a linear equation: y - y₁ = m (x - x₁)
- Substitute one of the points and the slope: y - 4 = -2(x - (-1))
- Simplify to get the equation in slope-intercept form: y - 4 = -2x - 2 y = -2x + 2

40. **Question:** The circle shown below has a center at O and a radius of 10. If the area of sector AOB is 25π, what is the measure of ∠AOB in degrees?

    (Insert a diagram of a circle with center O, radius 10, and sector AOB shaded)

    Answer Choices:
    - (A) 45°
    - (B) 90°
    - (C) 180°
    - (D) 270°

Correct Answer: (B)

   Explanation:

- Area of the whole circle: $\pi r^2 = \pi (10)^2 = 100\pi$
- Sector AOB represents $(25\pi)/(100\pi) = 1/4$ of the circle's area.
- ∠AOB represents 1/4 of the circle's total degrees (360°).
- Measure of ∠AOB: (1/4) * 360° = 90°

41. **Question:** A rectangular box has dimensions of 5 cm, 8 cm, and 10 cm.

What is the length of the longest diagonal of the box?

   Answer Choices:
- (A) √119 cm
- (B) √189 cm
- (C) √289 cm
- (D) 13 cm

Correct Answer: (B)

   Explanation:

- Find the diagonal of the base of the box using the Pythagorean theorem: $\sqrt{(5^2 + 8^2)} = \sqrt{89}$ cm
- This diagonal forms a new right triangle with the height of the box. Use the Pythagorean theorem again to find the longest diagonal: $\sqrt{(\sqrt{89}^2 + 10^2)} = \sqrt{(89 + 100)} = \sqrt{189}$ cm

42. **Passage 1:**

    The "endowment effect" is the finding that people are more likely to retain an object they own than acquire that same object when they do not own it.

    Passage 2:

    This is often explained by "loss aversion," where the pain of losing something one owns is greater than the pleasure of gaining something new.

    Question: Which choice best describes the relationship between the two passages?

Answer Choices:

o (A) Passage 2 provides a specific example of the concept described in Passage 1.

o (B) Passage 2 offers a possible explanation for the phenomenon described in Passage 1.

o (C) Passage 2 presents a contrasting perspective to the one presented in Passage 1.

o (D) Passage 2 challenges the validity of the concept introduced in Passage 1.

Correct Answer: (B)

Explanation: Passage 1 describes the endowment effect, while Passage 2 offers a possible explanation for this effect by referencing the concept of "loss aversion."

43. **Sentence:** The "bias blind spot" is the cognitive bias of recognizing the impact of biases on the judgment of others, while failing to see the impact of biases on one's own judgment.

Question: Which choice most effectively combines the two sentences at the underlined portion?

Answer Choices:

1. (A) others, while failing

2. (B) others; failing

3. (C) others, but failing

4. (D) others while they fail

5.

Correct Answer: (A)

Explanation: The original sentence is already the most effective way to combine the two sentences. It uses a subordinate clause ("while failing...") to correctly show the relationship between the two ideas. The other options either create a grammatical error or change the meaning of the sentence.

44. **Sentence:** The "choice-supportive bias" is the tendency to retroactively ascribe positive attributes to an option one has selected and negative attributes to options not selected.

Question: Which choice most effectively combines the two sentences at the underlined portion?

Answer Choices:

6. (A) selected, while ascribing

7. (B) selected, ascribing

8. (C) selected; ascribing

9. (D) selected and ascribe

Correct Answer: (B)

Explanation: Using a comma and the present participle "ascribing" creates a concise and grammatically correct way to combine the sentences. The other options either create a run-on sentence or change the meaning.

45. **Question:** If the function f is defined by $f(x) = -x^2 + 6x - 5$, what is the maximum value of $f(x)$?

Answer Choices:

1. (A) -5
2. (B) 3
3. (C) 4
4. (D) 9

Correct Answer: (C)

Explanation:

5. The graph of the function is a parabola that opens downward (because the coefficient of the x^2 term is negative).
6. The maximum value occurs at the vertex of the parabola.
7. To find the x-coordinate of the vertex, use the formula $x = -b/2a$, where $a = -1$ and $b = 6$: $x = -6 / (2 * -1) = 3$
8. Substitute $x = 3$ into the function to find the maximum value: $f(3) = -(3)^2 + 6(3) - 5 = -9 + 18 - 5 = 4$

46. **Question:** What is the product of the solutions to the quadratic equation $3x^2 + 8x - 3 = 0$?

Answer Choices:

1. (A) -1
2. (B) -3/8

3. (C) 8/3
4. (D) 3

Correct Answer: (A)

Explanation:

5. For a quadratic equation in the standard form $ax^2 + bx + c = 0$, the product of the solutions is c/a.
6. In this case, $a = 3$ and $c = -3$, so the product of the solutions is $-3/3 = -1$.

47. **Question:** What is the equation of the line that is parallel to the line with equation $4x - 2y = 6$ and passes through the point (1, 3)?

Answer Choices:

1. (A) $y = 2x + 1$
2. (B) $y = 2x + 3$
3. (C) $y = (-1/2) x + 7/2$
4. (D) $y = (-1/2) x + 5/2$

Correct Answer: (A)

Explanation:

5. Rewrite the given equation in slope-intercept form to find its slope: $-2y = -4x + 6$ $y = 2x - 3$ The slope is 2.
6. Parallel lines have the same slope, so the slope of the line we're looking for is also 2.
7. Use the point-slope form of a linear equation: $y - y_1 = m (x - x_1)$

8. Substitute the given point (1, 3) and the slope (2): y - 3 = 2(x - 1)

9. Simplify to get the equation in slope-intercept form: y - 3 = 2x - 2 y = 2x + 1

48. **Question:** A circular swimming pool has a diameter of 20 feet. If a fence is to be built around the pool with a 3-foot wide walkway between the pool and the fence, what is the length of the fence?

Answer Choices:

1. (A) 26π feet

2. (B) 32π feet

3. (C) 52π feet

4. (D) 64π feet

Correct Answer: (A)

Explanation:

5. The radius of the pool is 10 feet.

6. The radius of the pool plus the walkway is 10 + 3 = 13 feet.

7. The diameter of the circle that the fence will create is 2 * 13 feet = 26 feet.

8. Circumference of the fence = πd = 26π feet

49. **Question:** A right triangle has a hypotenuse of length 10 and one leg of length 6. What is the area of the triangle?

Answer Choices:

1. (A) 12

2. (B) 24

3. (C) 30

4. (D) 48

Correct Answer: (B)

Explanation:

5. Use the Pythagorean theorem to find the length of the other leg: $6^2 + b^2 = 10^2$ 36 + b^2 = 100 b^2 = 64 b = 8

6. Area of a triangle = (1/2) * base * height = (1/2) * 6 * 8 = 24

50. **Question:** A data set consists of the following five numbers: 2, 5, 8, 11, and x. If the median of the data set is 8, what is the value of x?

Answer Choices:

o (A) 7

o (B) 8

o (C) 9

o (D) 10

Correct Answer: (B)

Explanation:

The median is the middle value when the data set is arranged in order. Since the median is 8, and the data set is already in order, x must be 8.

51. **Question:** What is the mode of the following data set: 2, 3, 3, 4, 5, 5, 5, 6, 7?

Answer Choices:

o (A) 3

- (B) 4
- (C) 5
- (D) 6

Correct Answer: (C)

Explanation:

The mode is the value that appears most frequently in the data set. In this case, the value 5 appears three times, which is more than any other value.

52. **Question:** A bag contains 3 red marbles, 4 blue marbles, and 5 green marbles. If a marble is selected at random, what is the probability that it is not red?

Answer Choices:

- (A) 1/4
- (B) 1/3
- (C) 3/4
- (D) ⅔

Correct Answer: (C)

Explanation:

- Number of favorable outcomes (not red marbles): 4 + 5 = 9
- Total number of possible outcomes: 3 + 4 + 5 = 12
- Probability (not red) = 9/12 = 3/4

53. **Question:** A fair coin is flipped three times. What is the probability of getting heads exactly twice?

Answer Choices:

- (A) 1/8
- (B) 3/8
- (C) 1/2
- (D) ⅝

Correct Answer: (B)

Explanation:

- List the possible outcomes: HHH, HHT, HTH, THH, HTT, THT, TTH, TTT (8 total outcomes)
- Count the favorable outcomes (exactly two heads): HHT, HTH, THH (3 favorable outcomes)
- Probability = (favorable outcomes) / (total outcomes) = 3/8

54. **Passage 1:**

The "mere-exposure effect" suggests that people tend to develop a preference for things merely because they are familiar with them.

Passage 2:

This effect has been demonstrated in various studies, showing that repeated exposure to a stimulus, such as a picture or a song, can increase liking for that stimulus.

Question: Which choice best describes the relationship between the two passages?

Answer Choices:

(A) Passage 2 provides a specific example of the concept described in Passage 1.

(B) Passage 2 presents a contrasting perspective to the one presented in Passage 1.

(C) Passage 2 explains the underlying causes of the phenomenon described in Passage 1.

(D) Passage 2 provides evidence to support the claim made in Passage 1.

Correct Answer: (D)

Explanation: Passage 1 states the concept of the mere-exposure effect, and Passage 2 supports this claim by mentioning studies that demonstrate the effect.

55. **Passage 1:**

The "misinformation effect" refers to the tendency for post-event information to interfere with the memory of the original event.

Passage 2:

This effect can have significant implications for eyewitness testimony, as even subtle suggestions or leading questions can alter a person's memory of an event.

Question: Which choice best describes the relationship between the two passages?

Answer Choices:

(A) Passage 2 provides a specific example of the concept described in Passage 1.

(B) Passage 2 presents a contrasting perspective to the one presented in Passage 1.

(C) Passage 2 explains the underlying causes of the phenomenon described in Passage 1.

(D) Passage 2 discusses the implications of the concept described in Passage 1.

Correct Answer: (D)

Explanation: Passage 1 defines the misinformation effect, and Passage 2 discusses the implications of this effect, particularly in the context of eyewitness testimony.

56. **Sentence:** The term "negativity bias" refers to the notion that, even when of equal intensity, things of a more negative nature (e.g. unpleasant thoughts, emotions, or social interactions; harmful/traumatic events) have a greater effect on one's psychological state and processes than neutral or positive things.

Question: Which choice completes the text so that it conforms to the conventions of Standard English?

Answer Choices:

(A) NO CHANGE

(B) nature (e.g.,

○ (C) nature, (e.g.

○ (D) nature: (e.g.,

Correct Answer: (B)

Explanation: The original sentence is grammatically correct, but the punctuation can be improved. The abbreviation "e.g." (for example) should be set off with commas, and the parentheses should enclose the entire list of examples.

57. **Sentence:** The "observer-expectancy effect" is a form of reactivity in which a researcher's cognitive bias causes them to subconsciously influence the participants of an experiment.

Question: Which choice completes the text so that it conforms to the conventions of Standard English?

Answer Choices:

○ (A) NO CHANGE

○ (B) bias causes them,

○ (C) bias, causes them

○ (D) bias; causes them

Correct Answer: (A)

Explanation: The original sentence is grammatically correct. The relative clause "in which a researcher's cognitive bias causes them to subconsciously influence the participants of an experiment"

correctly modifies the noun phrase "form of reactivity."

58. **Question:** If $2(3x - 1) = 16$, what is the value of x?

Answer Choices:

○ (A) 2

○ (B) 3

○ (C) 4

○ (D) 5

Correct Answer: (B)

Explanation:

○ Distribute the 2: $6x - 2 = 16$

○ Add 2 to both sides: $6x = 18$

○ Divide both sides by 6: $x = 3$

59. **Question:** What is the solution to the inequality $5 - 2x \geq 11$?

Answer Choices:

○ (A) $x \leq -3$

○ (B) $x \geq -3$

○ (C) $x \leq 3$

○ (D) $x \geq 3$

Correct Answer: (A)

Explanation:

○ Subtract 5 from both sides: $-2x \geq 6$

○ Divide both sides by -2 (and remember to flip the inequality sign): $x \leq -3$

60. **Question:** If $g(x) = x - 3$ and $h(x) = 2x + 1$, what is the value of $h(g(5))$?

Answer Choices:

o (A) 3

o (B) 5

o (C) 7

o (D) 9

Correct Answer: (B)

Explanation:

o Find the value of $g(5)$: $g(5) = 5 - 3 = 2$

o Substitute this value into $h(x)$: $h(g(5)) = h(2) = 2(2) + 1 = 4 + 1 = 5$

61. **Question:** What is the slope of a line that is perpendicular to the line represented by the equation $3x + 2y = 6$?

Answer Choices:

o (A) -3/2

o (B) -2/3

o (C) 2/3

o (D) 3/2

Correct Answer: (C)

Explanation:

o Rewrite the equation in slope-intercept form ($y = mx + b$): $2y = -3x + 6$ $y = (-3/2)x + 3$

o The slope of the given line is -3/2.

o The slopes of perpendicular lines are negative reciprocals of each other.

o The negative reciprocal of -3/2 is 2/3.

62. **Question:** A triangle has sides of length 5 cm, 12 cm, and 13 cm. What type of triangle is it?

Answer Choices:

o (A) Scalene

o (B) Isosceles

o (C) Equilateral

o (D) Right

Correct Answer: (D)

Explanation:

The side lengths satisfy the Pythagorean theorem ($5^2 + 12^2 = 13^2$), so it is a right triangle.

63. **Question:** What is the area of a circle with a circumference of 10π cm?

Answer Choices:

o (A) 5π cm²

o (B) 10π cm²

o (C) 25π cm²

o (D) 100π cm²

Correct Answer: (C)

Explanation:

o Circumference of a circle = $2\pi r$, where r is the radius.

o 10π cm = $2\pi r$

o $r = 5$ cm

- Area of a circle = $\pi r^2 = \pi$ (5 cm)^2 = 25π cm^2

64. **Question:** What is the volume of a sphere with a radius of 3 cm?

    Answer Choices:

    - (A) 9π cm^3
    - (B) 12π cm^3
    - (C) 27π cm^3
    - (D) 36π cm^3

    Correct Answer: (D)

    Explanation:

    Volume of a sphere = $(4/3)\pi r^3 = (4/3)\pi(3$ cm)^3 = 36π cm^3

65. **Question:** A data set consists of the following five numbers: 4, 7, 10, 13, and x. If the mean of the data set is 10, what is the value of x?

    Answer Choices:

    - (A) 10
    - (B) 14
    - (C) 16
    - (D) 20

    Correct Answer: (C)

    Explanation:

    - Sum of the numbers = 4 + 7 + 10 + 13 + x = 34 + x
    - Mean = (Sum of the numbers) / (Number of numbers) = (34 + x) / 5 = 10
    - Solve for x: 34 + x = 50 x = 16

66. **Question:** What is the median of the following data set: 3, 5, 8, 11, 14, 17?

    Answer Choices:

    - (A) 8
    - (B) 9.5
    - (C) 11
    - (D) 12.5

    Correct Answer: (B)

    Explanation:

    The median is the average of the two middle numbers when the data set is arranged in order. In this case, the middle numbers are 8 and 11, so the median is (8 + 11) / 2 = 9.5.

67. **Question:** A bag contains 5 red marbles, 4 blue marbles, and 3 green marbles. If a marble is selected at random, what is the probability that it is blue or green?

    Answer Choices:

    - (A) 1/4
    - (B) 1/3
    - (C) 7/12
    - (D) ⅔

    Correct Answer: (C)

    Explanation:

    - Number of favorable outcomes (blue or green marbles): 4 + 3 = 7
    - Total number of possible outcomes: 5 + 4 + 3 = 12

o Probability (blue or green) = 7/12

68. **Question:** A fair coin is flipped four times. What is the probability of getting tails exactly three times?

Answer Choices:

o (A) 1/16

o (B) 1/4

o (C) 3/8

o (D) ½

Correct Answer: (B)

Explanation:

o There are 2 possible outcomes for each flip (heads or tails), so there are 2 * 2 * 2 * 2 = 16 total possible outcomes.

o The favorable outcomes are: HTTT, THTT, TTHT, TTTH (4 favorable outcomes).

o Probability = (favorable outcomes) / (total outcomes) = 4/16 = 1/4

69. **Passage 1:**

The "framing effect" is a cognitive bias in which people react to a particular choice in different ways depending on how it is presented.

Passage 2:

For example, people are more likely to choose a product described as "90% fat-free" than one described as "10% fat," even though the two descriptions are equivalent.

Question: Which choice best describes the relationship between the two passages?

Answer Choices:

o (A) Passage 2 provides a specific example of the concept described in Passage 1.

o (B) Passage 2 presents a contrasting perspective to the one presented in Passage 1.

o (C) Passage 2 explains the underlying causes of the phenomenon described in Passage 1.

o (D) Passage 2 challenges the validity of the concept introduced in Passage 1.

Correct Answer: (A)

Explanation: Passage 1 defines the framing effect, and Passage 2 provides a concrete example of how this effect influences people's choices by framing the same information in different ways.

70. **Sentence:** The "gambler's fallacy" is the mistaken belief that, if something happens more frequently than normal during some period, it will happen less frequently in the future, or that, if something happens less frequently than normal during some period, it will happen more frequently in the future (presumably as a means of balancing nature).

Question: Which choice completes the

text so that it conforms to the conventions of Standard English?

Answer Choices:

o (A) NO CHANGE

o (B) future, or, that if

o (C) future. Or that if

o (D) future; or that, if

Correct Answer: (A)

Explanation: The original sentence is grammatically correct and effectively uses punctuation. The commas and conjunctions are correctly placed to show the relationship between the different parts of the sentence.

71. **Sentence:** The "hot-hand fallacy" is the sometimes fallacious belief that a person who has experienced success with a random event has a greater chance of further success in additional attempts.

Question: Which choice completes the text so that it conforms to the conventions of Standard English?

Answer Choices:

o (A) NO CHANGE

o (B) event, has

o (C) event has,

o (D) event; has

Correct Answer: (A)

Explanation: The original sentence is grammatically correct. The relative clause "who has experienced success with a random event" correctly modifies the noun "person."

72. **Question:** If the function f is defined by $f(x) = -2x^2 + 8x - 3$, what is the value of $f(3)$?

Answer Choices:

o (A) -3

o (B) 3

o (C) 9

o (D) 15

Correct Answer: (B)

Explanation:

Substitute $x = 3$ into the function: $f(3) = -2(3)^2 + 8(3) - 3 = -18 + 24 - 3 = 3$

73. **Question:** What is the sum of the solutions to the quadratic equation $2x^2 - 7x + 3 = 0$?

Answer Choices:

o (A) -7/2

o (B) -3/2

o (C) 3/2

o (D) 7/2

Correct Answer: (D)

Explanation:

- For a quadratic equation in the standard form $ax^2 + bx + c = 0$, the sum of the solutions is $-b/a$.
- In this case, $a = 2$ and $b = -7$, so the sum of the solutions is $-(-7)/2 = 7/2$.

74. **Question:** A line passes through the points (-3, 1) and (1, 7). What is the equation of the line?

    Answer Choices:
    - (A) $y = (3/2) x + 11/2$
    - (B) $y = (3/2) x - 7/2$
    - (C) $y = (-2/3) x + 1$
    - (D) $y = (-2/3) x + 7$
    - **Correct Answer:** (A)

    Explanation:
    - Find the slope: $m = (y_2 - y_1) / (x_2 - x_1) = (7 - 1) / (1 - (-3)) = 6 / 4 = 3/2$
    - Use the point-slope form of a linear equation: $y - y_1 = m (x - x_1)$
    - Substitute one of the points and the slope: $y - 1 = (3/2) (x - (-3))$
    - Simplify to get the equation in slope-intercept form: $y - 1 = (3/2) x + 9/2$ $y = (3/2) x + 11/2$

75. **Question:** A circular garden has a radius of 12 feet. A path 3 feet wide is built around the garden. What is the area of the path?

    Answer Choices:
    - (A) 39π square feet
    - (B) 69π square feet

- (C) 144π square feet
- (D) 225π square feet

Correct Answer: (B)

Explanation:

- Area of the garden: $\pi r^2 = \pi (12 \text{ feet})^2 = 144\pi$ square feet
- Radius of the garden plus the path: 12 feet + 3 feet = 15 feet
- Area of the garden plus the path: $\pi (15 \text{ feet})^2 = 225\pi$ square feet
- Area of the path: 225π square feet - 144π square feet = 81π square feet

76. **Question:** A cone has a radius of 4 cm and a height of 9 cm. What is its volume?

    Answer Choices:
    - (A) 12π cm³
    - (B) 36π cm³
    - (C) 48π cm³
    - (D) 144π cm³

Correct Answer: (C)

Explanation:

Volume of a cone = $(1/3)\pi r^2 h = (1/3)\pi(4 \text{ cm})^2(9 \text{ cm}) = 48\pi$ cm³

77. **Question:** The table below shows the number of students who participated in different extracurricular activities.

    | Activity | Number of Students | |----------------|--------------------|| Sports | 50 || Music | 30 || Drama | 20 || Debate | 10 |

If a student is selected at random, what is the probability that the student participates in music or drama?

Answer Choices:

o (A) 1/5

o (B) 1/4

o (C) 1/2

o (D) ⅗

Correct Answer: (C)

Explanation:

o Number of favorable outcomes (music or drama): 30 + 20 = 50

o Total number of possible outcomes: 50 + 30 + 20 + 10 = 110

o Probability (music or drama) = 50/110 = 5/11

78. **Passage 1:**

The "illusion of control" is the tendency for people to overestimate their ability to control events. It occurs when someone feels a sense of agency in a situation, despite there being no evidence to support the notion that they are actually in control.

Passage 2:

This illusion can lead people to engage in risky behaviors, such as gambling or investing in volatile markets, believing they have more control over the outcomes than they actually do.

Question: Which choice best describes the relationship between the two passages?

Answer Choices:

o (A) Passage 2 provides a specific example of the concept described in Passage 1.

o (B) Passage 2 presents a contrasting perspective to the one presented in Passage 1.

o (C) Passage 2 explains the underlying causes of the phenomenon described in Passage 1.

o (D) Passage 2 discusses the potential consequences of the concept described in Passage 1.

Correct Answer: (D)

Explanation: Passage 1 defines the illusion of control, and Passage 2 explains the potential negative consequences of this illusion, such as engaging in risky behaviors.

79. **Sentence:** The term "information bias" refers to the tendency to seek information even when it cannot affect action.

Question: Which choice completes the text so that it conforms to the conventions of Standard English?

Answer Choices:

o (A) NO CHANGE

o (B) information, even

- ○ (C) information. Even
- ○ (D) information even,

Correct Answer: (A)

Explanation: The original sentence is grammatically correct. The adverb "even" correctly modifies the adverbial clause "when it cannot affect action."

80. **Question:** If $5(2x - 3) = 15$, what is the value of x?

Answer Choices:

- ○ (A) 1.5
- ○ (B) 2
- ○ (C) 3
- ○ (D) 6

Correct Answer: (C)

Explanation:

- ○ Distribute the 5: $10x - 15 = 15$
- ○ Add 15 to both sides: $10x = 30$
- ○ Divide both sides by 10: $x = 3$

81. **Question:** What is the solution to the inequality $7 - 4x < 19$?

Answer Choices:

- ○ (A) $x < -3$
- ○ (B) $x > -3$
- ○ (C) $x < 3$
- ○ (D) $x > 3$

Correct Answer: (B)

Explanation:

- ○ Subtract 7 from both sides: $-4x < 12$
- ○ Divide both sides by -4 (and remember to flip the inequality sign): $x > -3$

82. **Question:** If $3x + 2y = 13$ and $x - y = 1$, what is the value of x?

Answer Choices:

- ○ (A) 2
- ○ (B) 3
- ○ (C) 4
- ○ (D) 5

Correct Answer: (B)

Explanation:

- ○ Solve the second equation for x: $x = y + 1$
- ○ Substitute this value of x into the first equation: $3(y + 1) + 2y = 13$
- ○ Simplify and solve for y: $3y + 3 + 2y = 13$ $5y = 10\ y = 2$
- ○ Substitute the value of y back into the equation $x = y + 1$: $x = 2 + 1 = 3$

83. **Question:** If $f(x) = -x^2 + 5x - 2$ and $g(x) = 2x - 1$, what is the value of $f(g(3))$?

Answer Choices:

- ○ (A) -12
- ○ (B) -7
- ○ (C) 4
- ○ (D) 13

Correct Answer: (B)

Explanation:

- Find the value of $g(3)$: $g(3) = 2(3) - 1 = 6 - 1 = 5$
- Substitute this value into $f(x)$: $f(g(3)) = f(5) = -(5)^2 + 5(5) - 2 = -25 + 25 - 2 = -2$

84. **Question:** What is the equation of a line that passes through the point (3, -1) and has a slope of -2/3?

    Answer Choices:

    - (A) $y = (-2/3)x + 1$
    - (B) $y = (-2/3)x - 3$
    - (C) $y = (3/2)x - 11/2$
    - (D) $y = (3/2)x - 7/2$

Correct Answer: (A)

Explanation:

- Use the point-slope form of a linear equation: $y - y_1 = m(x - x_1)$
- Substitute the given values: $y - (-1) = (-2/3)(x - 3)$
- Simplify to get the equation in slope-intercept form: $y + 1 = (-2/3)x + 2$ $y = (-2/3)x + 1$

85. **Question:** A triangle has sides of length 7 cm, 24 cm, and 25 cm. What is the area of the triangle?

    Answer Choices:

    - (A) 84 cm²
    - (B) 168 cm²
    - (C) 336 cm²
    - (D) 420 cm²

Correct Answer: (A)

Explanation:

- Recognize that this is a right triangle ($7^2 + 24^2 = 25^2$).
- The legs of the right triangle are the base and height.
- Area of a triangle = (1/2) * base * height = (1/2) * 7 cm * 24 cm = 84 cm²

86. **Question:** A circle has a diameter of 16 cm. What is its area?

    Answer Choices:

    - (A) 8π cm²
    - (B) 16π cm²
    - (C) 64π cm²
    - (D) 256π cm²

Correct Answer: (C)

Explanation:

- Radius of the circle = diameter / 2 = 16 cm / 2 = 8 cm
- Area of a circle = $\pi r^2 = \pi (8 \text{ cm})^2 = 64\pi$ cm²

87. **Question:** A rectangular prism has a length of 12 cm, a width of 5 cm, and a height of 4 cm. What is its surface area?

    Answer Choices:

    - (A) 94 cm²
    - (B) 188 cm²

- (C) 240 cm²
- (D) 480 cm²

Correct Answer: (B)

Explanation:

Surface area of a rectangular prism = 2(lw + lh + wh) = 2(12 cm * 5 cm + 12 cm * 4 cm + 5 cm * 4 cm) = 2(60 cm² + 48 cm² + 20 cm²) = 2(128 cm²) = 256 cm²

88. **Question:** The data set 3, 6, 9, 12, 15, and x has a mean of 11. What is the value of x?

Answer Choices:

- (A) 11
- (B) 15
- (C) 21
- (D) 25

Correct Answer: (C)

Explanation:

- Sum of the numbers = 3 + 6 + 9 + 12 + 15 + x = 45 + x
- Mean = (Sum of the numbers) / (Number of numbers) = (45 + x) / 6 = 11
- Solve for x: 45 + x = 66 x = 21

89. **Question:** What is the range of the following data set: 2, 5, 7, 10, 12, 15?

Answer Choices:

- (A) 7
- (B) 8
- (C) 10

- (D) 13

Correct Answer: (D)

Explanation:

The range is the difference between the largest and smallest values in the data set. In this case, the range is 15 - 2 = 13.

90. **Question:** A recipe calls for 3 cups of flour and 2 cups of sugar. If you want to make one-third of the recipe, how much sugar will you need?

Answer Choices:

- (A) 1/3 cup
- (B) 2/3 cup
- (C) 1 cup
- (D) 1 1/3 cups

Correct Answer: (B)

Explanation:

To make one-third of the recipe, divide the amount of sugar by 3: 2 cups / 3 = 2/3 cup

91. **Question:** A car travels 240 miles at an average speed of 40 miles per hour. How long does it take the car to complete the journey?

Answer Choices:

- (A) 4 hours
- (B) 5 hours
- (C) 6 hours

○ (D) 7 hours

Correct Answer: (C)

Explanation:

Time = Distance / Speed = 240 miles / 40 miles per hour = 6 hours

92. **Question:** A store is having a sale where all items are 30% off. If a jacket originally costs $100, how much will it cost during the sale?

Answer Choices:

○ (A) $30

○ (B) $60

○ (C) $70

○ (D) $75

Correct Answer: (C)

Explanation:

○ Calculate the discount: $100 * 30/100 = $30

○ Subtract the discount from the original price: $100 - $30 = $70

93. **Question:** If $2^x = 64$, what is the value of x?

Answer Choices:

○ (A) 5

○ (B) 6

○ (C) 7

○ (D) 8

Correct Answer: (B)

Explanation:

64 is the same as 2 x 2 x 2 x 2 x 2 x 2 or 2^6. Therefore, x = 6

94. **Question:** What is the value of $(-3)^4$?

Answer Choices:

○ (A) -81

○ (B) -12

○ (C) 12

○ (D) 81

Correct Answer: (D)

Explanation:

$(-3)^4$ = -3 x -3 x -3 x -3 = 81

95. **Question:** If $\sqrt{x} = 11$, what is the value of x?

Answer Choices:

○ (A) 11

○ (B) 22

○ (C) 121

○ (D) 1331

Correct Answer: (C)

Explanation:

$\sqrt{x} = 11$ means x = 11^2 = 121

96. **Question:** What is the volume of a cube with a side length of 6 cm?

Answer Choices:

○ (A) 36 cm³

○ (B) 72 cm³

- ○ (C) 108 cm³
- ○ (D) 216 cm³

Correct Answer: (D)

Explanation:

Volume of a cube = side³ = 6 cm * 6 cm * 6 cm = 216 cm³

97. **Question:** A bag contains 4 red marbles, 5 blue marbles, and 6 green marbles. What is the probability of randomly selecting a blue marble?

Answer Choices:
- ○ (A) 1/3
- ○ (B) 1/5
- ○ (C) 4/15
- ○ (D) 5/15

Correct Answer: (A)

Explanation:

- ○ Number of favorable outcomes (blue marbles): 5
- ○ Total number of possible outcomes: 4 + 5 + 6 = 15
- ○ Probability = 5/15 = 1/3

98. **Passage:**

The "representativeness heuristic" is used when making judgments about the probability of an event under uncertainty.

Question: As used in the passage, what does the word "uncertainty" most nearly mean?

Answer Choices:
- ○ (A) Doubt
- ○ (B) Fear
- ○ (C) Indecision
- ○ (D) Disbelief

Correct Answer: (A)

Explanation:

In this context, "uncertainty" refers to a state of doubt or lack of sureness about the probability of an event.

99. **Passage:**

The "restraint bias" is the tendency to overestimate one's ability to show restraint in the face of temptation.

Question: Which choice best states the main idea of the text?

(A) The "restraint bias" is a cognitive bias that affects only a small percentage of the population.

(B) The "restraint bias" can be easily overcome with increased awareness and education.

(C) The "restraint bias" describes the tendency to overestimate one's ability to resist temptation.

(D) The "restraint bias" is a psychological phenomenon that has no real-world applications.

Correct Answer: (C)

Explanation:

The main idea of the text is that the "restraint bias" describes the tendency to overestimate one's ability to resist temptation.

100. **Passage:**

The "rhyme-as-reason effect" is a cognitive bias whereupon a saying or aphorism is judged as more accurate or truthful when it is rewritten to rhyme.

Question: Which choice best describes the function of the underlined sentence in the text as a whole?

(A) It provides an example of the "rhyme-as-reason effect" in action.

(B) It explains the origins of the term "rhyme-as-reason effect."

(C) It defines the term "rhyme-as-reason effect."

(D) It contrasts the "rhyme-as-reason effect" with other cognitive biases.

Correct Answer: C)

Explanation:

The underlined sentence provides a definition of the term "rhyme-as-reason effect," explaining how rhyming can influence people's judgments about the truthfulness of statements.

101. **Sentence:** The term "risk compensation" refers to the tendency to take greater risks when perceived safety increases.

Question: Which choice completes the text so that it conforms to the conventions of Standard English?

- (A) NO CHANGE
- (B) risks, when
- (C) risks when,
- (D) risks. When

Correct Answer: (A)

Explanation: The original sentence is grammatically correct. The adverbial clause "when perceived safety increases" correctly modifies the verb "take."

102. **Question:** If $3(x - 2) + 5 = 14$, what is the value of x?

(A) 1

(B) 3

(C) 5

(D) 7

Correct Answer: (C)

Explanation:

1. Distribute the 3: $3x - 6 + 5 = 14$

2. Combine like terms: $3x - 1 = 14$

3. Add 1 to both sides: $3x = 15$

4. Divide both sides by 3: $x = 5$

103. **Question:** What is the solution to the inequality $2x - 5 \leq 3x + 2$?

(A) $x \geq -7$

(B) $x \leq -7$

(C) $x \geq 7$

(D) $x \leq 7$

Correct Answer: (A)

Explanation:

1. Subtract 2x from both sides: $-5 \leq x + 2$

2. Subtract 2 from both sides: $-7 \leq x$

3. Rewrite with x on the left side: $x \geq -7$

104. **Question:** If $2x + y = 8$ and $x - y = 1$, what is the value of y?

(A) 1

(B) 2

(C) 3

(D) 4

Correct Answer: (B)

Explanation:

1. Add the two equations together: $3x = 9$

2. Solve for x: $x = 3$

3. Substitute the value of x into either original equation to solve for y. Using the first equation: $2(3) + y = 8$

   $6 + y = 8$

   $y = 2$

105. **Question:** If $f(x) = 3x - 2$ and $g(x) = x^2 + 1$, what is the value of $g(f(2))$?

(A) 10

(B) 17

(C) 20

(D) 26

Correct Answer: (B)

Explanation:

1. Find the value of f (2): f (2) = 3(2) - 2 = 6 - 2 = 4

2. Substitute this value into g(x): g (f (2)) = g (4) = 4^2 + 1 = 16 + 1 = 17

106. **Question:** What is the equation of a line that passes through the point (-2, 1) and has a slope of 1/2?

(A) y = (1/2) x

(B) y = (1/2) x + 2

(C) y = 2x + 5

(D) y = 2x - 3

Correct Answer: (B)

Explanation:

1. Use the point-slope form of a linear equation: y - y_1 = m (x - x_1)

2. Substitute the given values: y - 1 = (1/2) (x - (-2))

3. Simplify to get the equation in slope-intercept form: y - 1 = (1/2) x + 1

    y = (1/2) x + 2

107. **Question:** A triangle has sides of length 9 cm, 12 cm, and 15 cm. What type of triangle is it?

(A) Scalene

(B) Isosceles

(C) Equilateral

(D) Right

Correct Answer: (D)

Explanation:

The side lengths satisfy the Pythagorean theorem (9^2 + 12^2 = 15^2), so it is a right triangle.

108. **Question:** What is the circumference of a circle with an area of 16π cm²?

(A) 4π cm

(B) 8π cm

(C) 16π cm

(D) 32π cm

Correct Answer: (B)

Explanation:

1. Area of a circle = πr^2, where r is the radius.

2. 16π cm² = πr^2

3. $r^2 = 16$ cm²

4. $r = 4$ cm

5. Circumference of a circle $= 2\pi r = 2\pi (4$ cm$) = 8\pi$ cm

109. **Question:** What is the volume of a cone with a radius of 2 cm and a height of 6 cm?

(A) 4π cm³

(B) 8π cm³

(C) 12π cm³

(D) 24π cm³

Correct Answer: (B)

Explanation:

Volume of a cone $= (1/3) \pi r^2 h = (1/3) \pi (2$ cm$)^2 (6$ cm$) = 8\pi$ cm³

110. **Question:** A data set consists of the following five numbers: 5, 8, 11, 14, and x. If the median of the data set is 11, what is the value of x?

(A) 10

(B) 11

(C) 12

(D) 13

Correct Answer: (B)

Explanation:

The median is the middle value when the data set is arranged in order. Since the median is 11, and the data set is already in order, x must be 11.

111. **Question:** What is the mode of the following data set: 1, 2, 2, 3, 4, 4, 4, 5, 6?

(A) 2

(B) 3

(C) 4

(D) 5

Correct Answer: (C)

Explanation:

The mode is the value that appears most frequently in the data set. In this case, the value 4 appears three times, which is more than any other value.

112. **Question:** A bag contains 6 red marbles, 3 blue marbles, and 2 green marbles. If a marble is selected at random, what is the probability that it is not blue?

(A) 1/11

(B) 3/11

(C) 8/11

(D) 10/11

Correct Answer: (C)

Explanation:

Number of favorable outcomes (not blue marbles): 6 + 2 = 8

Total number of possible outcomes: 6 + 3 + 2 = 11

Probability (not blue) = 8/11

113. **Question:** A fair coin is flipped five times. What is the probability of getting heads exactly three times?

(A) 5/16

(B) 5/32

(C) 1/2

(D) 10/32

Correct Answer: (A)

Explanation:

1. There are 2 possible outcomes for each flip (heads or tails), so there are 2 * 2 * 2 * 2 * 2 = 32 total possible outcomes.

2. To find the number of favorable outcomes (exactly three heads), we can use combinations: $^5C_3 = 10$ favorable outcomes.

3. Probability = (favorable outcomes) / (total outcomes) = 10/32 = 5/16

114. *Passage 1*:

In the world of conservation, the introduction of non-native species has become a topic of concern. Species introduced to environments without their natural predators often disrupt local ecosystems, leading to the extinction of native species.

Passage 2:

Some conservationists argue that the introduction of non-native species is not always harmful. They claim that non-native species can sometimes fill ecological roles that have been left vacant due to the extinction of other species.

Question:

How do the authors of Passage 1 and Passage 2 differ in their view of non-native species?

- A) Passage 1 sees non-native species as a threat, while Passage 2 sees them as potentially beneficial.
- B) Passage 1 believes all non-native species should be eradicated, while Passage 2 sees them as harmless.
- C) Both passages argue that non-native species should be accepted.
- D) Both passages argue for stronger enforcement against the introduction of non-native species.

Answer: A) Passage 1 sees non-native species as a threat, while Passage 2 sees them as potentially beneficial.

Explanation: Passage 1 focuses on the potential harm that non-native species can bring to ecosystems, while Passage 2 presents an argument that non-native species may sometimes have positive effects, depending on the context.

115. *Original Text*:

The city planners, working diligently over the last few years, made many changes to the design of the town, adding bike paths, widening streets, and installing new traffic lights.

Question:

Which revision best clarifies the purpose of the sentence?

- A) The city planners made a lot of changes, including some to the design of the town.
- B) The city planners, having worked over the last few years, designed new roads, paths, and improved traffic lights.
- C) Over the past few years, city planners worked to improve traffic systems and enhance pedestrian safety by installing new traffic lights, adding bike paths, and widening streets.
- D) New traffic lights, bike paths, and wider streets were put in place by the city planners, making the town safer.

Answer: C) Over the past few years, city planners worked to improve traffic systems and enhance pedestrian safety by installing new traffic lights, adding bike paths, and widening streets.

Explanation: This option clarifies the purpose of the planners' actions, linking them to the goals of improving traffic systems and safety.

116. Solve the following system of inequalities:

$y < 2x + 3 y < 2x + 3$

$y > -x - 1 y > -x - 1$

Which region represents the solution to this system?

- A) The region below the line
  $y=2x+3y=2x+3$ and above the line
  $y=-x-1y=-x-1$
- B) The region above the line
  $y=2x+3y=2x+3$ and above the line
  $y=-x-1y=-x-1$
- C) The region below the line
  $y=2x+3y=2x+3$ and below the line
  $y=-x-1y=-x-1$
- D) The region above the line
  $y=2x+3y=2x+3$ and below the line
  $y=-x-1y=-x-1$

Answer: A) The region below the line
$y=2x+3y=2x+3$ and above the line
$y=-x-1y=-x-1$.

Explanation: The first inequality defines
the area below the line $y=2x+3y=2x+3$,
and the second defines the area above the
line $y=-x-1y=-x-1$. The solution is the
overlap of these regions.

117. *Passage 1*:

The influence of classical literature in
shaping modern narratives is undeniable.
From Shakespeare's plays to Greek
mythology, ancient texts have provided
frameworks for storytelling that are still
relevant today.

Passage 2:

While classical literature serves as a
foundation for much of modern
storytelling, some argue that it limits
creativity. They believe that clinging to
established narratives prevents writers
from exploring new, innovative forms of
expression.

Question:

Which of the following best describes the
relationship between the two passages?

- A) Passage 1 argues that classical
  literature limits creativity, while Passage 2
  agrees.
- B) Passage 1 views classical literature as a
  positive influence, while Passage 2
  highlights its restrictive nature.
- C) Both passages believe classical
  literature should be the sole influence on
  modern storytelling.
- D) Passage 1 dismisses classical literature,
  while Passage 2 defends it.

Answer: B) Passage 1 views classical
literature as a positive influence, while
Passage 2 highlights its restrictive nature.
Explanation: Passage 1 speaks of classical
literature's lasting influence, while
Passage 2 presents a counter-argument
about its potential to restrict creativity.

118. The concert was scheduled for Saturday.
It rained heavily. The event was canceled.

Question:

Which of the following best combines the sentences to maintain clarity and conciseness?

- A) The concert was scheduled for Saturday, but it was canceled because of heavy rain.
- B) Because it rained heavily, the Saturday concert was canceled.
- C) Although the concert was scheduled for Saturday, the event was canceled due to rain.
- D) Saturday's concert, which was scheduled, was canceled due to heavy rain.

Answer: A) The concert was scheduled for Saturday, but it was canceled because of heavy rain.

Explanation: This option combines the sentences in a clear and concise manner without unnecessary repetition.

119. The diameter of a circular garden is 14 feet. What is the area of the garden?

- A) $49\pi49\pi$ square feet
- B) $98\pi98\pi$ square feet
- C) $154\pi154\pi$ square feet
- D) $196\pi196\pi$ square feet

Answer: B) $98\pi98\pi$ square feet

Explanation: The area of a circle is given by the formula $A=\pi r2A=\pi r2$. The radius is half of the diameter, so $r=7r=7$. Therefore, $A=\pi\times72=98\pi A=\pi\times72=98\pi$.

120. A study showed the following data on high school students' participation in extracurricular activities:

Activity	Percentage of Students Participating
Sports	45%
Music	25%
Theater	15%
Academic Clubs	30%

Question:

Based on the data, which of the following statements is true?

- A) More students participate in music than in academic clubs.

- B) Theater has the lowest participation among the listed activities.
- C) Sports have the same participation rate as theater and academic clubs combined.
- D) Academic clubs have higher participation than sports.

Answer: B) Theater has the lowest participation among the listed activities.
Explanation: The table shows that 15% of students participate in theater, which is lower than any other activity.

121. Many experts believe that students who participate in extracurricular activities are more likely to succeed academically. According to recent studies, students in sports and music programs have shown improvement in both grades and discipline.

Question:

Which of the following pieces of evidence would best strengthen the argument in the text?

- A) A survey of 100 students found that 60% preferred sports to music.
- B) A study of over 10,000 students found that those in extracurricular activities had an average GPA of 3.5, compared to 3.0 for those who did not participate.

- C) School administrators report that extracurricular activities are more popular now than they were five years ago.
- D) Teachers often encourage students to join extracurricular activities to improve social skills.

Answer: B) A study of over 10,000 students found that those in extracurricular activities had an average GPA of 3.5, compared to 3.0 for those who did not participate.
Explanation: This piece of evidence provides specific data showing the academic benefits of extracurricular participation, directly supporting the argument.

122. A jar contains 6 red marbles, 4 blue marbles, and 5 green marbles. If one marble is selected at random, what is the probability that it will be either red or green?

- A) 515155
- B) 615156
- C) 11151511
- D) 10151510

Answer: C) 11151511
Explanation: There are a total of 6+4+5=156+4+5=15 marbles. The number of favorable outcomes (red or

green) is 6+5=116+5=11, so the probability is 11151511.

123. *Excerpt from a novel*:

"The sun sank below the horizon, painting the sky in hues of orange and purple. The trees stood like silent sentinels, their leaves rustling in the gentle breeze."

Question:

Which literary device is most evident in this passage?

- A) Simile
- B) Personification
- C) Metaphor
- D) Hyperbole

Answer: B) Personification

Explanation: The passage gives human-like qualities to trees by describing them as "silent sentinels," which is an example of personification.

124. *Original Text*:

The museum exhibit showcases various artifacts. These artifacts are from ancient Egypt. They were discovered during an archaeological dig in 1922.

Question:

Which revision best improves the flow of the sentences?

- A) Discovered during an archaeological dig in 1922, the museum exhibit showcases various ancient Egyptian artifacts.
- B) The museum exhibit features artifacts that were discovered in 1922 during an archaeological dig in ancient Egypt.
- C) The museum showcases artifacts from ancient Egypt that were discovered in a 1922 archaeological dig.
- D) Various ancient Egyptian artifacts were showcased in a museum exhibit, all discovered in 1922.

Answer: C) The museum exhibit showcases artifacts from ancient Egypt that were discovered in a 1922 archaeological dig. *Explanation*: This option combines the ideas smoothly and maintains clarity and conciseness.

125. The following graph shows the growth of a bacterial population over time:

Graph: Time vs. Population Growth]

Question:

Which of the following best describes the trend shown in the graph?

- A) The population grows at a constant rate.

B) The population initially grows slowly, then accelerates as time progresses.

C) The population grows and then declines sharply.

D) The population remains constant throughout the period shown.

Answer: B) The population initially grows slowly, then accelerates as time progresses.

Explanation: The graph shows an exponential growth curve, where the population increases at an accelerating rate over time.

125.

A rectangular garden has a length of 1010 meters and a width of 66 meters. What is the area of the garden?

- A) 1616 square meters
- B) 6060 square meters
- C) 100100 square meters
- D) 3636 square meters

Answer: B) 6060 square meters

Explanation: The area of a rectangle is calculated using the formula Area=length × width Area =length × width. Therefore, the area is 10 m×6 m=60 square meters 10m×6m= 60 square meters.

126. *Excerpt from a poem*:

"The wind whispered secrets through the trees, while the stars blinked like eyes watching over the world below."

Question:

Which literary device is primarily used in this excerpt?

- A) Simile
- B) Personification
- C) Metaphor
- D) Alliteration

Answer: B) Personification

Explanation: The wind is described as "whispering secrets," which gives it human-like qualities, thus exemplifying personification.

127. The athlete trained hard every day. She wanted to qualify for the national championship. Her determination was evident in her performance.

Question:

Which of the following revisions best combines the sentences while maintaining clarity?

- A) The athlete trained hard every day because she wanted to qualify for the national championship, and her determination was evident in her performance.

- B) The athlete, training hard every day, wanted to qualify for the national championship, and her performance showed determination.
- C) Training hard every day, the athlete wanted to qualify for the national championship; her determination was evident.
- D) The athlete wanted to qualify for the national championship, so she trained hard every day, and her determination was evident in her performance.

Answer: D) The athlete wanted to qualify for the national championship, so she trained hard every day, and her determination was evident in her performance.

Explanation: This option clearly shows the cause (wanting to qualify) and the effect (training hard and showing determination) without losing clarity.

128. A student must score at least 8585 on two exams to pass a class. If the first exam score is xx and the second exam score is yy, which of the following inequalities represents the passing requirement?

- A) $x+y \geq 85x+y \geq 85$

- B) $x \geq 85x \geq 85$ and $y \geq 85y \geq 85$
- C) $x+y \leq 85x+y \leq 85$
- D) $x \leq 85x \leq 85$ or $y \leq 85y \leq 85$

Answer: B) $x \geq 85x \geq 85$ and $y \geq 85y \geq 85$

Explanation: To pass the class, the student must score at least 8585 on both exams, hence both xx and yy must be greater than or equal to 8585.

129. *Passage*:

In recent years, renewable energy sources such as solar and wind have gained traction due to their environmental benefits. Studies indicate that transitioning to these energy forms could significantly reduce greenhouse gas emissions and decrease reliance on fossil fuels.

Question:

What is the main idea of the passage?

- A) Renewable energy sources are more expensive than fossil fuels.
- B) The environmental benefits of renewable energy justify the transition away from fossil fuels.
- C) Solar energy is the most efficient form of energy available.
- D) Wind energy is less reliable than fossil fuels.

Answer: B) The environmental benefits of renewable energy justify the transition away from fossil fuels.

Explanation: The passage emphasizes the environmental advantages of renewable energy sources, advocating for their increased use to combat climate change.

130. Many experts advocate for vegetarian diets, claiming they are healthier than diets including meat. Studies have shown that individuals who consume primarily plant-based foods often have lower cholesterol levels.

Question:

Which of the following pieces of evidence would best strengthen the argument in the text?

- A) Many people enjoy meat dishes at restaurants.
- B) A survey found that vegetarians report feeling more energetic than those who eat meat.
- C) The number of vegetarians is increasing in various countries.
- D) Some people believe that meat is an essential part of a balanced diet.

Answer: B) A survey found that vegetarians report feeling more energetic than those who eat meat.

Explanation: This evidence directly supports the claim about the health benefits of a vegetarian diet, strengthening the argument.

131. A box contains 3 blue, 5 red, and 2 green marbles. What is the probability of randomly selecting a red marble from the box?

- A) 1551
- B) 1221
- C) 510105
- D) 510105

Answer: C) 510105

Explanation: The total number of marbles is 3+5+2=103+5+2=10. The probability of selecting a red marble is 510=12105=21.

132. *Excerpt from a novel:*

"As the storm raged outside, the old house creaked and groaned, its walls whispering secrets of a forgotten past."

Question:

Which literary device is primarily used in this excerpt?

- A) Simile
- B) Imagery
- C) Personification
- D) Hyperbole

Answer: C) Personification

Explanation: The house is described as "whispering secrets," attributing it with human-like qualities, which is a clear example of personification.

133. The team of researchers conducted a study that was extensive and thorough to find out the effects of sleep on academic performance.

Question:

Which of the following revisions best improves the clarity of the sentence?

- A) The researchers conducted a comprehensive study on how sleep affects academic performance.
- B) The extensive research conducted by the team showed sleep's effects on academic performance.
- C) The study, which was extensive, conducted by the team found the effects of sleep on academic performance.
- D) The team conducted a study that was thorough to determine how sleep impacts academic performance.

Answer: A) The researchers conducted a comprehensive study on how sleep affects academic performance.

Explanation: This revision simplifies the sentence while maintaining clarity, making it more direct and effective.

134.

Solve the quadratic equation $x^2-5x+6=0$. What are the values of x?

- A) 2 and 3
- B) -2 and -3
- C) 1 and 6
- D) 0 and 5

Answer: A) 2 and 3

Explanation: The equation can be factored as $(x-2)(x-3)=0$, giving the solutions $x=2$ and $x=3$.

135. *Passage*:

Research shows that engaging in regular physical activity can lead to a variety of health benefits. Not only does it reduce the risk of chronic diseases, but it also improves mental health and enhances overall well-being.

Question:

Which statement best summarizes the main idea of the passage?

- A) Physical activity is only beneficial for physical health.
- B) Regular exercise is crucial for preventing chronic diseases.

- C) Engaging in regular physical activity provides both physical and mental health benefits.
- D) Mental health can be improved by medication rather than exercise.

Answer: C) Engaging in regular physical activity provides both physical and mental health benefits.

Explanation: The passage emphasizes that physical activity contributes to both physical and mental well-being.

136. The novel was praised for its intricate plot. It also features complex characters and vivid settings. The author spent years writing it.

Question:

Which of the following revisions best combines these sentences?

- A) The author spent years writing the novel, which was praised for its intricate plot, complex characters, and vivid settings.
- B) The novel features complex characters and vivid settings, and it was praised for its intricate plot, which the author spent years writing.
- C) The author spent years writing the novel, which has an intricate plot, complex characters, and vivid settings, and it was praised.
- D) Praised for its intricate plot, complex characters, and vivid settings, the novel took years for the author to write.

Answer: A) The author spent years writing the novel, which was praised for its intricate plot, complex characters, and vivid settings.

Explanation: This revision clearly combines the ideas and maintains the focus on the novel's qualities and the author's effort.

137. Solve the following system of equations:

1. $2x+3y=12$
2. $x-y=1$

What are the values of x and y?

- A) $x=3, y=2$
- B) $x=2, y=3$
- C) $x=4, y=0$
- D) $x=1, y=3$

Answer: A) $x=3, y=2$

Explanation: Solving the second equation for x gives $x=y+1$. Substituting into the first equation: $2(y+1)+3y=12$ leads to $2y+2+3y=12$, or

$5y+2=125y+2=12$, so $5y=105y=10$ and $y=2y=2$. Thus, $x=3x=3$.

138.

Excerpt from a story:

"The thunder growled ominously as the clouds gathered, heavy with the promise of rain."

Question:

Which literary device is primarily used in this excerpt?

- A) Simile
- B) Personification
- C) Hyperbole
- D) Alliteration

Answer: B) Personification

Explanation: The thunder is described as "growling," attributing it with human-like qualities, which is an example of personification.

139. The committee has decided to move forward with the project. This project has a lot of potential for improving community engagement and benefits the local economy.

Question:

Which of the following revisions best clarifies the purpose of the sentence?

- A) The committee has decided to advance the project that will significantly improve community engagement and benefit the local economy.
- B) The committee decided to move forward, and this project benefits community engagement and local economy.
- C) The committee has made a decision about the project; it could improve engagement and benefit the economy.
- D) The project that the committee has decided to move forward with will improve community engagement and the local economy.

Answer: A) The committee has decided to advance the project that will significantly improve community engagement and benefit the local economy.

Explanation: This option is clear, direct, and effectively communicates the committee's decision and the project's purpose.

140. A recipe calls for a ratio of 2 parts flour to 1-part sugar. If you have 8 cups of flour, how many cups of sugar are needed?

- A) 2 cups
- B) 4 cups

- C) 8 cups
- D) 10 cups

Answer: B) 4 cups

Explanation: The ratio of flour to sugar is 2:1. Therefore, if there are 8 cups of flour, the amount of sugar needed is 8 cups of flour2=4 cups of sugar28 cups of flour=4 cups of sugar.

141. *Passage*:

The introduction of electric vehicles (EVs) is seen as a pivotal step in reducing carbon emissions. Studies indicate that EVs produce significantly less pollution over their lifetime compared to traditional gasoline-powered cars.

Question:

What is the primary focus of the passage?

- A) The advantages of gasoline-powered cars over EVs.
- B) The role of electric vehicles in reducing pollution.
- C) The increase in gasoline prices affecting car sales.
- D) The environmental impact of manufacturing cars.

Answer: B) The role of electric vehicles in reducing pollution.

Explanation: The passage discusses how EVs contribute to lower carbon emissions compared to traditional vehicles, highlighting their environmental benefits.

142. Many people argue that public transportation is essential for urban areas. They believe it reduces traffic congestion and pollution.

Question:

Which of the following evidence would best support the argument in the text?

- A) Cities with limited public transportation options often have higher levels of traffic congestion.
- B) Public transportation systems are expensive to maintain.
- C) Some people prefer using their own vehicles over public transit.
- D) Public transportation is used by a small percentage of the population.

Answer: A) Cities with limited public transportation options often have higher levels of traffic congestion.

Explanation: This evidence directly supports the claim about the necessity of public transportation in reducing traffic and pollution.

143.

A triangle has a base of 1212 cm and a

height of 55 cm. What is the area of the triangle?

- A) 3030 cm²
- B) 6060 cm²
- C) 2424 cm²
- D) 1515 cm²

Answer: A) 3030 cm²

Explanation: The area of a triangle is calculated using the formula Area=12×base×heightArea=21× base × height. Therefore, the area is 12×12 cm×5 cm=30 cm221 ×12cm×5cm=30cm2.

144. *Excerpt from a novel:*

"She felt as if she were walking through a dream, each step taking her deeper into the mysteries of her own heart."

Question:

What does the excerpt suggest about the character's state of mind?

- A) She is confused and lost.
- B) She is feeling empowered and confident.
- C) She is experiencing a sense of nostalgia.
- D) She is in a reflective and introspective mood.

Answer: D) She is in a reflective and introspective mood.

Explanation: The phrase "walking through a dream" and "mysteries of her own heart" suggests that she is in a contemplative state, exploring her feelings and thoughts.

145. The committee will review the proposal that was submitted last week during the next meeting scheduled for Thursday.

Question:

Which of the following revisions best improves the clarity and conciseness of the sentence?

- A) During the next meeting on Thursday, the committee will review last week's proposal.
- B) The committee will review last week's proposal at the meeting scheduled for Thursday.
- C) The committee will review the proposal submitted last week at the next meeting, which is scheduled for Thursday.
- D) The proposal submitted last week will be reviewed by the committee in their next meeting on Thursday.

Answer: A) During the next meeting on Thursday, the committee will review last week's proposal.

Explanation: This revision is concise and clearly states the timing and subject of the review without unnecessary words.

146. Solve the system of equations:

1. 3x+4y=243x+4y=24
2. 2x−y=12x−y=1

What are the values of xx and yy?

- A) x=3, y=3x=3, y=3
- B) x=2, y=4x=2, y=4
- C) x=4, y=3x=4, y=3
- D) x=1, y=5x=1, y=5

Answer: C) x=4,y=3x=4,y=3

Explanation: To solve, substitute yy from the second equation into the first:
From 2x−y=12x−y=1, we get y=2x−1y=2x−1.
Substituting into the first equation:
3x+4(2x−1)=243x+4(2x−1)=24 gives 3x+8x−4=243x+8x−4=24 or 11x=2811x=28, thus x=4x=4 and y=3y=3.

147. *Passage*:

Urbanization is a key driver of economic growth. However, it also poses challenges such as increased pollution and housing shortages. Addressing these issues requires innovative urban planning strategies that prioritize sustainability and livability.

Question:

What is the primary concern expressed in the passage?

- A) Urbanization has no effect on economic growth.
- B) Urbanization leads to positive outcomes without any drawbacks.
- C) Urbanization creates significant challenges that must be managed effectively.
- D) Innovative planning is unnecessary for successful urbanization.

Answer: C) Urbanization creates significant challenges that must be managed effectively.
Explanation: The passage emphasizes the problems associated with urbanization, highlighting the need for effective management strategies.

148. Some experts suggest that reducing screen time for children can lead to better physical health. They argue that outdoor play encourages physical activity, which is essential for children's well-being.

Question:

Which of the following evidence would best support the argument in the text?

- A) Studies show that children today spend more time indoors than ever before.
- B) Children who engage in outdoor play regularly are less likely to be overweight.
- C) Many parents are concerned about their children's screen time.
- D) Reducing screen time is difficult for most families.

Answer: B) Children who engage in outdoor play regularly are less likely to be overweight.

Explanation: This evidence directly connects outdoor play with physical health outcomes, supporting the argument about the benefits of reducing screen time.

149. A recipe requires a ratio of 33 cups of flour to 22 cups of sugar. If you want to make a larger batch using 1212 cups of flour, how many cups of sugar will you need?

- A) 44 cups
- B) 66 cups
- C) 88 cups
- D) 1010 cups

Answer: B) 88 cups

Explanation: The ratio of flour to sugar is 3:23:2. If you have 1212 cups of flour, you can set up the proportion: $32=12x23=x12$, where xx is the amount of sugar needed. Cross-multiplying gives $3x=243x=24$, so $x=8x=8$.

150. *Passage*:

In many cultures, storytelling is a vital means of preserving history and values. Oral traditions often serve as a bridge connecting generations, allowing for the transmission of knowledge and cultural identity.

Question:

What theme is primarily conveyed in the passage?

- A) Storytelling is an outdated form of communication.
- B) Oral traditions are important for maintaining cultural heritage.
- C) Written texts are more effective than oral traditions.
- D) Knowledge is best transmitted through modern technology.

Answer: B) Oral traditions are important for maintaining cultural heritage.

Explanation: The passage highlights the significance of storytelling in preserving history and values within cultures.

151.

If $4x-7=94x-7=9$, what is the value of xx?

- A) 11
- B) 22
- C) 44
- D) 55

Answer: B) 44

Explanation: To solve for xx, first add 77 to both sides:

4x=164x=16. Then, divide both sides by 44:

x=4x=4.

152. *Excerpt from a novel*:

"Despite the harsh words exchanged, Emily could see the flicker of doubt in Mark's eyes. It was a moment of vulnerability that revealed the layers of his guarded persona."

Question:

What does the passage suggest about Mark's character?

- A) He is entirely confident and unyielding.
- B) He struggles with self-doubt despite his outward demeanor.
- C) He is indifferent to Emily's feelings.
- D) He is always honest with his emotions.

Answer: B) He struggles with self-doubt despite his outward demeanor.

Explanation: The "flicker of doubt" in

Mark's eyes suggests that he has insecurities, contrasting with his guarded behavior.

153. There are many advantages to living in a city, such as access to a variety of cultural events, which are plentiful, and public transportation that is available and convenient.

Question:

Which of the following revisions best improves the clarity of the sentence?

- A) Living in a city has many advantages, including access to plentiful cultural events and convenient public transportation.
- B) Many advantages exist in city living, such as a variety of cultural events and public transportation that is available.
- C) Access to a variety of cultural events and convenient public transportation are among the many advantages of city living.
- D) A city has many advantages, like public transportation, which is convenient, and cultural events, which are plentiful.

Answer: A) Living in a city has many advantages, including access to plentiful cultural events and convenient public transportation.

Explanation: This revision is clear and

concise, directly stating the benefits of living in a city.

154. A car travels at a speed of 6060 miles per hour. How far will it travel in 33 hours?

- A) 120120 miles
- B) 180180 miles
- C) 240240 miles
- D) 300300 miles

Answer: B) 180180 miles

Explanation: Distance is calculated using the formula Distance= Speed × Time Distance = Speed × Time. Therefore, the distance traveled is
60 miles/hour×3 hours=180 miles
60miles/hour×3 hours=180 miles.

155. *Passage*:

"The struggle for equality has been a long and arduous journey. Activists have fought tirelessly for the rights of marginalized communities, seeking to dismantle the systemic barriers that have long oppressed them."

Question:

What theme is primarily conveyed in the passage?

- A) Activism is not effective in bringing about change.

- B) The fight for equality is ongoing and requires persistence.
- C) Marginalized communities do not need advocates.
- D) Systemic barriers are easily dismantled.

Answer: B) The fight for equality is ongoing and requires persistence.
Explanation: The passage highlights the continuous effort of activists in the struggle for equality, indicating that the journey is still in progress.

156. In the event that the weather is bad, the picnic that is planned for Saturday will be postponed until next week.

Question:

Which of the following revisions best improves the conciseness of the sentence?

- A) If the weather is bad, Saturday's picnic will be postponed until next week.
- B) In case of bad weather, the picnic will be postponed to next week.
- C) If the weather does not cooperate, the picnic planned for Saturday will be rescheduled.
- D) The picnic planned for Saturday will be delayed until next week if the weather is bad.

Answer: A) If the weather is bad, Saturday's picnic will be postponed until next week.
Explanation: This option is concise and eliminates unnecessary phrases while maintaining the original meaning.

157. A recipe calls for 2332 cups of milk for every 1441 cup of sugar. How much milk is needed if 11 cups of sugar is used?

- A) 4334 cups
- B) 2552 cups
- C) 3223 cups
- D) 22 cups

Answer: A) 4334 cups

Explanation: The ratio of milk to sugar is 23:1432:41. To find the amount of milk needed for 11 cup of sugar, set up a proportion:
$2/31/4=x$ $11/42/3=1x$. Thus,
$x=23\times4=83=43x=32\times4=38=34$ cups.

158. *Passage*:

"James stood at the edge of the cliff, staring into the abyss below. The weight of his choices pressed heavily upon him as he contemplated his next move."

Question:

What does this passage suggest about James's state of mind?

- A) He is excited about his future.

- B) He feels uncertain and burdened by his decisions.
- C) He is indifferent to his surroundings.
- D) He is confident and ready to take risks.

Answer: B) He feels uncertain and burdened by his decisions.
Explanation: The mention of "the weight of his choices" implies that he is reflecting on difficult decisions, suggesting uncertainty and pressure.

159. The increase in temperature over the years is a significant concern. Scientists warn that if global temperatures continue to rise, the consequences for the planet will be severe.

Question:

Which of the following sentences would best strengthen the argument in the text?

- A) Many people enjoy warm weather and find it pleasant.
- B) Research indicates that higher temperatures lead to more extreme weather events and rising sea levels.
- C) Some regions are experiencing milder winters than in previous decades.
- D) Weather patterns are often unpredictable.

Answer: B) Research indicates that higher temperatures lead to more extreme weather events and rising sea levels. *Explanation:* This evidence directly supports the claim about the serious consequences of rising global temperatures.

160. A bag contains 5 red balls, 3 green balls, and 2 blue balls. If one ball is drawn at random, what is the probability that it is not green?

- A) 1331
- B) 2552
- C) 4554
- D) 1551

Answer: C) 4554

Explanation: The total number of balls is 5+3+2=105+3+2=10. The number of balls that are not green is 5+2=75+2=7. Therefore, the probability of not drawing a green ball is 710107.

161.

What is the volume of a rectangular prism with a length of 44 cm, a width of 33 cm, and a height of 55 cm?

- A) 6060 cm³
- B) 1212 cm³
- C) 2020 cm³
- D) 1515 cm³

Answer: A) 6060 cm³

Explanation: The volume of a rectangular prism is calculated using the formula Volume= length × width × height Volume= length × width × height. Therefore, the volume is 4 cm×3 cm×5 cm=60 cm 34 cm×3cm×5cm=60cm3.

162. *Excerpt from a story:*

"Amidst the chaos of the city, Sarah found solace in her little bookstore. It was a refuge where stories came alive and the burdens of the world faded away."

Question:

What theme is primarily conveyed in this excerpt?

- A) The negative aspects of urban life.
- B) The importance of community in city living.
- C) The power of literature to provide comfort and escape.
- D) The challenges of running a small business.

Answer: C) The power of literature to provide comfort and escape.
Explanation: The passage emphasizes how the bookstore serves as a refuge for

Sarah, highlighting literature's ability to offer solace.

163. The weather was very hot. We decided to go swimming in the lake. The cool water would help us feel better.

Question:

Which of the following revisions best combines these sentences?

- A) The hot weather made us decide to go swimming in the lake, as the cool water would help us feel better.
- B) Since the weather was hot, we decided to go swimming in the lake because it would help us feel better.
- C) We decided to go swimming in the lake because the weather was very hot, and the cool water would help us.
- D) It was very hot outside, so we went swimming in the lake to feel better in the cool water.

Answer: D) It was very hot outside, so we went swimming in the lake to feel better in the cool water.

Explanation: This option combines the ideas smoothly while maintaining clarity and logical flow.

164. Solve the inequality $3x+5<14$. What is the solution set for x?

- A) $x<3$
- B) $x<5$
- C) $x>3$
- D) $x>5$

Answer: A) $x<3$

Explanation: To solve for x, subtract 5 from both sides:
$3x<9$. Then divide both sides by 3: $x<3$.

165. *Passage*:

"After years of hard work and persistence, Mia finally received the promotion she had been striving for. The moment was bittersweet; she felt joy but also a tinge of guilt for leaving her colleagues behind."

Question:

What does the passage suggest about Mia's feelings regarding her promotion?

- A) She is solely happy about her achievement.
- B) She regrets her hard work and effort.
- C) She experiences mixed emotions, feeling both joy and guilt.
- D) She is indifferent to her colleagues' feelings.

Answer: C) She experiences mixed emotions, feeling both joy and guilt.

Explanation: The passage indicates that

while Mia is happy about her promotion, she also feels guilty about leaving her colleagues behind, demonstrating mixed emotions.

166. In the event of a fire, the safety of the people who are in the building is the first priority.

Question:

Which of the following revisions best improves the clarity and conciseness of the sentence?

- A) The first priority during a fire is the safety of people in the building.
- B) The safety of the people in the building is a priority during a fire.
- C) During a fire, ensuring that people in the building are safe is the priority.
- D) In case of fire, people in the building must be prioritized for safety.

Answer: A) The first priority during a fire is the safety of people in the building. *Explanation:* This revision is clear and concise, directly stating the priority without unnecessary words.

167. A store is having a sale where all items are discounted by 20%20%. If an item originally costs $50- $50, what is the sale price?

- A) $30$30
- B) $40$40
- C) $45$45
- D) $50$50

Answer: B) $40$40

Explanation: To find the sale price, calculate 20%20% of 5050: $0.20 \times 50 = 10$. $0.20 \times 50 = 10$. Subtract this from the original price: $50 - 10 = 40$. $50 - 10 = 40$.

168. *Passage:*

"Throughout history, artists have used their work to comment on social issues. From paintings that depict struggle to music that speaks of hope, the creative arts have been a powerful means of expression."

Question:

What theme is primarily conveyed in the passage?

- A) The arts have no impact on society.
- B) Artists often ignore social issues in their work.
- C) Creative arts serve as a powerful form of social commentary.
- D) Art is only valuable for aesthetic purposes.

Answer: C) Creative arts serve as a powerful form of social commentary.

Explanation: The passage emphasizes the role of artists in addressing social issues through their creative works.

169. The committee discussed the budget for the next year. They considered various proposals. The proposals were submitted by different departments.

Question:

Which of the following revisions best combines these sentences?

- A) The committee discussed the budget for next year and considered various proposals submitted by different departments.
- B) Various proposals were discussed by the committee for the next year's budget, which came from different departments.
- C) The committee considered the budget for next year, and they discussed various proposals that were submitted by different departments.
- D) The committee considered different departments' proposals as they discussed the next year's budget.

Answer: A) The committee discussed the budget for next year and considered various proposals submitted by different departments.

Explanation: This revision combines the ideas effectively and maintains clarity and flow.

170. A recipe requires 22 cups of flour for every 33 cups of sugar. How many cups of sugar are needed if 88 cups of flour are used?

- A) 44 cups
- B) 66 cups
- C) 1212 cups
- D) 1616 cups

Answer: C) 1212 cups

Explanation: Set up the proportion $23=8x32=x8$, where xx is the cups of sugar needed. Cross-multiplying gives $2x=242x=24$, thus $x=12x=12$.

171. The ages of five friends are 2222, 2424, 2626, 2222, and 3030. What is the mean age of the friends?

- A) 2222
- B) 2424
- C) 2525
- D) 2626

Answer: B) 2424

Explanation: To calculate the mean, add the ages: $22+24+26+22+30=12422+24+26+22+30$

=124. Then divide by the number of friends: 1245=245124=24.

172. *Excerpt from a story*:

"As he stepped onto the stage, his heart raced, and a wave of doubt washed over him. But as he looked into the crowd, he remembered why he was there, and determination replaced fear."

Question:

What does this passage reveal about the character's emotional journey?

- A) He is completely confident and prepared.
- B) He experiences initial fear but overcomes it with determination.
- C) He is indifferent to the outcome of his performance.
- D) He is excited and eager to perform without any doubts.

Answer: B) He experiences initial fear but overcomes it with determination.
Explanation: The passage describes his transition from doubt to determination, illustrating his emotional growth.

173. There are several reasons why students should consider studying abroad. This includes gaining new perspectives and experiencing different cultures.

Question:

Which of the following revisions best improves the clarity of the sentence?

- A) Studying abroad provides several advantages, such as gaining new perspectives and experiencing different cultures.
- B) There are many reasons for students to study abroad, including new perspectives and cultural experiences.
- C) Students can gain many perspectives and experience different cultures by studying abroad.
- D) Several reasons exist for students to study abroad, such as experiencing various cultures and gaining perspectives.

Answer: A) Studying abroad provides several advantages, such as gaining new perspectives and experiencing different cultures.
Explanation: This revision clearly outlines the benefits of studying abroad in a concise manner.

174. If two angles are complementary and one angle measures 35∘35∘, what is the measure of the other angle?

- A) 55∘55∘
- B) 65∘65∘
- C) 75∘75∘

- D) 85∘85∘

Answer: B) 55∘55∘

Explanation: Complementary angles add up to 90∘90∘. Therefore, the other angle is 90∘−35∘=55∘90∘−35∘=55∘.

175. *Passage*:

"The discovery of new technologies has transformed how we communicate, creating both opportunities for connection and challenges regarding privacy and authenticity."

Question:

What theme is primarily conveyed in the passage?

- A) Technology only creates problems in communication.
- B) New technologies enhance communication without any drawbacks.
- C) The impact of technology on communication is complex, with both positive and negative aspects.
- D) Traditional communication methods are superior to modern technologies.

Answer: C) The impact of technology on communication is complex, with both positive and negative aspects.

Explanation: The passage highlights that while technology enhances communication, it also introduces challenges.

176. The researchers conducted a study. The study examined the effects of sleep on academic performance. They collected data from various schools.

Question:

Which of the following revisions best combines these sentences?

- A) The researchers conducted a study that examined the effects of sleep on academic performance, collecting data from various schools.
- B) The researchers conducted a study, and the study examined how sleep affects academic performance and collected data from schools.
- C) Conducting a study, the researchers examined the effects of sleep on academic performance, and they collected data from various schools.
- D) The study that the researchers conducted examined the effects of sleep on academic performance and gathered data from schools.

Answer: A) The researchers conducted a study that examined the effects of sleep on academic performance, collecting data from various schools.

Explanation: This option effectively combines the ideas while maintaining clarity and conciseness.

177. If you invest $2000$2000 at an interest rate of 5%5% per year, how much interest will you earn after 33 years?

- A) $300$300
- B) $150$150
- C) $100$100
- D) $250$250

Answer: A) $300$300

Explanation: The formula for simple interest is Interest= P × r × t Interest = P × r × t. Therefore, the interest earned is 2000×0.05×3=3002000×0.05×3=300.

178. *Passage*:

"Feeling isolated in the bustling city, John volunteered at the local shelter. Each smile he received in return made him feel connected to others, easing his loneliness."

Question:

What motivates John to volunteer at the shelter?

- A) He wants to gain work experience.
- B) He seeks to alleviate his feelings of isolation.
- C) He is forced to volunteer by his friends.
- D) He is looking for a way to make money.

Answer: B) He seeks to alleviate his feelings of isolation.

Explanation: The passage indicates that volunteering helps John feel connected and reduces his loneliness, demonstrating his motivation.

179. The environmental changes that are occurring are alarming. They can lead to severe consequences for future generations.

Question:

Which of the following revisions makes the statement more impactful?

- A) The alarming environmental changes we face pose serious threats to future generations.
- B) Environmental changes are alarming and can affect future generations.
- C) It is alarming that environmental changes may have consequences for future generations.
- D) The changes in the environment are quite alarming and could lead to problems in the future.

Answer: A) The alarming environmental changes we face pose serious threats to future generations.

Explanation: This revision uses stronger language and directly addresses the urgency of the issue.

180. If 55 pounds of apples cost $10$10, how much would 88 pounds cost at the same rate?

- A) $12$12
- B) $16$16
- C) $18$18
- D) $20$20

Answer: B) $16$16

Explanation: The cost per pound is 105=2510=2 dollars. Therefore, 88 pounds would cost 2×8=162×8=16 dollars.

181.

In a recipe, the ratio of oil to vinegar is 3:13:1. If you use 99 tablespoons of oil, how many tablespoons of vinegar do you need?

- A) 33
- B) 66
- C) 99
- D) 1212

Answer: A) 33

Explanation: The ratio 3:13:1 means for every 33 parts of oil, there is 11 part of vinegar. If you have 99 tablespoons of oil, you can set up the proportion: 31=9x13=x9, where xx is the amount of vinegar. Cross-multiplying gives 3x=93x=9, thus x=3x=3.

182. *Passage*:

"The old oak tree stood tall and proud in the center of the park, a silent witness to generations of laughter and tears that echoed around its roots."

Question:

What theme is primarily conveyed in the passage?

- A) Nature is indifferent to human emotions.
- B) Memories and experiences shape our connection to nature.
- C) Trees can live forever.
- D) Parks are often neglected by the community.

Answer: B) Memories and experiences shape our connection to nature.

Explanation: The passage illustrates how the oak tree is intertwined with the human experiences that occur around it, emphasizing the connection between nature and human emotion.

183. The festival was a huge success. Many people attended. There were numerous food stalls and entertainment options available.

Question:

Which of the following revisions best combines these sentences?

- A) The festival was a huge success, with many people attending and numerous food stalls and entertainment options available.
- B) Many people attended the festival, and it was a huge success with entertainment options and food stalls.
- C) The festival, which was a huge success, attracted many attendees, and there were many food stalls.
- D) A huge success, the festival had many people attend, with food stalls and entertainment available.

Answer: A) The festival was a huge success, with many people attending and numerous food stalls and entertainment options available.
Explanation: This revision combines all ideas smoothly and maintains clarity.

184. A pair of shoes costs $80$80. If they are on sale for 25%25% off, what is the sale price?

- A) $60$60
- B) $70$70
- C) $75$75
- D) $80$80

Answer: A) $60$60
Explanation: The discount is 25%25% of 8080:
$0.25 \times 80 = 200.25 \times 80 = 20$. Therefore, the sale price is $80-20=6080-20=60$.

185. *Passage*:

"Determined to prove herself, Clara spent countless nights studying and practicing for the upcoming competition, hoping to finally earn her mother's approval."

Question:

What motivates Clara in this passage?

- A) A desire to win the competition.
- B) The need for personal achievement.
- C) The hope for her mother's approval.
- D) A wish to outshine her peers.

Answer: C) The hope for her mother's approval.
Explanation: The passage explicitly states that Clara's motivation stems from wanting to earn her mother's approval.

186. The committee decided to make changes to the policy. They felt that it was outdated. This would benefit the employees.

Question:

Which of the following revisions best combines and clarifies these sentences?

- A) The committee decided to update the outdated policy, believing it would benefit the employees.
- B) The committee felt that the policy was outdated, so they decided to change it for the benefit of the employees.
- C) An outdated policy was decided to be changed by the committee to benefit employees.
- D) The committee decided to make changes to the policy, which they felt was outdated, to benefit the employees.

Answer: A) The committee decided to update the outdated policy, believing it would benefit the employees.
Explanation: This revision clearly states the action taken and its purpose concisely.

187. A rectangular garden has a length of 1010 meters and a width of 44 meters. What is the perimeter of the garden?

- A) 2828 meters
- B) 4040 meters
- C) 3030 meters
- D) 2020 meters

Answer: A) 2828 meters
Explanation: The perimeter PP of a rectangle is calculated using the formula $P=2$ (length + width)$P=2$ (length + width). Therefore, $P=2(10+4)=28P=2(10+4)=28$ meters.

188. *Excerpt from a poem:*

"The stars danced playfully in the night sky, their twinkling laughter echoing through the silence."

Question:

Which literary device is primarily used in this excerpt?

- A) Hyperbole
- B) Personification
- C) Simile
- D) Metaphor

Answer: B) Personification
Explanation: The stars are described as "dancing" and "laughing," attributing human qualities to non-human elements, which is personification.

189. The findings of the study were significant and should be taken seriously by policymakers.

Question:

Which of the following revisions makes the statement more impactful?

- A) Policymakers must take the significant findings of the study seriously.
- B) The study's significant findings should be considered by policymakers.
- C) Policymakers are urged to take the important findings of the study seriously.
- D) The findings of the study are significant and deserve serious consideration by policymakers.

Answer: C) Policymakers are urged to take the important findings of the study seriously.

Explanation: This revision uses more assertive language, emphasizing the urgency for policymakers to consider the findings.

190. If $7x-14=0$, what is the value of x?

- A) 0
- B) 2
- C) 3
- D) 4

Answer: B) 2

Explanation: To solve for x, add 14 to both sides:

$7x=14$. Then divide both sides by 7:

$x=2$.

191. *Passage*:

"With every challenge she faced, Maria grew more resilient. Each setback was a lesson learned, pushing her closer to her dreams."

Question:

What does the passage suggest about Maria's character?

- A) She gives up easily when faced with challenges.
- B) She becomes discouraged by setbacks.
- C) She learns and grows stronger from her experiences.
- D) She avoids challenges to protect herself.

Answer: C) She learns and grows stronger from her experiences.

Explanation: The passage indicates that setbacks contribute positively to her resilience and determination.

192. The park was crowded with people. They were enjoying the warm weather. The children were playing games.

Question:

Which of the following revisions best combines these sentences?

- A) The park was crowded with people enjoying the warm weather, and children were playing games.
- B) People crowded the park to enjoy the warm weather and play games with children.
- C) Enjoying the warm weather, people crowded the park while children played games.
- D) The park, crowded with people enjoying warm weather, had children playing games.

Answer: A) The park was crowded with people enjoying the warm weather, and children were playing games.

Explanation: This option effectively combines the ideas while maintaining clarity.

193.

A bag contains 44 red marbles, 66 blue marbles, and 22 green marbles. What is the probability of drawing a red marble?

- A) 1331
- B) 1221
- C) 2332
- D) 1551

Answer: A) 1331

Explanation: The total number of marbles is 4+6+2=124+6+2=12. The probability of drawing a red marble is 4 (red marbles)12 (total marbles) =1312 (total marbles)4 (red marbles) =31.

194. *Passage:*

"After years of living in the shadows of her famous siblings, Lily decided to carve out her own identity by pursuing her passion for painting."

Question:

What motivates Lily to pursue painting?

- A) The desire for fame and recognition.
- B) A need to escape her family's expectations.
- C) An interest in art that is separate from her family.
- D) The wish to prove herself better than her siblings.

Answer: B) A need to escape her family's expectations.

Explanation: The passage indicates that Lily wants to establish her own identity, suggesting she is motivated by a desire to break free from her family's influence.

195. The results of the experiment were surprising. They were unexpected and not what we thought would happen.

Question:

Which of the following revisions best combines these sentences for clarity?

- A) The results of the experiment were surprising and not what we expected.
- B) Unexpected and surprising, the results of the experiment were not what we thought would happen.
- C) The experiment's results were not what we thought, and they were surprising.
- D) Surprising results from the experiment were unexpected and not what we anticipated.

Answer: A) The results of the experiment were surprising and not what we expected. *Explanation:* This option clearly combines the ideas while maintaining straightforwardness.

196. A recipe requires 3443 cups of sugar for every 2332 cups of flour. How much sugar is needed if 22 cups of flour are used?

- A) 11 cup
- B) 112121 cups
- C) 22 cups
- D) 214241 cups

Answer: B) 112121 cups

Explanation: Set up a proportion based on the original ratio: $3/42/3=x22/33/4=2x$, where xx is the amount of sugar needed. Cross-multiplying gives $3\cdot2=4x/33\cdot2=4x/3$. Solving gives $x=34\times21=32=1.5x=43\times12=23=1.5$, which is 112121 cups.

197. *Passage*:

"In the depths of winter, the small community banded together, sharing resources and warmth. Their resilience in the face of adversity revealed the strength of their bonds."

Question:

What theme is primarily conveyed in the passage?

- A) Adversity can tear communities apart.
- B) Cooperation and unity strengthen community ties during difficult times.
- C) Winter is the harshest season for communities.
- D) Individualism is more important than community support.

Answer: B) Cooperation and unity strengthen community ties during difficult times.

Explanation: The passage illustrates how

the community's collaboration during adversity enhances their connections.

198. The committee has decided that they will hold the meeting next week on Tuesday.

Question:

Which of the following revisions best improves the conciseness of the sentence?

- A) The committee will hold the meeting next Tuesday.
- B) The committee has decided to hold the meeting next week on Tuesday.
- C) The committee will meet next week on Tuesday.
- D) The committee has decided that the meeting will be next Tuesday.

Answer: A) The committee will hold the meeting next Tuesday.
Explanation: This revision eliminates unnecessary words while clearly conveying the same information.

199. A cyclist travels at a speed of 1515 miles per hour. How far will they travel in 44 hours?

- A) 3030 miles
- B) 4545 miles
- C) 6060 miles
- D) 7575 miles

Answer: C) 6060 miles
Explanation: Distance is calculated using the formula Distance= Speed × Time Distance= Speed × Time. Therefore, the distance traveled is
15 miles/hour×4 hours=60 miles 15 miles/hour×4 hours=60 miles.

200. *Passage*:

"After much deliberation, Alex finally decided to take the leap and start his own business, despite the risks involved. He knew this was a chance he couldn't pass up."

Question:

What does this passage suggest about Alex's character?

- A) He is impulsive and does not consider risks.
- B) He is cautious and avoids making difficult decisions.
- C) He is thoughtful and willing to take calculated risks for his dreams.
- D) He is indifferent to the success of his business.

Answer: C) He is thoughtful and willing to take calculated risks for his dreams.
Explanation: The passage indicates that Alex has carefully considered his decision

and recognizes the importance of pursuing

his dreams despite the risks.

PRACTICE 3

1. *Passage 1:*

Science and exploration – Over the centuries, exploration has led to some of the greatest scientific discoveries. Scientists like Darwin changed the world by documenting unfamiliar species, creating new theories of evolution. Many of the world's most significant scientific advancements have resulted from a combination of curiosity and determination.

Passage 2:

The cost of exploration – While exploration has led to significant discoveries, it also comes with ethical and environmental costs. Human exploration has often resulted in the destruction of ecosystems and the extinction of species.

Question:

How do the authors of Passage 1 and Passage 2 differ in their view of scientific exploration?

- A) Both passages see exploration as entirely positive.

- B) Passage 1 focuses on the benefits of exploration, while Passage 2 highlights its negative consequences.

- C) Passage 1 argues that exploration should be limited, while Passage 2 encourages more exploration.

- D) Both passages highlight the destructive effects of exploration.

Answer: B) Passage 1 focuses on the benefits of exploration, while Passage 2 highlights its negative consequences. *Explanation:* Passage 1 highlights exploration's scientific achievements, while Passage 2 discusses the environmental and ethical costs, showing the two different perspectives.

2. *Passage:*

In 1903, the Wright brothers made history by flying the first powered aircraft. What is often overlooked, however, is the years of research and countless failed attempts that led up to that day. Their story is one of perseverance and dedication to a singular goal.

Question:

Which of the following best captures the main idea of the passage?

- A) The Wright brothers' success was inevitable.
- B) The Wright brothers' success was the result of years of hard work and persistence.
- C) The Wright brothers failed many times before finally giving up.
- D) The Wright brothers were only successful due to luck.

Answer: B) The Wright brothers' success was the result of years of hard work and persistence.
Explanation: The passage emphasizes the perseverance and dedication that led to the Wright brothers' successful flight.

3. The project team was able to complete their work on time, even though it took longer than expected to complete.

Question:

Which revision best improves the clarity and conciseness of the sentence?

- A) The project team managed to finish their work, even though it took longer than anticipated.
- B) Although it took longer than expected, the project team were able to complete their work on time.
- C) Despite taking longer than expected, the project team completed the work on time.
- D) The team was able to finish the project on time, though it took a long time to complete.

Answer: C) Despite taking longer than expected, the project team completed the work on time.
Explanation: This option is the clearest and most concise, eliminating unnecessary words while maintaining the meaning.

4. Many athletes who compete in professional sports has trained for years to reach the top of their game.

Question:

Which of the following corrects the verb agreement error in the sentence?

- A) Many athletes who compete in professional sports have trained for years to reach the top of their game.
- B) Many athletes who competes in professional sports has trained for years to reach the top of their game.

- C) Many athletes who compete in professional sports had trained for years to reach the top of their game.
- D) Many athletes who compete in professional sports was trained for years to reach the top of their game.

Answer: A) Many athletes who compete in professional sports have trained for years to reach the top of their game.
Explanation: The verb "have" agrees with the plural subject "athletes."

5. If 2x+5=152x+5=15, what is the value of xx?

- A) 55
- B) 1010
- C) 00
- D) 33

Answer: D) 33

Explanation: Subtract 55 from both sides to get 2x=102x=10. Divide by 22, so x=5x=5.

6. A rectangle has a length of 1010 cm and a width of 44 cm. What is the area of the rectangle?

- A) 14 cm214cm2
- B) 20 cm220cm2
- C) 40 cm240cm2
- D) 24 cm224cm2

Answer: C) 40 cm240cm2

Explanation: The area of a rectangle is calculated using the formula Area= length × width Area= length × width, so 10 cm×4 cm=40 cm210cm×4cm=40cm2.

7. *Passage*:

"The vastness of space has always intrigued humanity. From the first stargazers to modern astrophysicists, people have long sought to understand the universe and their place in it."

Question:

What is the main point of the passage?

- A) The vastness of space is too complex for humanity to understand.
- B) Interest in space has only recently become popular.
- C) Humanity has always been curious about space and has made great strides in understanding it.
- D) Space exploration is unnecessary and expensive.

Answer: C) Humanity has always been curious about space and has made great strides in understanding it.
Explanation: The passage emphasizes humanity's long-standing curiosity

about space and the progress made by modern scientists.

8. *Passage*:

"The city council is debating whether to invest in public parks or improve the local roads. Both options have strong support, but funds are limited, and a decision must be made soon."

Question:

What issue is the city council facing?

- A) A decision about how to allocate limited funds between two important projects.
- B) Deciding whether to eliminate public parks.
- C) Convincing residents to support road improvements.
- D) Finding more funds for future projects.

Answer: A) A decision about how to allocate limited funds between two important projects.
Explanation: The passage outlines the city council's dilemma in choosing between public parks and road improvements due to limited funds.

9. The new library opened last week, and many residents have already started

borrowing books, attending events, and using the study rooms.

Question:

Which of the following sentences best maintains the meaning and improves conciseness?

- A) The new library opened last week, with many residents already borrowing books, attending events, and using the study rooms.
- B) The library was newly opened last week, and many residents have already started borrowing books, attending events, and using the study rooms.
- C) Last week the new library was opened, and a lot of residents have already started using the study rooms, borrowing books, and attending events.
- D) The new library opened last week, and already many residents are borrowing books, attending events, and using the study rooms.

Answer: A) The new library opened last week, with many residents already borrowing books, attending events, and using the study rooms.
Explanation: This option is the most concise while maintaining the meaning and structure of the original sentence.

10. Because of the rain that fell steadily all day, the soccer game had to be postponed until another day.

Question:

Which of the following revisions best improves the conciseness of the sentence?

- A) The soccer game was postponed because it rained steadily all day.
- B) The rain that fell steadily all day forced the soccer game to be postponed until another day.
- C) Due to the steady rain all day, the soccer game was postponed.
- D) The steady rain caused the soccer game to be postponed until another day.

Answer: C) Due to the steady rain all day, the soccer game was postponed.
Explanation: This revision is the clearest and most concise, avoiding unnecessary repetition.

11. At the conference, the keynote speaker was amazing; she spoke about the importance of staying motivated and how to succeed despite challenges.

Question:

Which of the following revisions best maintains the meaning and tone of the sentence while improving its conciseness?

- A) The keynote speaker at the conference was great, talking about motivation and how to overcome challenges.
- B) At the conference, the keynote speaker impressed the audience by discussing how to stay motivated and succeed despite challenges.
- C) The keynote speaker spoke wonderfully at the conference about the need for staying motivated and succeeding in the face of challenges.
- D) At the conference, the keynote speaker impressed by talking about staying motivated and overcoming challenges.

Answer: D) At the conference, the keynote speaker impressed by talking about staying motivated and overcoming challenges.
Explanation: This option effectively captures the original meaning while reducing wordiness.

12. Solve the inequality:
$3x-4\leq8 3x-4\leq8$

- A) $x\leq4 x\leq4$
- B) $x\geq4 x\geq4$

- C) $x \geq -4 x \geq -4$
- D) $x \leq -4 x \leq -4$

Answer: A) $x \leq 4 x \leq 4$

Explanation: First, add 44 to both sides: $3x \leq 12 3x \leq 12$. Then, divide both sides by 33:

$x \leq 4 x \leq 4$.

13. What is the area of a triangle with a base of 66 cm and a height of 44 cm?

- A) 10 cm210cm2
- B) 12 cm212cm2
- C) 24 cm224cm2
- D) 48 cm248cm2

Answer: B) 12 cm212cm2

Explanation: The area of a triangle is calculated using the formula Area=12×base×heightArea=21×base×height. Therefore, $12 \times 6 \times 4 = 12$ cm221×6×4=12cm2.

14. If the cost of 33 apples is $6$6, how much would 77 apples cost at the same rate?

- A) $10$10
- B) $12$12
- C) $14$14
- D) $16$16

Answer: C) $14$14

Explanation: The cost per apple is

$63 = 236 = 2$ dollars. Therefore, 77 apples would cost $7 \times 2 = 147 \times 2 = 14$ dollars.

15. Solve for xx:

$4(x-3) = 8 4(x-3) = 8$

- A) $x = 2 x = 2$
- B) $x = 3 x = 3$
- C) $x = 5 x = 5$
- D) $x = 4 x = 4$

Answer: A) $x = 5 x = 5$

Explanation: First, distribute the 44: $4x - 12 = 8 4x - 12 = 8$. Add 1212 to both sides:

$4x = 20 4x = 20$. Then, divide by 44:

$x = 5 x = 5$.

16. *Passage*:

"The small village, nestled in the mountains, was often cut off from the outside world during the harsh winter months. Despite this, the villagers remained cheerful and self-sufficient, relying on one another to survive."

Question:

What is the central idea of the passage?

- A) The villagers were unhappy with their isolation.
- B) The harsh winters made life in the village impossible.

- C) The village is isolated but remains resilient and self-reliant.
- D) The villagers struggled to survive each winter without help.

Answer: C) The village is isolated but remains resilient and self-reliant.

Explanation: The passage describes how the villagers manage to remain cheerful and self-sufficient despite being cut off during the winter months.

17. *Passage*:

"As the clock ticked closer to midnight, the streets became quieter and quieter. The lights in the buildings flickered out one by one, leaving only the dim glow of the streetlamps to guide the few remaining people home."

Question:

What atmosphere does the passage create?

- A) A sense of fear and danger.
- B) A feeling of excitement and energy.
- C) A calm, quiet, and peaceful atmosphere.
- D) A sense of urgency and movement.

Answer: C) A calm, quiet, and peaceful atmosphere.

Explanation: The passage describes the quieting of the streets and the gradual fading of lights, creating a calm and peaceful mood.

18. A lot of people believe that exercising regularly is important for maintaining good health, while others don't think it's necessary at all.

Question:

Which of the following revisions best improves the clarity and conciseness of the sentence?

- A) Many people believe regular exercise is important for health, while others disagree.
- B) A lot of people believe that exercising often is vital to good health, though some don't agree.
- C) A number of people think exercise is necessary, but some people don't think it's that important.
- D) Some believe that exercising regularly is necessary for maintaining health, but others believe it is not.

Answer: A) Many people believe regular exercise is important for health, while others disagree.

Explanation: This revision eliminates

unnecessary words and makes the sentence clearer and more concise.

19. During the meeting, the team discussed several strategies that they might consider implementing next quarter.

Question:

Which revision best improves the sentence for conciseness?

- A) The team discussed many strategies that they considered for next quarter during the meeting.
- B) During the meeting, the team discussed various strategies they could implement next quarter.
- C) The team discussed several strategies for implementation during next quarter at the meeting.
- D) Several strategies were discussed by the team in the meeting to be used next quarter.

Answer: B) During the meeting, the team discussed various strategies they could implement next quarter.
Explanation: This version eliminates unnecessary words and streamlines the sentence for clarity.

20. Solve for x:

$x^2 - 16 = 0$

- A) $x = 4$
- B) $x = -4$
- C) $x = 0$
- D) $x = \pm 4$

Answer: D) $x = \pm 4$
Explanation: The equation can be factored as $(x-4)(x+4) = 0$, so the solutions are $x = 4$ and $x = -4$.

21. Simplify the expression:

$4x^2 + 2x - 6 + 3x^2 - 4x + 9$

- A) $7x^2 - 2x + 3$
- B) $7x^2 + 6x + 15$
- C) $7x^2 - 2x + 15$
- D) $5x^2 - 2x - 3$

Answer: C) $7x^2 - 2x + 15$
Explanation: Combine like terms: $4x^2 + 3x^2 = 7x^2$, $2x - 4x = -2x$, and $-6 + 9 = 3$.

22. What is the value of x in the equation $2x + 7 = 21$?

- A) 7
- B) 9
- C) 5
- D) 6

Answer: C) 77

> *Explanation:* Subtract 77 from both sides: $2x=142x=14$, then divide by 22: $x=7x=7$.

23. A rectangular field has a length of 30 meters and a width of 20 meters. What is the perimeter of the field?

- A) 50 meters
- B) 100 meters
- C) 60 meters
- D) 80 meters

Answer: B) 100 meters

> *Explanation:* The perimeter PP of a rectangle is calculated using the formula $P=2(\text{length}+\text{width})P=2(\text{length}+\text{width})$. Therefore, $P=2(30+20)=100 \text{ meters}P=2(30+20)=100\text{meters}$.

24. Solve for yy in the equation $3y-4=2y+53y-4=2y+5$.

- A) $y=1y=1$
- B) $y=2y=2$
- C) $y=9y=9$
- D) $y=-1y=-1$

Answer: C) $y=9y=9$

> *Explanation:* Subtract 2y2y from both sides: $y-4=5y-4=5$. Then, add 44 to both sides: $y=9y=9$.

25. What is the slope of the line that passes through the points $(1,2)(1,2)$ and $(4,6)(4,6)$?

- A) 1221
- B) 22
- C) 11
- D) 4334

Answer: B) 22

> *Explanation:* The formula for the slope is $y2-y1x2-x1x2-x1y2-y1$. So, $6-24-1=434-16-2=34$.

26. *Passage*:

> "A farmer's fields stretched far beyond the horizon. He planted seeds year after year, hoping each season would bring a good harvest. But this year, the rains came late, and the crops began to wither under the hot sun."

Question:

What is the main theme of the passage?

- A) The importance of modern farming techniques.
- B) The challenges farmers face due to unpredictable weather.
- C) The joy of working on a farm.
- D) The beauty of a well-maintained field.

Answer: B) The challenges farmers face due to unpredictable weather.

Explanation: The passage highlights how the farmer's crops were affected by the late arrival of rain, emphasizing the struggles farmers endure due to changing weather.

27. *Passage*:

"From her perch on the balcony, Sara could see the whole city spread out before her. The setting sun cast a golden glow over the buildings, making them seem almost magical."

Question:

What mood does the passage create?

- A) Tense and suspenseful.
- B) Joyful and magical.
- C) Boring and routine.
- D) Dark and mysterious.

Answer: B) Joyful and magical.

Explanation: The passage describes a serene and beautiful scene, with the sun creating a "golden glow" that evokes a sense of magic and wonder.

28. *Passage*:

"The professor paced back and forth in the classroom, his voice rising as he explained the complexities of quantum mechanics. The students listened intently, some scribbling notes while others stared in awe."

Question:

What is the primary focus of the passage?

- A) The professor's frustration with his students.
- B) The students' struggle to understand quantum mechanics.
- C) The professor's passion for teaching.
- D) The difficulty of quantum mechanics.

Answer: C) The professor's passion for teaching.

Explanation: The passage emphasizes the professor's animated teaching style and how engaged the students are, which reflects his enthusiasm for the subject.

29. *Passage*:

"The wind howled through the narrow streets, rattling windows and sending loose papers flying. People hurried to find shelter as the storm approached."

Question:

What is the atmosphere created by the passage?

- A) Calm and peaceful.
- B) Dark and eerie.
- C) Tense and foreboding.
- D) Joyful and carefree.

Answer: C) Tense and foreboding.

Explanation: The howling wind and the people rushing to find shelter suggest an incoming storm, creating a tense and foreboding mood.

30. *Passage:*

"As the plane soared higher into the sky, the landscape below shrank into tiny patches of green and brown. The clouds enveloped the wings, creating a sense of serenity and detachment from the world below."

Question:

What feeling is conveyed by the passage?

- A) Anxiety and fear.
- B) Serenity and detachment.
- C) Excitement and anticipation.
- D) Confusion and chaos.

Answer: B) Serenity and detachment.

Explanation: The passage describes a calm and peaceful scene of the plane ascending, evoking a sense of detachment from the earth below.

31. The new regulations requires businesses to submit their tax forms electronically.

Question:

Which of the following corrects the verb agreement error in the sentence?

- A) The new regulations require businesses to submit their tax forms electronically.
- B) The new regulations required businesses to submit their tax forms electronically.
- C) The new regulations has required businesses to submit their tax forms electronically.
- D) The new regulation require businesses to submit their tax forms electronically.

Answer: A) The new regulations require businesses to submit their tax forms electronically.

Explanation: "Regulations" is plural, so the verb should be "require" rather than "requires."

32. Despite her injury, the runner continued to participate in the race, finishing in third place.

Question:

Which of the following revisions best improves the conciseness of the sentence?

- A) The runner, despite being injured, continued the race and finished in third place.
- B) Despite being injured, the runner continued the race and finished third.
- C) Although she was injured, the runner participated in the race and came in third place.
- D) The runner finished in third place despite continuing to participate while being injured.

Answer: B) Despite being injured, the runner continued the race and finished third.
Explanation: This revision eliminates unnecessary words while maintaining the original meaning.

33. Many students who attend college learn valuable skills, make lifelong friendships, and often find career opportunities.

Question:

Which of the following revisions best improves the clarity and conciseness of the sentence?

- A) Attending college helps many students learn valuable skills, make friendships, and find career opportunities.
- B) Many students who attend college often learn skills, make lifelong friendships, and find career opportunities.
- C) College students often learn valuable skills, make lifelong friendships, and find career opportunities.
- D) Many college students learn skills, make friends for life, and find job opportunities.

Answer: C) College students often learn valuable skills, make lifelong friendships, and find career opportunities.
Explanation: This version is clear and concise while maintaining the meaning of the original sentence.

34. Because of the fact that the road was closed, we had to take a different route to get to the concert.

Question:

Which of the following revisions best improves the conciseness of the sentence?

- A) Because of the road closure, we had to take a different route to the concert.
- B) Due to the fact that the road was closed, we had to take a different route to get to the concert.
- C) The road closure made us take a different route to get to the concert.
- D) Because of the fact the road was closed, we had to take a different route.

Answer: A) Because of the road closure, we had to take a different route to the concert.

Explanation: This revision eliminates unnecessary words while keeping the original meaning intact.

35. There were many problems that arose during the planning process, and these issues delayed the project's completion.

Question:

Which of the following revisions best improves clarity and conciseness?

- A) Many problems that came up during the planning process delayed the project.
- B) The project was delayed because of the numerous problems that arose during the planning process.
- C) Many problems arose during the planning process, delaying the project's completion.
- D) Numerous problems arose during planning, delaying the project.

Answer: C) Many problems arose during the planning process, delaying the project's completion.

Explanation: This version combines the ideas clearly and concisely.

36. The company issued a statement saying that it plans to release a new version of its software next year.

Question:

Which of the following revisions best improves the sentence for clarity and conciseness?

- A) The company said it would release new software next year.
- B) The company plans to release a new version of its software next year.
- C) A statement was issued by the company about a new software version coming next year.
- D) The company issued a statement about releasing software next year.

Answer: B) The company plans to release a new version of its software next year.

Explanation: This revision eliminates unnecessary wording and directly states the information.

37. Solve for xx:

$3x-9=123x-9=12$

- A) x=5x=5
- B) x=3x=3
- C) x=7x=7
- D) x=6x=6

Answer: D) x=7x=7

Explanation: Add 99 to both sides to get $3x=213x=21$, then divide by 33 to get x=7x=7.

38. The sum of two numbers is 2424. One of the numbers is 1414. What is the other number?

- A) 1010
- B) 1212
- C) 88
- D) 99

Answer: A) 1010

Explanation: Subtract 1414 from 2424 to find the other number: $24-14=1024-14=10$.

39. Simplify the expression:

$5(3x+4)-2x5(3x+4)-2x$

- A) 15x+415x+4
- B) 13x+2013x+20
- C) 17x+417x+4
- D) 13x+1213x+12

Answer: B) 13x+2013x+20

Explanation: First distribute the 55: $15x+2015x+20$, then subtract 2x2x: $15x-2x+20=13x+2015 x-2 x+20$ $=13x+20$.

40. Solve the equation:

$7x+3=317x+3=31$

- A) x=2x=2
- B) x=3x=3
- C) x=4x=4
- D) x=6x=6

Answer: D) x=4x=4

Explanation: Subtract 33 from both sides: $7x=287x=28$, then divide by 77: x=4x=4.

41. *Passage*:

"As the storm clouds rolled in, the sky darkened, and the first drops of rain began to fall. The streets emptied quickly as people rushed to take shelter."

Question:

What mood does the passage create?

- A) Calm and peaceful.
- B) Excitement and anticipation.
- C) Tense and foreboding.
- D) Joyful and carefree.

Answer: C) Tense and foreboding.

Explanation: The description of darkening skies and people hurrying to take shelter suggests an approaching storm, creating a tense atmosphere.

42. *Passage*:

"Though the town was small, it had a strong sense of community. Neighbors frequently stopped by to check on one another, and people gathered in the town square every weekend to share stories and laugh together."

Question:

What theme is primarily conveyed in the passage?

- A) The importance of community and togetherness.
- B) The struggle of living in a small town.
- C) The isolation experienced by rural towns.

- D) The challenges of maintaining relationships.

Answer: A) The importance of community and togetherness.

Explanation: The passage focuses on how the townspeople interact and support each other, highlighting the value of community.

43. *Passage*:

"The clock ticked louder with each passing minute. Thomas stared at his notebook, waiting for inspiration to strike, but his mind remained frustratingly blank."

Question:

What feeling does the passage convey about Thomas's state of mind?

- A) Calm and patient.
- B) Eager and confident.
- C) Frustrated and anxious.
- D) Relaxed and unhurried.

Answer: C) Frustrated and anxious.

Explanation: The description of Thomas staring at a blank notebook while hearing the ticking clock suggests his growing frustration and anxiety.

44. *Passage*:

"On the surface, their friendship seemed

perfect, but beneath it lay unresolved tension that neither of them wanted to confront."

Question:

What does the passage suggest about the friendship between the two characters?

- A) It is strong and unwavering.
- B) It is in danger of falling apart.
- C) It is genuine and honest.
- D) It is built on mutual trust and respect.

Answer: B) It is in danger of falling apart.

Explanation: The phrase "unresolved tension" suggests that there are hidden issues in their friendship that could lead to problems.

45. *Passage*:

"The roaring river cut through the mountains like a jagged scar, carving deeper into the earth with every passing year."

Question:

Which literary device is used in the phrase "cut through the mountains like a jagged scar"?

- A) Simile.
- B) Metaphor.
- C) Personification.
- D) Alliteration.

Answer: A) Simile.

Explanation: A simile is a comparison using "like" or "as." In this case, the river is compared to a scar using the word "like."

46. The team of engineers is planning to build a new bridge that will cross the river and connect the two sides of the city.

Question:

Which of the following revisions best improves the conciseness of the sentence?

- A) The team of engineers is planning to build a bridge across the river to connect both sides of the city.
- B) The engineers are planning to build a bridge over the river to connect the two sides of the city.
- C) The engineers plan to build a bridge across the river to connect the two sides of the city.
- D) The team is planning to construct a new bridge that will span the river and connect both sides of the city.

Answer: C) The engineers plan to build a bridge across the river to connect the two sides of the city.

Explanation: This option is the most

concise and maintains the meaning of the original sentence.

47. The report, which was published last year, detailed the effects of climate change on coastal regions.

Question:

Which revision best improves the clarity of the sentence?

- A) The report published last year detailed the effects of climate change on coastal regions.
- B) Last year, the report detailed the effects of climate change on coastal regions.
- C) The report, published last year, detailed the effects of climate change on coastal regions.
- D) The report was published last year and detailed the effects of climate change on coastal regions.

Answer: A) The report published last year detailed the effects of climate change on coastal regions.
Explanation: This revision eliminates the unnecessary commas and maintains clarity.

48. In light of the new policies that were introduced, many employees have voiced concerns about the changes.

Question:

Which revision best improves the clarity and conciseness of the sentence?

- A) Due to new policies being introduced, many employees have voiced concerns about the changes.
- B) Many employees have voiced concerns about the changes since new policies were introduced.
- C) Since the introduction of new policies, many employees voiced their concerns.
- D) Many employees have voiced concerns due to the new policies that were introduced.

Answer: B) Many employees have voiced concerns about the changes since new policies were introduced.
Explanation: This version is both concise and maintains the clarity of the original sentence without redundant phrases.

49. The board of directors were pleased with the results of the annual report, but they noted that there were areas for improvement.

Question:

Which revision best corrects the subject-verb agreement error in the sentence?

- A) The board of directors was pleased with the results of the annual report, but they noted areas for improvement.
- B) The board of directors was pleased with the results of the annual report, but noted that there were areas for improvement.
- C) The board of directors were pleased with the results of the annual report, but noted some areas for improvement.
- D) The board of directors were pleased with the results of the annual report, noting areas for improvement.

Answer: A) The board of directors was pleased with the results of the annual report, but they noted areas for improvement.
Explanation: "Board of directors" is a singular entity, so the verb should be "was" to maintain subject-verb agreement.

50. The exhibit, which is filled with historical artifacts, it will remain open until the end of the month.

Question:

Which of the following revisions corrects the grammatical error in the sentence?

- A) The exhibit, which is filled with historical artifacts, will remain open until the end of the month.
- B) The exhibit, filled with historical artifacts, it will remain open until the end of the month.
- C) The exhibit filled with historical artifacts will remain open until the end of the month.
- D) The exhibit that is filled with historical artifacts it will remain open until the end of the month.

Answer: A) The exhibit, which is filled with historical artifacts, will remain open until the end of the month.
Explanation: The unnecessary "it" in the original sentence creates a grammatical error. Removing "it" corrects the sentence.

51. Solve for xx:
$5x+12=375x+12=37$

- A) $x=4x=4$
- B) $x=5x=5$
- C) $x=6x=6$
- D) $x=7x=7$

Answer: C) $x=5x=5$

Explanation: First, subtract 1212 from both sides:

$5x=255x=25$. Then divide by 55: $x=5x=5$.

52. If the sum of the angles in a triangle is always $180°180°$, what is the measure of the third angle in a triangle where two of the angles are $40°40°$ and $70°70°$?

- A) $30°30°$
- B) $60°60°$
- C) $70°70°$
- D) $80°80°$

Answer: A) $70°70°$

Explanation: The sum of the two angles is $40°+70°=110°40°+70°=110°$. Therefore, the third angle is $180°-110°=70°180°-110°=70°$.

53. What is the value of $3x-23x-2$ when $x=5x=5$?

- A) 1313
- B) 1212
- C) 1111
- D) 1515

Answer: A) 1313

Explanation: Substitute 55 for xx: $3(5)-2=15-2=133(5)-2=15-2=13$.

54. What is the slope of the line passing through the points $(2,5)(2,5)$ and $(4,9)(4,9)$?

- A) 22
- B) 33
- C) 4224
- D) 9229

Answer: A) 22

Explanation: Use the slope formula: $m=\frac{y2-y1}{x2-x1}=\frac{9-5}{4-2}=\frac{4}{2}=2m=\frac{x2-x1}{y2-y1}=\frac{4-2}{9-5}=\frac{2}{4}=2$.

55. *Passage*:

"Her hands trembled as she clutched the letter. The words on the page seemed to blur, and she could feel her heart pounding in her chest."

Question:

What is the emotional state of the character based on the passage?

- A) Calm and focused.
- B) Nervous and anxious.
- C) Happy and excited.
- D) Sad and reflective.

Answer: B) Nervous and anxious.

Explanation: The character's trembling hands and rapid heartbeat suggest nervousness and anxiety.

56. *Passage*:

"Despite the chaos in the streets, people still managed to smile as they passed each other. The sense of community was stronger than ever."

Question:

What does the passage suggest about the community?

- A) The community is falling apart.
- B) The community remains strong despite challenges.
- C) The community does not care about what is happening around them.
- D) The community is struggling to maintain order.

Answer: B) The community remains strong despite challenges.

Explanation: The passage highlights how people continue to smile and connect with one another even in difficult circumstances, indicating their strength and resilience.

57. *Passage*:

"As the boat drifted farther from the shore, she felt a deep sense of peace wash over her. The gentle rocking of the waves and the vast, open sky made her feel free."

Question:

What mood does the passage create?

- A) Peaceful and serene.
- B) Tense and suspenseful.
- C) Chaotic and confusing.
- D) Angry and bitter.

Answer: A) Peaceful and serene.

Explanation: The description of the gentle waves and open sky, combined with the character's sense of peace, creates a calm and serene mood.

58. *Passage*:

"The sunlight filtered through the trees, casting dappled shadows on the forest floor. Birds chirped overhead, and a soft breeze carried the scent of pine."

Question:

What atmosphere is created by the passage?

- A) Dark and ominous.
- B) Peaceful and natural.
- C) Eerie and suspenseful.
- D) Chaotic and disorganized.

Answer: B) Peaceful and natural.

Explanation: The description of sunlight, birds chirping, and a soft breeze evokes a calm and peaceful natural atmosphere.

59. Although the test was difficult, the students who had studied hard managed to pass, while those who had not struggled.

Question:

Which of the following revisions best improves the sentence's clarity and conciseness?

- A) Despite the difficulty of the test, the students who studied hard passed, while others struggled.
- B) The test was difficult, but the students who studied passed, while others did not.
- C) Although difficult, the students who studied passed the test, while others who did not struggled.
- D) The difficult test was passed by those who studied hard, while others struggled.

Answer: A) Despite the difficulty of the test, the students who studied hard passed, while others struggled.
Explanation: This revision keeps the meaning intact while improving clarity and conciseness.

60. The festival, which is held annually, attracts thousands of visitors from all over the country, who come to enjoy music, food, and art.

Question:

Which of the following revisions best improves clarity and conciseness?

- A) The festival is held annually and attracts thousands of visitors from across the country, who come for the music, food, and art.
- B) The festival, held annually, attracts thousands of visitors from across the country to enjoy music, food, and art.
- C) Annually held, the festival attracts thousands of visitors from all over, who come to enjoy the music, food, and art.
- D) Every year, the festival attracts thousands of visitors from across the country, where they come to enjoy the music, food, and art.

Answer: B) The festival, held annually, attracts thousands of visitors from across the country to enjoy music, food, and art.

61. The restaurant served the best food in town, but it's location was inconvenient for many people.

Question:

Which revision best corrects the possessive error in the sentence?

- A) The restaurant served the best food in town, but its location was inconvenient for many people.
- B) The restaurant served the best food in town, but the location was inconvenient for many people.
- C) The restaurant served the best food in town, but its inconvenient location was problematic.
- D) The restaurant served the best food in town, but its location was inconvenient to most people.

Answer: A) The restaurant served the best food in town, but its location was inconvenient for many people.
Explanation: The possessive form of "its" is needed here, rather than the contraction "it's" (which means "it is").

62. The committee debated the proposal for hours; ultimately deciding to delay their final decision until the next meeting.

Question:

Which of the following revisions best corrects the punctuation error in the sentence?

- A) The committee debated the proposal for hours ultimately deciding to delay their final decision until the next meeting.
- B) The committee debated the proposal for hours, ultimately deciding to delay their final decision until the next meeting.
- C) The committee debated the proposal for hours: ultimately deciding to delay their final decision until the next meeting.
- D) The committee debated the proposal for hours but decided to delay their final decision until the next meeting.

Answer: B) The committee debated the proposal for hours, ultimately deciding to delay their final decision until the next meeting.
Explanation: The semicolon should be replaced with a comma to properly connect the independent and dependent clauses.

63. Each of the athletes are required to attend a mandatory meeting before the competition.

Question:

Which revision best corrects the subject-verb agreement error?

- A) Each of the athletes is required to attend a mandatory meeting before the competition.
- B) Every athlete are required to attend a mandatory meeting before the competition.
- C) All of the athletes is required to attend a mandatory meeting before the competition.
- D) Each athlete are required to attend a mandatory meeting before the competition.

Answer: A) Each of the athletes is required to attend a mandatory meeting before the competition.

Explanation: "Each" is a singular subject, so the verb should be "is," not "are."

64. If $5x-3=17$, what is the value of x?

- A) 22
- B) 44
- C) 33
- D) 55

Answer: D) 55

Explanation: Add 33 to both sides to get $5x=20$. Then divide by 55 to get $x=4$.

65. What is the area of a rectangle with a length of 88 meters and a width of 66 meters?

- A) 40 m240m2
- B) 48 m248m2
- C) 60 m260m2
- D) 72 m272m2

Answer: B) 48 m248m2

Explanation: The area of a rectangle is calculated as Area= length × width Area= length × width. Thus, $8×6=48$ m2$8×6=48$m2.

66. Solve for x in the equation $2x+3=15$$2x+3=15$.

- A) x=6x=6
- B) x=8x=8
- C) x=5x=5
- D) x=7x=7

Answer: A) x=6x=6

Explanation: Subtract 33 from both sides to get $2x=12$$2x=12$. Then divide by 22: x=6x=6.

67. A triangle has sides measuring 55, 1212, and 1313. Is this a right triangle?

- A) Yes
- B) No
- C) Maybe

- D) Not enough information

Answer: A) Yes

Explanation: According to the Pythagorean theorem, if $a^2+b^2=c^2$, then the triangle is a right triangle. Here, $5^2+12^2=25+144=169=13^2$, so it is a right triangle.

68. *Passage:*

"After years of hard work and dedication, she finally achieved her dream of becoming a doctor. The journey had been long and difficult, but the reward was worth every challenge."

Question:

What theme does this passage emphasize?

- A) The importance of perseverance in achieving one's goals.
- B) The need for natural talent to succeed in life.
- C) The difficulty of balancing personal and professional life.
- D) The unpredictability of life's challenges.

Answer: A) The importance of perseverance in achieving one's goals.

Explanation: The passage focuses on the character's hard work and dedication, emphasizing how perseverance led to achieving her dream.

69. *Passage:*

"The air was thick with tension as the two competitors faced off in the final match of the tournament. The crowd held its breath, waiting for the first move."

Question:

What mood does the passage create?

- A) Calm and peaceful.
- B) Tense and suspenseful.
- C) Happy and celebratory.
- D) Sad and reflective.

Answer: B) Tense and suspenseful.

Explanation: The description of thick tension and the crowd holding its breath suggests an atmosphere of suspense and anticipation.

70. *Passage:*

"As the storm rolled in, dark clouds blotted out the sun, and a cold wind swept through the village. People hurried indoors, securing windows and doors as the first drops of rain began to fall."

Question:

What atmosphere does the passage convey?

- A) Calm and peaceful.
- B) Frantic and chaotic.
- C) Ominous and threatening.
- D) Happy and carefree.

Answer: C) Ominous and threatening.

Explanation: The dark clouds, cold wind, and people hurrying indoors suggest an impending storm, creating a foreboding atmosphere.

71. *Passage:*

"Her laughter echoed through the empty halls, a bright contrast to the somber paintings that lined the walls. She didn't seem to notice the heavy silence around her."

Question:

What contrast is highlighted in the passage?

- A) The contrast between silence and noise.
- B) The contrast between light and darkness.
- C) The contrast between joy and sadness.
- D) The contrast between art and nature.

Answer: C) The contrast between joy and sadness.

Explanation: The joyful laughter of the character contrasts with the somber atmosphere created by the paintings and the heavy silence.

72. We recommend that everyone brings their own water bottle to the event, since it will be a hot day.

Question:

Which revision best corrects the pronoun-verb agreement error in the sentence?

- A) We recommend that everyone bring their own water bottle to the event, since it will be a hot day.
- B) We recommend that everyone brings their own water bottle to the event because it will be a hot day.
- C) We recommend that everyone bring their own water bottles to the event, since it will be a hot day.
- D) We recommend that everyone bring his or her water bottle to the event, since it will be a hot day.

Answer: A) We recommend that everyone bring their own water bottle to the event, since it will be a hot day.

Explanation: The correct form is "bring"

in the subjunctive mood, since it follows the verb "recommend."

73. It is important for students to stay on top of their assignments and to manage their time effectively.

Question:

Which revision best improves the conciseness of the sentence?

- A) It's important for students to stay on top of assignments and manage their time well.
- B) It is important for students to stay on top of assignments and manage their time.
- C) Students must manage their time effectively and stay on top of assignments.
- D) Staying on top of assignments and time management is important for students.

Answer: A) It's important for students to stay on top of assignments and manage their time well.
Explanation: This revision eliminates unnecessary wording while maintaining clarity.

74.

Original Text:

The concert tickets, that were sold online, were much more expensive than the ones sold at the venue.

Question:

Which revision best corrects the error in the sentence?

- A) The concert tickets, which were sold online, were much more expensive than those sold at the venue.
- B) The concert tickets that were sold online were much more expensive than those sold at the venue.
- C) The concert tickets that sold online were much more expensive than those at the venue.
- D) The concert tickets, which sold online, were more expensive than the ones at the venue.

Answer: A) The concert tickets, which were sold online, were much more expensive than those sold at the venue.
Explanation: "Which" is the correct relative pronoun to introduce a non-restrictive clause, and "those" is more concise than "the ones."

75. Even though the plan was carefully thought out, it still had a number of unforeseen problems that we did not predict.

Question:

Which of the following revisions best improves the conciseness of the sentence?

- A) Even though the plan was carefully thought out, it still encountered unforeseen problems.
- B) The plan, though carefully thought out, encountered some unforeseen problems.
- C) Even though carefully thought out, the plan had unforeseen problems we did not expect.
- D) Despite being carefully planned, the project had unforeseen problems that we did not predict.

Answer: A) Even though the plan was carefully thought out, it still encountered unforeseen problems.
Explanation: This version removes redundant phrasing like "we did not predict" while maintaining the original meaning.

76. One of the most important factors in the success of the project were the people who worked on it.

Question:

Which revision best corrects the subject-verb agreement error?

- A) One of the most important factors in the success of the project was the people who worked on it.
- B) One of the most important factors in the success of the project were the team members who worked on it.
- C) One of the most important factors in the success of the project was the dedication of the people who worked on it.
- D) One of the important factors in the project's success were the people who worked on it.

Answer: C) One of the most important factors in the success of the project was the dedication of the people who worked on it.
Explanation: The singular subject "one of the most important factors" requires a singular verb like "was," and this revision clarifies the meaning.

77. Solve for xx:
$6x-2=16$ $6x-2=16$

- A) $x=2$ $x=2$
- B) $x=3$ $x=3$
- C) $x=4$ $x=4$

- D) $x=5$

Answer: C) $x=3$

Explanation: Add 2 to both sides to get $6x=18$. Then divide by 6: $x=3$.

78. What is the perimeter of a square with a side length of 5 meters?

- A) 10 meters
- B) 15 meters
- C) 20 meters
- D) 25 meters

Answer: C) 20 meters

Explanation: The perimeter of a square is 4 times the side length: $4\times5=20$ meters.

79.

What is the value of x in the equation $4x+5=21$?

- A) $x=3$
- B) $x=4$
- C) $x=5$
- D) $x=6$

Answer: B) $x=4$

Explanation: Subtract 5 from both sides to get $4x=16$. Then divide by 4 to get $x=4$.

80. A circle has a radius of 7 cm. What is the circumference of the circle? Use $\pi\approx3.14$.

- A) 21.98 cm
- B) 30.2 cm
- C) 43.96 cm
- D) 49.1 cm

Answer: C) 43.96 cm

Explanation: The formula for the circumference of a circle is $2\pi r$. Substituting the radius $r=7$, we get $2\times3.14\times7=43.96$ cm.

81. If a rectangle has an area of 36 cm² and a length of 9 cm, what is the width of the rectangle?

- A) 2 cm
- B) 3 cm
- C) 4 cm
- D) 5 cm

Answer: B) 4 cm

Explanation: The area of a rectangle is calculated by Area = length × width. Solving for the width: $36\text{ cm}^2=9\text{ cm}\times\text{width}$, so the width is $\frac{36}{9}=4$ cm.

82. A train travels 120 miles in 2 hours. What is the train's average speed?

- A) 40 miles per hour40miles per hour
- B) 50 miles per hour50miles per hour
- C) 60 miles per hour60miles per hour
- D) 70 miles per hour70miles per hour

Answer: C) 60 miles per hour60miles per hour

Explanation: Average speed is calculated by dividing the distance traveled by the time:

120 miles2 hours=60 miles per hour2hours120miles=60miles per hour.

83. Solve for yy in the equation 5y+3=185y+3=18.

- A) y=3y=3
- B) y=5y=5
- C) y=4y=4
- D) y=2y=2

Answer: A) y=3y=3

Explanation: Subtract 33 from both sides to get 5y=155y=15. Then divide by 55: y=3y=3.

84. Passage:

"After years of conflict, the country finally found peace. The people could now walk freely in the streets without fear of violence or war."

Question:

What is the main theme of the passage?

- A) The devastation caused by war.
- B) The importance of walking freely.
- C) The relief and hope brought by peace.
- D) The long struggle to achieve victory.

Answer: C) The relief and hope brought by peace.

Explanation: The passage focuses on the newfound peace and how it has brought a sense of relief to the people.

85. Passage:

"The sun set slowly over the horizon, casting a golden glow across the fields. The farmers finished their work for the day, their faces tired but content."

Question:

What mood is created by the passage?

- A) Peaceful and calm.
- B) Energetic and lively.
- C) Sad and reflective.
- D) Tense and anxious.

Answer: A) Peaceful and calm.

Explanation: The description of the sunset and the farmers' contentment creates a peaceful and calm atmosphere.

86. Passage:

"Even after countless failures, Thomas continued to experiment with his invention. His determination never wavered, and he refused to give up on his dream."

Question:

What quality of Thomas is highlighted in the passage?

- A) His intelligence.
- B) His generosity.
- C) His determination.
- D) His creativity.

Answer: C) His determination.

Explanation: The passage emphasizes Thomas's perseverance and refusal to give up, highlighting his determination.

87. *Passage*:

"The air was thick with the smell of freshly baked bread. The bakery bustled with activity as customers came in and out, eager to grab their favorite treats."

Question:

What sensory detail is primarily used in the passage?

- A) Sight.
- B) Sound.
- C) Smell.
- D) Taste.

Answer: C) Smell.

Explanation: The passage focuses on the smell of freshly baked bread, appealing to the sense of smell.

88. *Passage*:

"Maria stood in the crowded room, her heart racing as she prepared to deliver her speech. She took a deep breath, hoping the audience wouldn't notice her shaking hands."

Question:

What emotion is Maria feeling in the passage?

- A) Excitement.
- B) Confidence.
- C) Nervousness.
- D) Indifference.

Answer: C) Nervousness.

Explanation: Maria's racing heart and shaking hands suggest that she is feeling nervous.

89. In order to achieve success, it is necessary for people to work hard, be persistent, and stay focused on their goals.

Question:

Which of the following revisions best improves the conciseness of the sentence?

- A) To achieve success, people must work hard, persist, and stay focused.
- B) Achieving success requires working hard, being persistent, and focusing on your goals.
- C) In order to succeed, hard work, persistence, and focus are required.
- D) Success is achieved through hard work, persistence, and focus.

Answer: A) To achieve success, people must work hard, persist, and stay focused. *Explanation:* This revision eliminates unnecessary words and simplifies the sentence while maintaining its original meaning.

90.

Original Text:

The coach emphasized that the key to victory lies in teamwork, effective communication, and practice, although players often overlook this advice.

Question:

Which of the following revisions best improves the conciseness of the sentence?

- A) The coach emphasized that victory depends on teamwork, communication, and practice, but players often overlook this advice.
- B) The coach emphasized that victory relies on teamwork, communication, and practice, though players sometimes ignore this advice.
- C) The key to victory, the coach emphasized, lies in teamwork, communication, and practice, which players tend to overlook.
- D) Victory, the coach emphasized, lies in teamwork, communication, and practice, but players often don't listen to this advice.

Answer: A) The coach emphasized that victory depends on teamwork, communication, and practice, but players often overlook this advice. *Explanation:* This version improves conciseness by eliminating unnecessary words without losing the original meaning.

91. During the meeting, the group discussed several important topics, but they decided that they needed more time to make a decision.

Question:

Which of the following revisions best

improves the clarity and conciseness of the sentence?

- A) The group discussed several important topics but decided more time was needed to make a decision.
- B) The group discussed important topics but needed more time to make a decision.
- C) During the meeting, important topics were discussed, but more time was needed for a decision.
- D) Several important topics were discussed, but the group decided they needed more time to make a decision.

Answer: B) The group discussed important topics but needed more time to make a decision.

Explanation: This version is clear and concise, eliminating redundant wording.

92. Many people believe that regular exercise is beneficial to your health and can help to improve mood and increase energy levels.

Question:

Which of the following revisions best improves the conciseness of the sentence?

- A) Regular exercise is believed to be beneficial to health, improving mood and increasing energy levels.
- B) Many believe regular exercise benefits health and improves mood and energy levels.
- C) Regular exercise is beneficial to health and can improve mood and increase energy.
- D) Exercise helps improve mood, energy, and is generally good for health.

Answer: B) Many believe regular exercise benefits health and improves mood and energy levels.

Explanation: This revision eliminates unnecessary words, keeping the sentence concise and clear.

93. If $3x-4=11$, what is the value of x?

- A) $x=7$
- B) $x=5$
- C) $x=4$
- D) $x=6$

Answer: A) $x=5$

Explanation: Add 4 to both sides: $3x=15$. Divide by 3: $x=5$.

94. What is the area of a triangle with a base of 8 cm and a height of 6 cm?

- A) 24 cm224cm2
- B) 30 cm230cm2
- C) 36 cm236cm2
- D) 48 cm248cm2

Answer: D) 24 cm224cm2

Explanation: The area of a triangle is 12×base×height21×base × height. Thus, 12×8×6=24 cm221×8×6=24cm2.

95. The ratio of boys to girls in a classroom is 2:32:3. If there are 1212 boys, how many girls are there?

- A) 1515
- B) 1616
- C) 1818
- D) 2020

Answer: C) 1818

Explanation: The ratio of boys to girls is 2:32:3, so if there are 1212 boys, there are 122×3=18212×3=18 girls.

96. What is the value of 4x+2=184x+2=18?

- A) x=3x=3
- B) x=4x=4
- C) x=5x=5
- D) x=6x=6

Answer: B) x=4x=4

Explanation: Subtract 22 from both

sides: 4x=164x=16. Divide by 44: x=4x=4.

97. A rectangle has a length of 1212 meters and a width of 44 meters. What is its perimeter?

- A) 16 meters 16 meters
- B) 24 meters24meters
- C) 32 meters32meters
- D) 40 meters40meters

Answer: C) 32 meters32meters

Explanation: The perimeter of a rectangle is calculated by 2(length+width)=2(12+4)=32 meters2(length+width)=2(12+4)=32meters.

98. *Passage*:

"The sky turned a deep orange as the sun dipped below the horizon. The sound of waves crashing against the shore filled the air, creating a peaceful symphony."

Question:

What atmosphere does the passage create?

- A) Tense and suspenseful.
- B) Peaceful and serene.
- C) Sad and melancholic.

- D) Chaotic and confusing.

Answer: B) Peaceful and serene.

Explanation: The description of the sunset and the sound of waves creates a calm, peaceful atmosphere.

99. *Passage*:

"The students gathered in the library, huddled over their books, deep in concentration. The only sound was the rustling of pages and the occasional whisper."

Question:

What mood is created by the passage?

- A) Quiet and focused.
- B) Noisy and chaotic.
- C) Bored and uninterested.
- D) Tense and anxious.

Answer: A) Quiet and focused.

Explanation: The passage emphasizes the students' concentration and the quiet atmosphere of the library, creating a mood of focus.

100. *Passage*:

"As the clock struck midnight, the streets fell silent. A cold wind swept through the empty alleys, and the city seemed to hold its breath."

Question:

What mood is conveyed by the passage?

- A) Joyful and energetic.
- B) Tense and eerie.
- C) Bored and uninterested.
- D) Calm and peaceful.

Answer: B) Tense and eerie.

Explanation: The description of the silent streets and the cold wind creates an eerie, tense atmosphere.

101.

Passage:

"The rain poured down in sheets, drenching everything in sight. Despite the downpour, the little girl continued to dance in the puddles, laughing and spinning."

Question:

What is the main contrast in the passage?

- A) The contrast between the rain and the girl's joy.
- B) The contrast between the rain and the city's silence.

- C) The contrast between the girl and the cold.
- D) The contrast between the rain and the puddles.

Answer: A) The contrast between the rain and the girl's joy.

Explanation: The passage contrasts the gloomy rain with the girl's happiness as she dances and laughs, emphasizing her joy despite the downpour.

102. *Passage*:

"Every morning, the town woke up to the sound of church bells ringing in the distance. The streets slowly came to life as shopkeepers opened their doors and people hurried to work."

Question:

What mood does the passage create?

- A) Tense and anxious.
- B) Calm and peaceful.
- C) Busy and frantic.
- D) Sad and reflective.

Answer: B) Calm and peaceful.

Explanation: The passage describes a peaceful, routine morning with the sound of church bells and the slow awakening of the town.

103. In the past decade, renewable energy has grown rapidly, but it still only makes up a small percentage of the world's energy production.

Question:

Which of the following revisions best improves the clarity and conciseness of the sentence?

- A) Renewable energy has grown rapidly in the past decade, but it still makes up a small percentage of the world's energy production.
- B) In the last ten years, renewable energy grew rapidly, but it only makes up a small part of global energy production.
- C) Renewable energy is growing, but in the past decade, it only made up a small part of global energy production.
- D) Despite rapid growth over the past decade, renewable energy still accounts for only a small part of global energy production.

Answer: D) Despite rapid growth over the past decade, renewable energy still accounts for only a small part of global energy production.

Explanation: This version eliminates

redundancy and is more concise while maintaining the meaning.

104. It's important for everyone to take responsibility for their own actions, especially in situations where there is shared responsibility.

Question:

Which of the following revisions best improves the conciseness of the sentence?

- A) Everyone should take responsibility for their actions, especially when responsibility is shared.
- B) It's important for people to take responsibility in situations where there is shared responsibility.
- C) It's crucial that people take responsibility for their actions, especially when others are involved.
- D) Taking responsibility is important, particularly in situations where responsibility is shared.

Answer: A) Everyone should take responsibility for their actions, especially when responsibility is shared.
Explanation: This version removes unnecessary wording and is more

concise while keeping the original meaning.

105. Solve for xx in the equation $2x+9=272x+9=27$.

- A) $x=8x=8$
- B) $x=7x=7$
- C) $x=9x=9$
- D) $x=10x=10$

Answer: B) $x=9x=9$
Explanation: Subtract 99 from both sides to get $2x=182x=18$. Then divide by 22 to get $x=9x=9$.

106. A rectangle has a length of 10 cm10cm and a width of 6 cm6cm. What is the area of the rectangle?

- A) 60 cm260cm2
- B) 16 cm216cm2
- C) 30 cm230cm2
- D) 40 cm240cm2

Answer: A) 60 cm260cm2
Explanation: The area of a rectangle is calculated by Area= length × width Area= length × width, so $10×6=60$ cm$210×6=60$cm2.

107. A recipe calls for 2332 cup of sugar for every 11 cup of flour. How much sugar is needed if 33 cups of flour are used?

- A) 2 cups2cups
- B) 1.5 cups1.5cups
- C) 2.5 cups2.5cups
- D) 3 cups3cups

Answer: A) 2 cups2cups

> *Explanation:* The ratio of sugar to flour is 23:132:1. If 33 cups of flour are used, the amount of sugar needed is $3 \times 23 = 2$ cups$3 \times 32 = 2$cups.

108. The perimeter of a square is 32 cm32cm. What is the length of each side of the square?

- A) 6 cm6cm
- B) 8 cm8cm
- C) 9 cm9cm
- D) 10 cm10cm

Answer: B) 8 cm8cm

> *Explanation:* The perimeter of a square is 44 times the length of one side, so each side is 324=8 cm432=8cm.

109. A car travels 180 miles in 3 hours. What is the car's average speed in miles per hour?

- A) 40 miles per hour40miles per hour
- B) 50 miles per hour50miles per hour
- C) 60 miles per hour 60 miles per hour
- D) 70 miles per hour70miles per hour

Answer: C) 60 miles per hour 60 miles per hour

> *Explanation:* The average speed is calculated by dividing the distance traveled by the time taken:
> 180 miles3 hours=60 miles per hour 3 hours 180 miles=60 miles per hour.

110. *Passage:*

"The streets were filled with people, their voices blending together in a cacophony of sound. Above, the sun shone brightly, casting long shadows on the busy marketplace."

Question:

What is the atmosphere of the passage?

- A) Quiet and peaceful.
- B) Busy and energetic.
- C) Dark and mysterious.
- D) Sad and reflective.

Answer: B) Busy and energetic.

> *Explanation:* The description of the crowded streets and the marketplace suggests a lively and energetic atmosphere.

111. *Passage:*

"Despite the many challenges he faced, Marcus refused to give up on his dream of becoming a musician. He spent countless hours practicing, knowing that perseverance was the key to success."

Question:

What is the main message of the passage?

- A) Marcus enjoys playing music for fun.
- B) Marcus understands the importance of hard work and perseverance.
- C) Marcus wants to quit but feels obligated to continue.
- D) Marcus believes success is a matter of luck.

Answer: B) Marcus understands the importance of hard work and perseverance.

Explanation: The passage emphasizes how Marcus's perseverance and dedication are central to his pursuit of becoming a musician.

112. *Passage*:

"The forest was silent except for the occasional rustle of leaves in the wind. The trees stood tall, their branches forming a canopy that blocked out most of the sunlight."

Question:

What mood is created by the passage?

- A) Calm and peaceful.
- B) Tense and foreboding.
- C) Joyful and lively.
- D) Dark and dangerous.

Answer: A) Calm and peaceful.

Explanation: The description of the quiet forest and the gentle rustling of leaves creates a calm and peaceful mood.

113.

Passage:

"The small village was nestled between two mountains, its red-roofed houses visible from afar. Smoke curled from the chimneys, and the sound of children playing echoed through the valley."

Question:

What is the tone of the passage?

- A) Dark and ominous.
- B) Peaceful and serene.
- C) Exciting and adventurous.
- D) Chaotic and loud.

Answer: B) Peaceful and serene.

Explanation: The description of the village, smoke from chimneys, and children playing creates a peaceful and calm tone.

114. Despite their differences, the two friends they were always there for each other during difficult times.

Question:

Which revision best corrects the grammatical error in the sentence?

- A) Despite their differences, the two friends were always there for each other during difficult times.
- B) Despite their differences, the two friends always were there for each other during difficult times.
- C) The two friends were there for each other during difficult times despite differences.
- D) Despite their differences, two friends were always there for each other during difficult times.

Answer: A) Despite their differences, the two friends were always there for each other during difficult times.
Explanation: The phrase "they were" is unnecessary. Removing it makes the sentence grammatically correct.

115. The conference begins at 9:00 AM in the morning, so please make sure to arrive on time.

Question:

Which revision best improves the sentence's clarity and conciseness?

- A) The conference begins at 9:00 AM, so please arrive on time.
- B) The conference starts at 9:00 AM, please make sure to be there on time.
- C) The conference will begin at 9:00 AM in the morning, so please arrive on time.
- D) The conference begins at 9:00 AM, so arrive early.

Answer: A) The conference begins at 9:00 AM, so please arrive on time.
Explanation: "AM in the morning" is redundant; "9:00 AM" is sufficient. This revision keeps the sentence clear and concise.

116. Her presentation was both informative and interesting, but it could have been improved by including more visuals and interactive elements.

Question:

Which of the following revisions best improves clarity while maintaining the meaning of the sentence?

- A) Her presentation was interesting and informative, but more visuals and interactive elements could have made it better.

- B) While her presentation was informative and interesting, it could have been better with more visuals and interactive elements.
- C) Although her presentation was informative and interesting, it would have been improved with more visuals and interactive elements.
- D) Her presentation was very informative, interesting, and could be improved by more visuals.

Answer: C) Although her presentation was informative and interesting, it would have been improved with more visuals and interactive elements.

Explanation: This version preserves the meaning and keeps the sentence clear without any awkward phrasing.

117. Solve for x:

$7x-4=24$

- A) $x=4$
- B) $x=5$
- C) $x=6$
- D) $x=8$

Answer: C) $x=4$

Explanation: Add 4 to both sides to get

$7x=28$, then divide by 7 to get $x=4$.

118. A triangle has angles measuring $40°$, $60°$, and $x°$. What is the value of x?

- A) $80°$
- B) $90°$
- C) $70°$
- D) $60°$

Answer: C) $80°$

Explanation: The sum of the angles in a triangle is always $180°$. Therefore, $40°+60°+x°=180°$. Solving for x gives $x=80°$.

119. If $y=5x-3$, what is the value of y when $x=4$?

- A) 17
- B) 15
- C) 12
- D) 14

Answer: A) 17

Explanation: Substitute $x=4$ into the equation:

$y=5(4)-3=20-3=17$.

120. The perimeter of a rectangle is $48\,cm$. If the length of the rectangle is 14 cm14cm, what is its width?

- A) 10 cm10cm
- B) 8 cm8cm
- C) 6 cm6cm
- D) 5 cm5cm

Answer: B) 10 cm10cm

Explanation: The perimeter PP of a rectangle is calculated by P=2(length + width)P=2(length + width). Plugging in the values:
48=2(14+width)48=2(14+width)
Divide by 22:
24=14+width24=14+width
width=10 cm width=10cm.

121. *Passage*:

"The tall trees swayed in the wind, their branches creaking as the storm approached. Dark clouds gathered overhead, and the once-bright sky became ominously gray."

Question:

What mood is created by the passage?

- A) Joyful and carefree.
- B) Calm and serene.
- C) Ominous and tense.
- D) Exciting and adventurous.

Answer: C) Ominous and tense.

Explanation: The description of dark clouds, creaking branches, and the approaching storm creates a tense, ominous mood.

122. *Passage*:

"Though the journey was long and exhausting, the breathtaking view from the mountaintop made every step worth it."

Question:

What theme does the passage convey?

- A) The importance of patience.
- B) The value of hard work and perseverance.
- C) The beauty of nature.
- D) The challenge of overcoming fear.

Answer: B) The value of hard work and perseverance.

Explanation: The passage emphasizes the reward that comes from persevering through a difficult journey, highlighting the theme of perseverance.

123. *Passage*:

"Every day, Samuel went to the park to feed the birds. He had done so for years, and each time, they flocked to him without hesitation, as if he were a part of their world."

Question:

What does the passage suggest about Samuel's relationship with the birds?

- A) The birds are afraid of Samuel.
- B) Samuel has a special bond with the birds.
- C) Samuel is indifferent to the birds.
- D) The birds only approach Samuel because of the food.

Answer: B) Samuel has a special bond with the birds.

Explanation: The passage suggests that Samuel and the birds share a connection, as the birds flock to him without hesitation.

124. *Passage*:

"As the sun rose over the city, casting its golden light on the rooftops, the streets began to fill with the sounds of people starting their day. There was a sense of new beginnings in the air."

Question:

What is the mood of the passage?

- A) Hopeful and energetic.
- B) Dark and somber.
- C) Mysterious and tense.

- D) Sad and reflective.

Answer: A) Hopeful and energetic.

Explanation: The description of the sunrise, golden light, and the sounds of people starting their day creates a mood of hope and energy.

125.

Passage:

"The ocean waves crashed against the rocks, sending mist into the air. Seagulls circled overhead, their calls blending with the rhythmic sound of the tide."

Question:

What atmosphere is created by the passage?

- A) Calm and serene.
- B) Chaotic and loud.
- C) Peaceful and rhythmic.
- D) Dark and foreboding.

Answer: C) Peaceful and rhythmic.

Explanation: The description of the waves and the seagulls, along with the rhythmic sound of the tide, creates a peaceful and natural atmosphere.

126. The students, who were tired after studying for hours, they decided to take a break before continuing their work.

Question:

Which revision best corrects the grammatical error in the sentence?

- A) The students, who were tired after studying for hours, decided to take a break before continuing their work.
- B) The tired students, who studied for hours, decided to take a break.
- C) The students, tired after studying for hours, took a break before continuing their work.
- D) The students decided to take a break after studying for hours, as they were very tired.

Answer: A) The students, who were tired after studying for hours, decided to take a break before continuing their work. *Explanation:* The phrase "they decided" is unnecessary. Removing it corrects the grammatical error.

127. The team, despite their best efforts, were unable to complete the project on time due to unforeseen complications.

Question:

Which revision best corrects the subject-verb agreement error in the sentence?

- A) The team, despite their best efforts, were unable to complete the project on time.
- B) The team, despite its best efforts, was unable to complete the project on time due to unforeseen complications.
- C) Despite their best efforts, the team was unable to complete the project on time due to complications.
- D) The team were unable to complete the project due to complications despite their best efforts.

Answer: B) The team, despite its best efforts, was unable to complete the project on time due to unforeseen complications. *Explanation:* "Team" is a collective noun and requires the singular verb "was."

128. Given the importance of the issue, we are asking all employees to submit their feedback by the end of the week.

Question:

Which revision best improves the clarity and conciseness of the sentence?

- A) Given the importance of the issue, all employees are being asked to submit their feedback by the end of the week.
- B) Due to how important this issue is, we are asking all employees to submit

their feedback before the end of the week.

- C) Because of the issue's significance, employees are asked to submit their feedback by week's end.
- D) All employees are asked to submit feedback by the week's end due to the issue's importance.

Answer: C) Because of the issue's significance, employees are asked to submit their feedback by week's end.

Explanation: This version is the most concise, eliminating unnecessary phrasing while retaining clarity.

129. If $5x+3=28$, what is the value of x?

- A) $x=4$
- B) $x=5$
- C) $x=6$
- D) $x=7$

Answer: D) $x=5$

Explanation: Subtract 33 from both sides to get $5x=25$, then divide by 55 to get $x=5$.

130. The perimeter of a rectangle is 4040 cm. If the length is 1212 cm, what is the width?

- A) 66 cm

- B) 88 cm
- C) 1010 cm
- D) 1414 cm

Answer: B) 88 cm

Explanation: The formula for the perimeter of a rectangle is $P=2(\text{length} + \text{width})$. Substituting $P=40$ and length$=12$:
$40=2(12+\text{width}) \Rightarrow 40=24+2\times\text{width} \Rightarrow \text{width}=8$ cm.

131. What is the value of x in the equation $3x-7=20$?

- A) $x=9$
- B) $x=10$
- C) $x=11$
- D) $x=12$

Answer: D) $x=9$

Explanation: Add 77 to both sides to get $3x=27$. Divide by 33: $x=9$.

132. If a triangle has sides measuring 33, 44, and 55 units, is this a right triangle?

- A) Yes
- B) No
- C) Maybe
- D) Not enough information

Answer: A) Yes

Explanation: Use the Pythagorean theorem: $a2+b2=c2a2+b2=c2$. In this case, $32+42=9+16=25=5232+42=9+16=25=52$, so it is a right triangle.

133. *Passage*:

"As the train pulled out of the station, she pressed her forehead against the glass window, watching the world blur by. Her mind was filled with memories of the city she was leaving behind."

Question:

What emotion is the character most likely feeling in the passage?

- A) Excitement
- B) Regret
- C) Indifference
- D) Nostalgia

Answer: D) Nostalgia

Explanation: The character is reflecting on memories of the city she's leaving behind, suggesting a feeling of nostalgia.

134. *Passage*:

"Though the sun had set hours ago, the city was still alive with activity. Neon signs flickered, and people crowded the streets, eager to enjoy the nightlife."

Question:

What atmosphere is created by the passage?

- A) Calm and serene
- B) Dark and foreboding
- C) Lively and energetic
- D) Quiet and peaceful

Answer: C) Lively and energetic

Explanation: The description of neon signs and crowded streets suggests an active, energetic atmosphere.

135. *Passage*:

"The old man's hands trembled as he held the letter. The words on the page seemed to swim before his eyes, but he continued reading, determined to make sense of them."

Question:

What is the primary focus of the passage?

- A) The difficulty of understanding the letter.
- B) The man's physical condition.
- C) The man's determination to understand the letter.
- D) The content of the letter.

Answer: C) The man's determination to understand the letter.

Explanation: The passage emphasizes the man's struggle and his determination to keep reading despite the difficulty.

136. *Passage:*

"The sky was overcast, and the wind whipped through the trees, making them sway dangerously. Dark clouds loomed in the distance, threatening to unleash a storm."

Question:

What mood is created by the passage?

- A) Peaceful and calm
- B) Dark and foreboding
- C) Joyful and light-hearted
- D) Confused and disorganized

Answer: B) Dark and foreboding

Explanation: The description of dark clouds and swaying trees suggests an ominous and foreboding atmosphere.

137. After the meeting, everyone returned back to their offices to finish their work.

Question:

Which of the following revisions best improves the conciseness of the sentence?

- A) After the meeting, everyone went back to their offices to finish their work.
- B) After the meeting, everyone returned to their offices to finish their work.
- C) After the meeting, everyone went back to finish their work in their offices.
- D) After the meeting, everyone was able to return to their offices and finish their work.

Answer: B) After the meeting, everyone returned to their offices to finish their work.

Explanation: "Returned back" is redundant. "Returned" by itself is sufficient.

138. Despite being warned about the risks, he still proceeded forward with his plans.

Question:

Which revision best improves the clarity and conciseness of the sentence?

- A) Even though he had been warned about the risks, he still proceeded forward with his plans.
- B) Despite being warned about the risks, he proceeded with his plans.
- C) Although warned of the risks, he continued to proceed with his plans.
- D) Though warned about the risks, he still moved forward with his plans.

Answer: B) Despite being warned about the risks, he proceeded with his plans. *Explanation:* The word "forward" is redundant after "proceeded." This revision eliminates unnecessary words and keeps the sentence concise.

139. Many of the students, regardless of their background, they were able to succeed in the challenging program.

Question:

Which revision best corrects the grammatical error in the sentence?

- A) Many of the students, regardless of their background, were able to succeed in the challenging program.
- B) Many of the students, they were able to succeed in the challenging program regardless of their background.
- C) Many of the students succeeded in the challenging program despite their background.
- D) Many students were able to succeed, regardless of background, in the challenging program.

Answer: A) Many of the students, regardless of their background, were able to succeed in the challenging program. *Explanation:* The phrase "they were" is unnecessary and causes a grammatical error. Removing it corrects the sentence.

140. After studying for several hours, the student, exhausted but determined, continued working on her assignment until midnight.

Question:

Which of the following revisions best improves the conciseness of the sentence?

- A) Exhausted but determined, the student kept working on her assignment until midnight, after studying for several hours.
- B) Although exhausted, the student continued working on her assignment until midnight after hours of studying.
- C) The student continued working on her assignment until midnight, exhausted but determined after studying for hours.
- D) The student, exhausted but determined, kept working on her assignment until midnight after hours of studying.

Answer: D) The student, exhausted but determined, kept working on her assignment until midnight after hours of studying.

Explanation: This version keeps the sentence clear and concise while maintaining the focus on the student's determination.

141. Solve for x:

$4x + 6 = 30$

- A) $x = 6$
- B) $x = 5$
- C) $x = 8$
- D) $x = 7$

Answer: B) $x = 6$

Explanation: Subtract 6 from both sides: $4x = 24$. Then divide by 4: $x = 6$.

142. The area of a rectangle is $72 cm^2$, and its length is $12 cm$. What is its width?

- A) $6 cm$
- B) $8 cm$
- C) $9 cm$
- D) $12 cm$

Answer: A) $6 cm$

Explanation: The area of a rectangle is Area = length × width. Substituting the values: $72 = 12 × width$. Solving for width: width $= 6 cm$.

143. If a triangle has two sides measuring $5 cm$ and $12 cm$, and the hypotenuse is $13 cm$, is this triangle a right triangle?

- A) Yes
- B) No
- C) Not enough information
- D) It depends

Answer: A) Yes

Explanation: According to the Pythagorean theorem, $a^2 + b^2 = c^2$. Substituting the side lengths: $5^2 + 12^2 = 25 + 144 = 169 = 13^2$, confirming it is a right triangle.

144. What is the value of x in the equation $3x - 5 = 16$?

- A) $x = 6$
- B) $x = 7$
- C) $x = 8$
- D) $x = 9$

Answer: D) $x = 7$

Explanation: Add 5 to both sides to get $3x = 21$, then divide by 3: $x = 7$.

145. *Passage*:

"As the sun dipped below the horizon, a

soft breeze carried the scent of blooming flowers through the air. The peaceful evening was a welcome end to a long day."

Question:

What is the mood created by the passage?

- A) Tense and suspenseful.
- B) Sad and reflective.
- C) Calm and peaceful.
- D) Dark and ominous.

Answer: C) Calm and peaceful.

Explanation: The description of the sunset, soft breeze, and blooming flowers suggests a peaceful, calm atmosphere.

146. *Passage*:

"After years of hard work, Emily finally achieved her dream of opening her own bakery. As she stood behind the counter on opening day, she couldn't help but smile."

Question:

What is the main emotion conveyed in the passage?

- A) Frustration
- B) Excitement
- C) Nervousness
- D) Satisfaction

Answer: D) Satisfaction

Explanation: The passage focuses on Emily's sense of accomplishment and fulfillment after achieving her long-time goal.

147. *Passage*:

"The forest was quiet, except for the occasional rustle of leaves as a light breeze stirred the treetops. Sunlight filtered through the dense canopy, casting dappled shadows on the ground below."

Question:

What mood does the passage create?

- A) Joyful and energetic
- B) Peaceful and serene
- C) Dark and ominous
- D) Sad and reflective

Answer: B) Peaceful and serene

Explanation: The description of the forest with light breezes and filtered sunlight creates a calm, peaceful atmosphere.

148. *Passage*:

"She clutched the letter in her hands, her eyes scanning the words again and again. Her heart raced as the meaning of the letter became clearer with each read."

Question:

What emotion is the character most likely feeling in the passage?

- A) Happiness
- B) Confusion
- C) Anxiety
- D) Indifference

Answer: C) Anxiety

Explanation: The character's racing heart and repeated reading suggest a sense of anxiety or nervousness about the letter's contents.

149. The new regulations that were introduced last year, they significantly impacted the way the company operates.

Question:

Which revision best corrects the sentence?

- A) The new regulations introduced last year significantly impacted the way the company operates.
- B) The new regulations, which were introduced last year, they significantly impacted the way the company operates.
- C) The new regulations introduced last year, they significantly impacted the company.
- D) The regulations from last year, they significantly impacted the company.

Answer: A) The new regulations introduced last year significantly impacted the way the company operates.
Explanation: The phrase "they" is unnecessary and creates redundancy. Removing it makes the sentence grammatically correct and concise.

150. After speaking to the committee, she said she would consider all of the options before she makes a final decision.

Question:

Which revision best improves clarity and conciseness?

- A) After talking to the committee, she said she would consider all options before making a decision.
- B) She said she would consider all of the options after talking to the committee before she makes a decision.
- C) After speaking to the committee, she would consider every option before making the final decision.

D) She said she would consider all options before making her final decision after talking to the committee.

Answer: A) After talking to the committee, she said she would consider all options before making a decision.

Explanation: This revision eliminates unnecessary words and creates a more concise, straightforward sentence.

151.

Original Text:

The teacher explained the lesson in such a way that all of the students, even those who usually struggled, they were able to understand it.

Question:

Which revision best corrects the grammatical error in the sentence?

- A) The teacher explained the lesson so well that all of the students, even those who usually struggled, were able to understand it.

- B) The teacher explained the lesson so that all the students, including those who struggled, they were able to understand it.

- C) The teacher explained the lesson so well that even the struggling students were able to understand it.

- D) The teacher explained the lesson in such a way that the struggling students were able to understand it.

Answer: A) The teacher explained the lesson so well that all of the students, even those who usually struggled, were able to understand it.

Explanation: The phrase "they were" is unnecessary. Removing it makes the sentence grammatically correct and maintains clarity.

152. She didn't know whether or not she could finish the project by the end of the week.

Question:

Which revision best improves the clarity and conciseness of the sentence?

- A) She didn't know if she could finish the project by the end of the week.

- B) She wasn't sure whether she could finish the project by the end of the week.

- C) She wasn't sure if she could finish the project by the week's end.

- D) She didn't know whether or not she could complete the project on time.

Answer: A) She didn't know if she could finish the project by the end of the week.

Explanation: "Whether or not" is redundant here; "if" simplifies the sentence while maintaining the original meaning.

153. The company's new initiative, which focuses on reducing waste and increasing efficiency, it has been well-received by both employees and customers.

Question:

Which revision best corrects the grammatical error in the sentence?

- A) The company's new initiative focuses on reducing waste and increasing efficiency and has been well-received by both employees and customers.

- B) The company's new initiative, focusing on reducing waste and increasing efficiency, it has been well-received by both employees and customers.

- C) The company's new initiative, which focuses on reducing waste and increasing efficiency, has been well-received by both employees and customers.

- D) The company's new initiative, which focuses on reducing waste and increasing efficiency, has been welcomed by customers.

Answer: C) The company's new initiative, which focuses on reducing waste and increasing efficiency, has been well-received by both employees and customers.

Explanation: The phrase "it has been" is unnecessary and redundant. Removing it corrects the grammatical error.

154. Solve for x:

$7x - 2 = 19$

- A) $x = 3$
- B) $x = 4$
- C) $x = 5$
- D) $x = 6$

Answer: D) $x = 3$

Explanation: Add 2 to both sides to get $7x = 21$. Divide by 7 to get $x = 3$.

155. What is the perimeter of a triangle with sides measuring 5 cm, 6 cm, and 7 cm?

- A) 18 cm

- B) 20 cm20cm
- C) 15 cm15cm
- D) 16 cm16cm

Answer: A) 18 cm18cm

Explanation: The perimeter of a triangle is the sum of its three sides: 5+6+7=18 cm5+6+7=18cm.

156. If the ratio of apples to oranges in a basket is 3:43:4 and there are 2424 oranges, how many apples are there?

- A) 1212
- B) 1818
- C) 2424
- D) 2020

Answer: B) 1818

Explanation: The ratio of apples to oranges is 3:43:4. If there are 2424 oranges, then the number of apples is 34×24=1843×24=18.

157. What is the area of a triangle with a base of 10 cm10cm and a height of 8 cm8cm?

- A) 40 cm240cm2
- B) 50 cm250cm2
- C) 80 cm280cm2
- D) 60 cm260cm2

Answer: A) 40 cm240cm2

Explanation: The area of a triangle is calculated using the formula 12×base×height21× base × height. So, 12×10×8=40 cm221×10×8=40cm2.

158. *Passage*:

"The snow fell lightly, blanketing the ground in a thick, soft layer of white. The world outside seemed to slow down, as if frozen in time."

Question:

What mood is created by the passage?

- A) Chaotic and tense.
- B) Peaceful and serene.
- C) Exciting and adventurous.
- D) Dark and foreboding.

Answer: B) Peaceful and serene.

Explanation: The description of the snow falling and the world slowing down creates a calm and peaceful atmosphere.

159. *Passage*:

"After hours of hiking through the dense forest, they finally reached the clearing. The sight of the vast, open meadow filled them with a sense of accomplishment and relief."

Question:

What is the main emotion conveyed in the passage?

- A) Fear
- B) Excitement
- C) Relief
- D) Confusion

Answer: C) Relief

Explanation: The passage emphasizes the characters' sense of accomplishment and relief after reaching their destination.

160. *Passage*:

"The streets were quiet as the storm approached. Dark clouds gathered overhead, and the air was heavy with the promise of rain."

Question:

What atmosphere is created by the passage?

- A) Dark and ominous.
- B) Joyful and light-hearted.
- C) Peaceful and quiet.
- D) Busy and energetic.

Answer: A) Dark and ominous.

Explanation: The dark clouds, quiet streets, and heavy air suggest an ominous, foreboding atmosphere.

161. *Passage*:

"As the boat drifted farther from shore, the waves grew stronger. The sky darkened, and the wind picked up, signaling that a storm was on its way."

Question:

What mood does the passage create?

- A) Calm and serene.
- B) Tense and suspenseful.
- C) Joyful and carefree.
- D) Reflective and thoughtful.

Answer: B) Tense and suspenseful.

Explanation: The description of the darkening sky, stronger waves, and increasing wind creates a tense and suspenseful mood, suggesting an approaching storm.

162. The committee members agreed to meet again next week to discuss the budget in more detail.

Question:

Which revision best corrects the grammatical error in the sentence?

- A) The committee members agreed to meet next week to discuss the budget in detail.

- B) The committee members agreed to meet again next week to discuss the budget in more detail.
- C) The committee agreed to meet next week in order to discuss the budget more closely.
- D) The committee members all agreed that they would meet next week and discuss the budget in more detail.

Answer: B) The committee members agreed to meet again next week to discuss the budget in more detail.
Explanation: The phrase "they agreed" is unnecessary. Removing it corrects the grammatical error.

163. The school principal believes that it is important for students to learn the value of hard work, and to set high standards for themselves.

Question:

Which revision best improves the clarity and conciseness of the sentence?

- A) The principal thinks students should learn the value of hard work and set high standards for themselves.
- B) The school principal believes students should work hard and set high standards for themselves.

- C) The principal thinks students should value hard work and setting high standards.
- D) The school principal believes students should learn to work hard and always set standards high.

Answer: A) The principal thinks students should learn the value of hard work and set high standards for themselves.
Explanation: This revision eliminates unnecessary wording while maintaining clarity and meaning.

164. She was extremely tired after the long day at work, however, she still found the energy to go for a run.

Question:

Which of the following revisions best corrects the sentence's punctuation?

- A) She was extremely tired after the long day at work. However, she still found the energy to go for a run.
- B) She was extremely tired after the long day at work; however, she still found the energy to go for a run.
- C) She was extremely tired after the long day at work, but however, she still found the energy to go for a run.

D) She was extremely tired after the long day at work however, she still found energy to go for a run.

Answer: B) She was extremely tired after the long day at work; however, she still found the energy to go for a run.
Explanation: A semicolon is needed to correctly separate two independent clauses followed by a transitional phrase like "however."

165. The meeting will start at 10:00 AM in the morning, so be sure to arrive on time.

Question:

Which revision best improves the sentence's conciseness?

- A) The meeting starts at 10:00 AM, so be sure to arrive on time.
- B) The meeting starts at 10:00 AM in the morning, so please be there on time.
- C) The meeting will begin at 10:00 AM in the morning, so make sure to arrive on time.
- D) The meeting starts at 10 AM, so be on time.

Answer: A) The meeting starts at 10:00 AM, so be sure to arrive on time.
Explanation: "AM in the morning" is

redundant. This revision simplifies the sentence while keeping its meaning clear.

166. Since many people forgot to RSVP to the event, we had to change the seating arrangements in order to accommodate everyone.

Question:

Which revision best improves the clarity and conciseness of the sentence?

- A) Since many forgot to RSVP to the event, we had to change the seating arrangements to accommodate everyone.
- B) Many people forgot to RSVP to the event, so we had to change seating arrangements to accommodate them.
- C) Due to many forgetting to RSVP, we had to change seating arrangements to accommodate all guests.
- D) We had to change the seating arrangements because many forgot to RSVP to the event to accommodate everyone.

Answer: A) Since many forgot to RSVP to the event, we had to change the seating arrangements to accommodate everyone.
Explanation: This version eliminates

unnecessary words, keeping the sentence concise while retaining its meaning.

167. Solve for xx:

$5x+4=245x+4=24$

- A) x=3x=3
- B) x=4x=4
- C) x=5x=5
- D) x=6x=6

Answer: C) x=4x=4

Explanation: Subtract 44 from both sides to get 5x=205x=20. Divide by 55 to get x=4x=4.

168. What is the area of a rectangle with a length of 9 cm9cm and a width of 7 cm7cm?

- A) 63 cm263cm2
- B) 45 cm245cm2
- C) 72 cm272cm2
- D) 81 cm281cm2

Answer: A) 63 cm263cm2

Explanation: The area of a rectangle is calculated by Area= length × width Area= length × width. Therefore, 9×7=63 cm29×7=63cm2.

169. If a car travels 240240 miles in 44 hours, what is the average speed of the car in miles per hour?

- A) 50 miles per hour50miles per hour
- B) 55 miles per hour55miles per hour
- C) 60 miles per hour60miles per hour
- D) 65 miles per hour65miles per hour

Answer: C) 60 miles per hour60miles per hour

Explanation: The average speed is calculated by dividing the distance by the time:

240 miles4 hours=60 miles per hour4hours240miles=60miles per hour.

170. What is the value of yy in the equation 3y−7=113y−7=11?

- A) y=5y=5
- B) y=6y=6
- C) y=7y=7
- D) y=8y=8

Answer: D) y=6y=6

Explanation: Add 77 to both sides to get 3y=183y=18, then divide by 33: y=6y=6.

171. *Passage*:

"As the sun began to set, the sky turned a brilliant shade of orange and pink, casting a warm glow over the fields below. The world seemed to slow down as evening approached."

Question:

What mood is created by the passage?

- A) Tense and suspenseful.
- B) Calm and peaceful.
- C) Dark and ominous.
- D) Exciting and energetic.

Answer: B) Calm and peaceful.

Explanation: The description of the sunset and the world slowing down suggests a calm and peaceful atmosphere.

172. *Passage*:

"Sarah had always been a perfectionist, but lately, the pressure of trying to meet everyone's expectations had begun to wear her down. She knew she needed a break."

Question:

What emotion is Sarah most likely feeling in the passage?

- A) Happiness
- B) Frustration
- C) Confusion
- D) Confidence

Answer: B) Frustration

Explanation: The passage suggests that Sarah is feeling overwhelmed and frustrated by the pressure to meet expectations.

173. *Passage*:

"The wind howled through the empty streets, and the once-bustling city now felt eerily quiet. Not a single light was on in the windows, and the darkness seemed to swallow everything whole."

Question:

What atmosphere is created by the passage?

- A) Dark and foreboding.
- B) Busy and energetic.
- C) Joyful and carefree.
- D) Calm and serene.

Answer: A) Dark and foreboding.

Explanation: The description of howling wind, empty streets, and darkness creates an eerie and foreboding atmosphere.

174. *Passage*:

"The classroom was buzzing with excitement as the students prepared for the annual science fair. Posters and models were scattered across the tables, and the chatter of eager voices filled the air."

Question:

What mood is created by the passage?

- A) Calm and peaceful.
- B) Joyful and energetic.
- C) Sad and reflective.
- D) Dark and ominous.

Answer: B) Joyful and energetic.

Explanation: The description of students' excitement and the busy classroom atmosphere creates a mood of joy and energy.

175.

Original Text:

Each of the team members have completed their individual parts of the project, and now they just need to compile everything.

Question:

Which revision best corrects the subject-verb agreement error?

- A) Each of the team members has completed their part of the project, and now they just need to compile everything.

- B) Each of the team members have completed their parts of the project, and now they need to compile everything.
- C) Each team member has completed their individual parts of the project, and now they just need to compile everything.
- D) Each of the team members has completed their individual parts, and now they just need to compile everything.

Answer: C) Each team member has completed their individual parts of the project, and now they just need to compile everything.

Explanation: "Each" is singular, so the verb should be "has." This revision corrects the subject-verb agreement and maintains clarity.

176. The construction of the new building was delayed due to several factors, including bad weather and a shortage of materials.

Question:

Which revision best improves the conciseness of the sentence?

- A) The construction of the new building was delayed due to various factors, including poor weather and a lack of materials.

- B) Bad weather and a shortage of materials delayed the construction of the new building.
- C) The construction was delayed by bad weather and a shortage of materials.
- D) The construction of the new building was slowed down by bad weather and a lack of materials.

Answer: B) Bad weather and a shortage of materials delayed the construction of the new building.

Explanation: This revision simplifies the sentence while maintaining its meaning and improves conciseness.

177. The researchers found a direct correlation between the amount of time students spent studying and their test scores, with those who studied more generally scoring higher.

Question:

Which of the following revisions best improves clarity and conciseness?

- A) The researchers found a direct correlation between time spent studying and test scores, with more study time leading to higher scores.

- B) The researchers discovered a correlation between how long students studied and their test scores, showing that studying longer resulted in better scores.
- C) The researchers discovered that studying more led to higher test scores, and they found a direct correlation between these factors.
- D) Students who studied more received higher scores, showing a direct correlation between study time and test performance.

Answer: A) The researchers found a direct correlation between time spent studying and test scores, with more study time leading to higher scores.

Explanation: This revision eliminates redundancy and improves the clarity and flow of the sentence.

178. What is the perimeter of a square with a side length of 12 cm12cm?

- A) 24 cm24cm
- B) 36 cm36cm
- C) 48 cm48cm
- D) 60 cm60cm

Answer: C) 48 cm48cm

Explanation: The perimeter of a square

is 4×side length4×side length. So, 4×12=48 cm4×12=48cm.

179. If $2x+5=17$2x+5=17, what is the value of xx?

- A) $x=6$x=6
- B) $x=4$x=4
- C) $x=5$x=5
- D) $x=7$x=7

Answer: B) $x=6$x=6

Explanation: Subtract 55 from both sides: $2x=12$2x=12. Then divide by 22: $x=6$x=6.

180. A triangle has angles measuring 35∘35∘, 45∘45∘, and x∘x∘. What is the value of xx?

- A) 90∘90∘
- B) 100∘100∘
- C) 95∘95∘
- D) 100∘100∘

Answer: C) 100∘100∘

Explanation: The sum of the angles in a triangle is 180∘180∘. So, 35∘+45∘+x∘=180∘35∘+45∘+x∘=180∘. Solving for xx gives x=100∘x=100∘.

181. A car travels 150150 miles in 33 hours. What is its average speed in miles per hour?

- A) 40 miles per hour40miles per hour
- B) 50 miles per hour50miles per hour
- C) 55 miles per hour55miles per hour
- D) 60 miles per hour60miles per hour

Answer: D) 50 miles per hour50miles per hour

Explanation: The average speed is calculated by dividing the distance by the time:

150 miles3 hours=50 miles per hour3hours150miles=50miles per hour.

182. *Passage*:

"The quiet library was filled with the soft rustle of pages turning, and the occasional cough echoed through the room. Everyone was focused on their studies, completely absorbed in their work."

Question:

What mood is created by the passage?

- A) Energetic and lively
- B) Peaceful and focused
- C) Dark and tense
- D) Sad and reflective

Answer: B) Peaceful and focused

Explanation: The description of the quiet atmosphere, soft sounds, and focused students creates a peaceful and focused mood.

183. *Passage*:

"After years of dreaming about starting her own business, she finally opened her bakery. The smell of fresh bread filled the air, and customers eagerly lined up outside the door."

Question:

What emotion is conveyed in the passage?

- A) Sadness
- B) Frustration
- C) Excitement
- D) Anxiety

Answer: C) Excitement

Explanation: The description of the bakery opening and eager customers suggests excitement and accomplishment.

184. *Passage*:

"As the rain poured down, the city streets glistened with reflections of the streetlights. The sound of rain on the pavement created a rhythmic melody that seemed to calm the bustling city."

Question:

What mood is created by the passage?

- A) Calm and serene
- B) Tense and suspenseful
- C) Chaotic and busy
- D) Exciting and energetic

Answer: A) Calm and serene

Explanation: The description of the rain, reflections, and rhythmic sounds creates a calming, peaceful atmosphere.

185. *Passage*:

"The sun was setting, casting long shadows across the park. The golden light filtered through the trees, and the air was filled with the sounds of laughter and conversation."

Question:

What mood is created by the passage?

- A) Sad and somber
- B) Joyful and peaceful
- C) Tense and ominous
- D) Quiet and mysterious

Answer: B) Joyful and peaceful

Explanation: The description of golden light, laughter, and conversation creates a joyful and peaceful mood.

186. Although the test was difficult, most students, they did well because they studied hard.

Question:

Which revision best corrects the grammatical error in the sentence?

- A) Although the test was difficult, most of the students did well because they studied hard.

- B) Most of the students, they did well on the test because they studied hard, even though it was difficult.

- C) The students did well on the test despite it being difficult because they studied hard.

- D) Although the test was hard, the students, they did well because they studied hard.

Answer: A) Although the test was difficult, most of the students did well because they studied hard.

Explanation: The phrase "they did" is unnecessary and creates a grammatical error. Removing it corrects the sentence.

187. The new park, which opened last week, it has quickly become a popular spot for families and children.

Question:

Which revision best corrects the grammatical error in the sentence?

- A) The new park, which opened last week, has quickly become a popular spot for families and children.

- B) The new park opened last week and has become a popular spot for families and children.

- C) The new park, opened last week, has quickly become a popular spot for families and children.

- D) The new park, which just opened last week, quickly became a popular spot for families.

Answer: A) The new park, which opened last week, has quickly become a popular spot for families and children.

Explanation: The phrase "it has" is redundant.

188.

Original Text:

Because of the fact that the presentation was so long, many attendees lost interest by the end.

Question:

Which of the following revisions best improves the clarity and conciseness of the sentence?

- A) Due to the length of the presentation, many attendees lost interest by the end.

- B) Because the presentation was very long, many attendees lost interest.
- C) The presentation was so long that by the end, many attendees lost interest.
- D) Because the presentation was lengthy, attendees lost interest by the end.

Answer: A) Due to the length of the presentation, many attendees lost interest by the end.

Explanation: This revision removes redundant phrasing like "Because of the fact that" and improves the sentence's clarity.

189. After carefully reviewing the data, the team they decided to revise their initial hypothesis.

Question:

Which revision best corrects the grammatical error in the sentence?

- A) After reviewing the data carefully, the team decided to revise their initial hypothesis.
- B) The team, after carefully reviewing the data, they decided to revise their initial hypothesis.
- C) After carefully reviewing the data, the team decided to revise their hypothesis.

- D) After carefully reviewing the data, the team, they decided to revise their hypothesis.

Answer: C) After carefully reviewing the data, the team decided to revise their hypothesis.

Explanation: The phrase "they decided" is unnecessary and causes a grammatical error. Removing it corrects the sentence.

190. The meeting has been rescheduled for next Friday, at which time we will discuss the budget.

Question:

Which revision best improves the conciseness of the sentence?

- A) The meeting is rescheduled for next Friday, and at that time we will discuss the budget.
- B) The meeting has been rescheduled for next Friday, when we will discuss the budget.
- C) The meeting is rescheduled for next Friday, when we plan to discuss the budget.
- D) The meeting has been moved to next Friday, at which time we will discuss the budget.

Answer: B) The meeting has been rescheduled for next Friday, when we will discuss the budget.

Explanation: This revision removes unnecessary words like "at which time" while maintaining the meaning of the sentence.

191. Solve for xx:

6x+3=276x+3=27

- A) x=3x=3
- B) x=4x=4
- C) x=5x=5
- D) x=6x=6

Answer: C) x=4x=4

Explanation: Subtract 33 from both sides to get 6x=246x=24, then divide by 66: x=4x=4.

192. The sum of two numbers is 4040. If one number is 1515, what is the other number?

- A) 2020
- B) 2525
- C) 3030
- D) 3535

Answer: B) 2525

Explanation: Subtract 1515 from 4040 to find the other number: 40−15=2540−15=25.

193. What is the value of xx in the equation 4x−7=174x−7=17?

- A) x=6x=6
- B) x=7x=7
- C) x=8x=8
- D) x=9x=9

Answer: D) x=6x=6

Explanation: Add 77 to both sides to get 4x=244x=24, then divide by 44 to get x=6x=6.

194. The perimeter of a rectangle is 64 cm64cm, and its length is 20 cm20cm. What is the width?

- A) 8 cm8cm
- B) 10 cm10cm
- C) 12 cm12cm
- D) 14 cm14cm

Answer: B) 12 cm12cm

Explanation: The formula for the perimeter of a rectangle is P=2(length + width)P=2(length + width). Substituting P=64P=64 and length=20length=20: 64=2(20+width)64=2(20+width), so width=12 width=12cm.

195. *Passage:*

"The wind picked up, sending leaves

swirling through the air. Dark clouds gathered on the horizon, and the first drops of rain began to fall."

Question:

What mood is created by the passage?

- A) Calm and peaceful
- B) Joyful and lighthearted
- C) Tense and ominous
- D) Confused and chaotic

Answer: C) Tense and ominous

Explanation: The description of the wind, swirling leaves, dark clouds, and rain suggests a tense and ominous mood.

196. *Passage*:

"The crowd cheered as the fireworks lit up the night sky. The air was filled with excitement, and everyone seemed to be in high spirits."

Question:

What is the mood of the passage?

- A) Sad and reflective
- B) Exciting and joyful
- C) Tense and suspenseful
- D) Calm and serene

Answer: B) Exciting and joyful

Explanation: The cheering crowd and

fireworks create an atmosphere of excitement and joy.

197. *Passage*:

"Despite the chaos around her, she remained calm. Her steady breathing and focused gaze showed that she was ready to face whatever came next."

Question:

What quality is emphasized about the character in the passage?

- A) Her intelligence
- B) Her confidence
- C) Her fear
- D) Her indecision

Answer: B) Her confidence

Explanation: The passage emphasizes the character's calm demeanor and readiness, suggesting confidence.

198. *Passage*:

"As the ship sailed farther from the shore, the water grew darker, and the waves began to rise. The vast ocean stretched out in all directions, seemingly endless."

Question:

What mood is created by the passage?

- A) Mysterious and adventurous

- B) Calm and peaceful
- C) Joyful and lighthearted
- D) Sad and reflective

Answer: A) Mysterious and adventurous

Explanation: The description of the endless ocean and rising waves creates a sense of mystery and adventure.

199. While some of the suggestions were useful, there was a lot of them that were unrealistic and impossible to implement.

Question:

Which revision best corrects the grammatical error in the sentence?

- A) While some suggestions were useful, many were unrealistic and impossible to implement.
- B) While some suggestions were useful, there were many that were unrealistic and impossible to implement.
- C) Though some of the suggestions were useful, most were unrealistic and impossible to implement.
- D) Some suggestions were useful, but many of them were too unrealistic to implement.

Answer: A) While some suggestions were useful, many were unrealistic and impossible to implement.

Explanation: The phrase "a lot of them" is wordy and can be replaced with "many" for conciseness and clarity.

200. The team finished the project ahead of schedule, which allowed them to take some extra time to review their work and make improvements.

Question:

Which of the following revisions best improves the conciseness of the sentence?

- A) The team finished the project early, which allowed them to take extra time to review and improve their work.
- B) The team completed the project ahead of schedule, giving them extra time to review and improve their work.
- C) The team finished ahead of schedule and used the extra time to review their work and make improvements.
- D) Finishing early gave the team extra time to review their work and make some improvements.

Answer: B) The team completed the project ahead of schedule, giving them extra time to review and improve their work.

Explanation: This revision improves conciseness while maintaining the original meaning of the sentence.

TIPS FOR CONTINUED LEARNING

Learning is a lifelong journey, and continued learning beyond the PSAT 8/9 is essential for academic success and personal growth. This section provides valuable tips and strategies to maintain your learning momentum and cultivate a love for acquiring knowledge.

1. Embrace Curiosity

Curiosity is the engine of learning. Cultivate a curious mindset by asking questions, exploring new topics, and seeking out different perspectives. Embrace the joy of discovery and allow yourself to be fascinated by the world around you.

2. Set Realistic Goals

Setting realistic goals can help you stay motivated and focused on your learning journey. Break down larger goals into smaller, more manageable steps. Celebrate your achievements along the way and don't be afraid to adjust your goals as your interests and priorities evolve.

3. Find Your Learning Style

Everyone learns differently. Discover your unique learning style, whether it's visual, auditory, kinesthetic, or a combination of different styles. Tailor your learning experiences to match your preferences for optimal comprehension and retention.

4. Explore Different Learning Resources

A wealth of learning resources is available beyond textbooks and traditional classroom settings. Explore online courses, documentaries, podcasts, museums, libraries, and community events to expand your knowledge and engage with different learning formats.

5. Cultivate a Reading Habit

Reading is a gateway to knowledge and imagination. Cultivate a regular reading habit by setting aside dedicated reading time each day or week. Explore different genres, authors, and perspectives to broaden your horizons and deepen your understanding of the world.

6. Engage in Active Recall

Active recall is a powerful technique for enhancing memory and retention. After learning something new, try to recall the information without looking at your notes or resources. This process strengthens neural connections and improves long-term memory.

7. Embrace Challenges

Learning often involves stepping outside your comfort zone and embracing challenges. Don't be afraid to tackle difficult topics or concepts. The process of overcoming challenges can lead to deeper understanding and a sense of accomplishment.

8. Connect with Others

Learning is often enhanced through collaboration and interaction with others. Join study groups, engage in discussions, or seek out mentors to share ideas, gain new perspectives, and learn from each other's experiences.

9. Practice Time Management

Effective time management is crucial for balancing your learning goals with other commitments. Create a schedule that allows for dedicated learning time, prioritize your tasks, and avoid procrastination to make the most of your learning opportunities.

10. Seek Feedback

Feedback can provide valuable insights into your strengths and areas for improvement. Don't hesitate to seek feedback from your teachers, mentors, or peers. Use their constructive criticism to refine your learning strategies and enhance your understanding.

11. Embrace Failure as a Learning Opportunity

Failure is an inevitable part of the learning process. Instead of viewing it as a setback, embrace it as a learning opportunity. Analyze your mistakes, identify areas for improvement, and use those lessons to grow and develop your skills.

12. Cultivate a Growth Mindset

A growth mindset is the belief that your abilities and intelligence can be developed through dedication and hard work. Embrace this mindset by viewing challenges as opportunities for growth and learning from your mistakes.

13. Stay Curious and Never Stop Learning

The pursuit of knowledge is a lifelong endeavor. Stay curious, embrace new learning opportunities, and never stop exploring the vast world of information and ideas.

CONCLUSION

Congratulations on completing your PSAT 8/9 preparation journey! You've learned valuable strategies, practiced essential skills, and gained the confidence to tackle the exam head-on. Remember, the PSAT 8/9 is just one step in your academic journey. Embrace the challenges ahead, continue to nurture your love for learning, and strive for excellence in all your endeavors.

Believe in yourself, stay focused, and approach the exam with a positive attitude. Your hard work and dedication will pave the way to success on the PSAT 8/9 and beyond. Good luck, and may your future be filled with endless possibilities!

GLOSSARY OF KEY TERMS

This glossary provides definitions for key terms and concepts relevant to the PSAT 8/9 and your broader academic journey.

1. Active Recall: A learning technique that involves actively retrieving information from memory, strengthening neural connections and improving retention.

2. Adaptive Testing: A testing method that adjusts the difficulty of questions based on the test-taker's performance, providing a more personalized assessment.

3. Analogy: A comparison between two things that are different but share similar characteristics, often used to explain complex concepts.

4. Anecdote: A short, personal story used to illustrate a point or provide an example.

5. Argument: A set of reasons or evidence presented in support of a claim or position.

6. Assumption: A belief or statement taken for granted without proof or evidence.

7. Bias: A prejudice or inclination that influences judgment or perspective.

8. Citation: A reference to a source of information, used to acknowledge the origin of ideas or data.

9. Claim: A statement or assertion that something is true or factual.

10. Coherence: The logical connection and flow of ideas in a piece of writing.

11. Conciseness: Expressing ideas clearly and effectively using as few words as possible.

12. Conclusion: A judgment or decision reached based on reasoning and evidence.

13. Connotation: The emotional or cultural association of a word, beyond its literal definition.

14. Context: The surrounding words, sentences, or circumstances that influence the meaning of a word or passage.

15. Counterargument: An argument presented in opposition to another argument.

16. Critical Thinking: The objective analysis and evaluation of information to form a judgment.

17. Deductive Reasoning: A logical process that starts with a general principle and applies it to a specific case to reach a conclusion.

18. Denotation: The literal dictionary definition of a word.

19. Diction: The choice and use of words in writing or speech.

20. Evidence: Facts, data, or information that support a claim or argument.

21. Figurative Language: Language that uses figures of speech, such as metaphors and similes, to create a non-literal meaning.

22. Generalization: A broad statement or conclusion based on specific instances or observations.

23. Genre: A category or type of literature or art, characterized by specific style, form, or content.

24. Grammar: The set of rules that govern the structure and use of language.

25. Inference: A conclusion reached based on reasoning and evidence.

26. Informational Text: Non-fiction writing that aims to convey factual information.

27. Irony: A literary device that uses language to express the opposite of its literal meaning.

28. Juxtaposition: Placing two or more things side by side for comparison or contrast.

29. Literary Device: A technique used in writing to create a specific effect or convey meaning.

30. Main Idea: The central point or message of a passage or text.

31. Metaphor: A figure of speech that compares two unlike things without using "like" or "as."

32. Mood: The atmosphere or feeling created in a literary work.

33. Narrative: A story or account of events.

34. Nuance: A subtle difference or distinction in meaning or expression.

35. Objective: Not influenced by personal feelings or opinions.

36. Parallelism: The use of similar grammatical structures to express related ideas.

37. Paraphrase: To express someone else's ideas in your own words.

38. Perspective: A particular attitude or way of considering something.

39. Plagiarism: The act of using someone else's work or ideas without giving proper credit.

40. Plot: The sequence of events that make up a story.

41. Precision: The quality of being exact and accurate.

42. Prediction: A statement about what might happen in the future.

43. Punctuation: The use of marks or symbols to clarify meaning and structure in writing.

44. Qualitative Data: Data that describes qualities or characteristics.

45. Quantitative Data: Data that can be measured or expressed numerically.

46. Rhetoric: The art of effective or persuasive speaking or writing.

47. Setting: The time and place in which a story takes place.

48. Simile: A figure of speech that compares two unlike things using "like" or "as."

49. Style: The way in which an author writes or expresses themselves.

50. Subjective: Influenced by personal feelings or opinions.

51. Summary: A brief statement of the main points of a text or passage.

52. Supporting Details: Facts, examples, or evidence that support the main idea.

53. Symbolism: The use of symbols to represent ideas or qualities.

54. Theme: The underlying message or idea of a literary work.

55. Thesis Statement: A sentence that summarizes the main point or argument of an essay or research paper.

56. Tone: The author's attitude or feeling towards the subject matter.

57. Transition: A word or phrase that connects ideas and creates a smooth flow between sentences or paragraphs.

58. Validity: The quality of being logically or factually sound.

59. Vocabulary: The body of words used in a particular language or subject.

60. Voice: The author's unique style and personality expressed in their writing.

Made in the USA
Las Vegas, NV
11 December 2024